Nudged

Nudged

Exploring your Creative Core

Derrick Trimble

DEUTERON GROUP

First paperback edition February 2020

Book and cover design by Derrick Trimble

ISBN 978-1-9163455-0-8 (paperback)
ISBN 978-1-9163455-1-5 (ebook)
ISBN 978-1-9163455-2-2 (audiobook)

For Mom and Dad,

I hope you are watching

Contents

Introduction

The game show is a cultural phenomenon that has captured the imagination of the masses since the inception of television. Contestants pit their skills against the house in a televised battle of odds-defying drama while sponsors ply their wares to mesmerised audiences during commercial breaks. Returning from the fast-talking sales salvo of the break to the live studio audience, contestants average Jane or Joe must act with lightning-fast decisiveness and accuracy to get a shot at a prize. A mix of chance and skill set the stage for the pleasant host and screened players' flirt with destiny. Meanwhile, an audience of dedicated home viewers keep ratings up to satisfy sponsor saturation measurements. The spectacle of watching somebody like yourself, somebody you may know, or an underdog win big is a powerful attraction.

Tipping Point is a British game show conceived from a popular arcade game. The amusement centre version is a lite form of gambling aimed to snag otherwise disposable loose change. A player will strategically select a slot to insert their coin. A rub for luck, a spin for action and the coin careens from the slot to join a growing mound of coins. A nearby ledge is poised to collect randomly landing coins as amassed sections cascade into a trough for collection. By nature of the game, winnings are small. Invariably, a portion of the winnings is fed back into the process by the player. Winning, in the end, and for this example, is not as crucial as that well-placed coin that nudges the pile forward.

Expectation, anticipation, and finally, satisfaction bring the plunking addiction to a close. Bored of the game, or out of coins, the competition ends. With its termination, the player will return to engage in the meaningful games of chance and skill that mark a life. A metaphor of our existence or a casual distraction? I am constantly aware of connections in daily activities. That is what I do. I draw parallels that have the potential to touch people and evoke meaningful change. We can easily miss the value of those moments of observation, like the tipping point arcade game, if we aren't looking. Too busy or checked out, we may squander rich insights of human nature, the universe in which we live, or the consequences of their interactions. Instead, we can find ourselves in a perpetual pattern of rinse and repeat. A nudge is an action that can dislodge you from that cycle. You are frequently nudged over the day to think and act to stimuli. Some nudges are uncomfortable. Other nudges are outright revolutionary, demanding a substantial investment of energy, resources, and self. Most nudges we receive are barely noticeable, ignored or put on the back burner for later consideration. We do far better when we don't allow the habit of nudge neglect to gain permanence in our attitude. An overdeveloped habit of ignoring nudges may have consequences. Over a lifetime, negligence of stimulating opportunities may become the basis for regret. A mental condition no person intentionally seeks to develop.

What if you had the tools to manage life's challenges and minimise regret? The rhythmic pitch of marketing legend Ron Popeil surfaces from memory in response to that proposition. "How much would you pay for that tool? Remember it helps manage not some, not bits, but all of life's challenges?" Then comes the increased value. "What would you pay for such a tool? Hundreds, thousands, maybe even millions?" After hawking some added value to the wonder tool, Popeil would introduce the pitch. "For today only you won't pay millions, not thousands, not hundreds. No, not even £39.99." With bated breath, audience excitement heightens. The brain of a bargain junky then floods with adrenaline. "Today, and every day, you can have this tool for FREE! The answer is already inside of you." All that for free? What's the catch? The catch is simple and immortalised by the Pitch King—"You must act now." Stale opportunities may give way to new opportunities, but the one that came wrapped in the moment is lost or won by an action.

Whether we recognise an opportunity when it arrives mostly depends on our ability to appreciate the use-by date of that moment. No matter how a prospect comes wrapped, regardless of its nature or eventual outcome, there is a single common thread that binds that occasion to every other opportunity we face. A prospect for change is the spark that ignites creative engagement. Creativity is then the accomplishment of an idea or the materialisation of something imagined. Deep within the crevices of your brain, imagination forms and morphs using the bits and pieces that you daily feed your mind as building blocks for a creation. At a state of saturation or urgency, your imagination will spill over as an action.

Every new action you take is rooted in your creative core and affected by new and established connections. That core and its processes become the instinctive drive directing every aspect of your decision-making. Your ability to create is intrinsically connected to these features of the human experience. Psychologists, scientists, and philosophers continue in their debate about the nature of creativity. We are fortunate to live in an era where the accumulated theoretical thought on creativity is met by technological advances to measure those theories. Over the past few decades, we've gained incredible insights into the brain and human behaviour. Those discoveries also challenge the premise of free-will—all but stripping consciousness to a state of organic automation. To some, your actions can be ascribed as nothing less than autonomic chain reactions set-off before your consciousness engages. Considering the complexities of the brain, this debate of choice and its relation to creativity will continue for some time. For those that recognise the value of creativity in their day-to-day living and seek to enhance their abilities, the debate is immaterial.

Even if we are non-unique automatons, as suggested in some circles, you can learn. Like building muscle, you experience life, and your response to those experiences can alter the physical dynamics of your brain. You can train your brain to think and respond differently through engagement and practise. The pathways for this kind of brain training are innumerable. Regardless of your age or any other personal factors, you have applied countless approaches to modifying your behaviours and ultimately the person of you. Reading this book is another pathway of your engaged brain training. With your consumption of the past 1080 words of this introduction, your mind weighed, tested, and analysed what I've written comparing the content to your thoughts. In other words, you've already been nudged. What does it mean to be nudged? At least what does it mean in the context of our applications of creativity?

Think about how you use a nudge in situations where boredom or apathy create a level of mental, if not also emotional, disengagement. A family member fidgeting during a religious service or a dinner might receive a gentle nudge to encourage an appearance of alertness. An audience member that succumbs to a moment of "resting his eyes" gets a nudge before his unconscious rest escalates into an embarrassing nasal growl. Perhaps, a partner receives a polite nudge in the side following an insensitive comment in an awkward social moment. To be nudged is to be metaphorically poked in the side to be made aware of a condition. Unfortunately, that kind of poking doesn't earn the long-term results that we want. An intrusive nudge of this type may instead evoke an emotional escalation. Good intentions may not matter much if the person receiving the nudge is offended. You want a nudge that has a positive and productive long-term impact. You want to create something that lasts.

For that purpose, let's take a wander back a few thousand years. History can give us a perspective that changes in the way humankind responds to challenges have not differed much over time. Ancient Greece provides plenty of examples for consideration. Foundations of thought in ancient Greece became the DNA of government, science, philosophy, and the arts in Western civilisation. Among the many names associated with influencing Greek thought, the son of a sculptor is perhaps most well-known. Until his death in 399 BCE, the philosopher Socrates sowed seeds of ideas that shaped much of the way the world thinks. Distinctions of thought between Socrates and his contemporary Plato remain the essence of philosophical debate. Of his teacher, Plato referred to Socrates as a 'gadfly' of the Athenian state. A gadfly being that annoying, biting, inescapable pest that relentlessly denies the harassed any form of rest. Undoubtedly, it was Socrates' likening of the state to that of "a great and noble steed" that fuelled his reputation as an irritation of the state. Plato suggested that Socrates saw it as his duty to provoke, or nudge, the State to apply reason to their actions.

Socrates applied a method of eliciting knowledge from his students that I liken to midwifery. He used questions to nudge a response and then build upon that response until a full thought was born. That approach to educating is called maieutic or the Socratic method. Following this methodology, the teacher-coach-trainer-tutor is more of a guide than an expert. Alternatively, education in the form of knowledge transfer is best known as the didactic approach, wherein the student is a passive receptacle. I mean that in a general sense. I appreciate the value of didactic teaching. It is used globally for transferring information. Where a student has limited experience or knowledge, there needs to be a cascading of information through knowledge transfer. Where a student has limited understanding, the didactic approach is the leading method of student education conducted around the world. Scientific theory and how-to instructions provide the bedrock for students to explore possibilities. And that is where the handover to a Socratic method and reason accelerate growth.

Midwifing a thought to fullness infers that conception has occurred. The role of the coach then is to excite that thought to another stage of development. Therein lies the action of being nudged; activating your reason to move an idea along. The Nudge Principle is how we participate in that moment. Going back to the Popeil tool illustration, what tools do you already have that will allow you to move a thought along at will? If you are going to drive a thought, what can you do to shape that thought for a purpose? What will be the outcome of that purpose? And ultimately, what form of action will that thought inspire?

A simple definition of creativity is to use the imagination or original thought to create something. One definition of creativity tags onto that 'something created' with qualifiers that the created must also be unique and have a value to somebody. If confined to the financial definition of value, then we'd have to bow to the axiom that a valued item or action is only as valuable as what somebody is willing to pay. The use of creativity in a business case depends on the exchange of monetary value for the created. We will address creativity as a business case as we progress. I think the definition of required value, or even being unique, is too narrow for our use. To strum the chords of the imagination of a broader audience, we are going to stick with the general definition of creativity that it is the process of creating something.

We are comfortable with the word creator when it comes to defining a person that creates. A creative is any person capable of original thought. You can wear the title creator when there is a creation. What you'll find in the Nudge Principle are nudges of creative movement that harness your imagination, develop original thoughts, and then to create something. While there is a solid argument in the business case scenario for having an end in mind—a something—the creative process can also be undermined by limitations. If a vision of a something is fixed in the mind, then the creative process can become restricted. You may be pre-ordaining an outcome instead of stimulating creative dynamism.

In a manufacturing mentality, you know that you must create a widget for A, so you will tick the boxes of X and Y and thereby create a functional widget. I want to encourage you to avoid falling into this trap of utilitarianism as we explore principles of creativity. Not that there isn't a place for methodology in the creative process—quite the contrary. Creativity is saturated with method. What I hope you gain from creativity comes at an individual level where creativity does something for you as a person. The tools you will use are tools from your toolbox. The utility comes later, once the imagination and original thought have achieved some maturity to stand on their own.

Tools in your imagination toolbox are more principles than tools. What you have at your disposal for crafting your imagination and original thought is priceless. Your Nudge journey will lead through familiar territory. You have functioned with these nudges your whole life. Perhaps unaware of their presence, you engage in each frequently day by day, maybe moment to moment. Creativity is developed and released from your creative core by the nudges of SEE, TELL, FLOW, PLAY, FEEL, BE and DO. Regardless of your view of your creativity, your creative core is continuously working out possibilities and using the resources of your creative core. The process is as old as human history.

One

Your Creative Core

1

The Creative Nomad

In the wake of the 2007 slip of the economy that led to a full-blown recession, I sought to recreate myself. My friend Nate convinced me that I should have a go at screenwriting. An ambitious independent filmmaker, he was also looking for a script to produce. Having not long before suffered the consequence of redundancy, I thought I'd give it a try. Within six months, I'd written four scripts. Awarded the confidence of my friend, I thought it was time to invest.

Together we attended the 2008 Screenwriters Expo in Los Angeles. Before the big event, my hopes of screenwriting glory reached ripeness with my bundle of untested scripts in hand. Although it was a lot of writing for a guy just getting started, it is was laughable achievement compared to that of the competition. Inspired by visions of acceptance awards at the Kodak Theater, we charged onward with abandon through workshops of screenwriting hope. If nothing else, we told ourselves we'd walk away with a better understanding of the industry. Throughout the weekend, I overheard other hungry hopefuls express their disdain for that sterile industrial term. Our nostalgic vision of filmmaking was more romantic than pragmatic. A weekend with industry experts would change all of our minds. Hollywood style film making is business. The infrastructure that makes Hollywood creative magic happen is called the industry.

Our time spent that weekend in Los Angeles was invaluable. Besides the repeated reality check that studios won't even touch an unsolicited script, there were axioms, unwritten rules, and jargon aplenty. (Please see the legal department for an explanation.) Carried along on the information wave with the "Don't copy an original concept" advice, was a writing rule about gaining audience attention within the first five to ten minutes. That is called The Hook. Professional speakers have a similar guide in an unsubstantiated 90-second rule. Regardless of the exact passage of time when a film or speaker begins to lose an audience, there is indeed a point where an audience member will emotionally invest or divest. A person might wonder how some films make it to the big screen if their filmmakers were following these same hard rules. What is not a surprise is the depth of creativity exercised in every aspect of a film's creation. Nate and I only scratched the surface of an enormous corporate landscape where creativity and business meet.

To ground our journey of creativity, let's explore the subject on the grand scale of the human story. The most excellent drama of history is the passage of humanity from era to era. Creativity is the constant of each forward step. How civilisation arrived at different stages of social development permeates every nuance of our collective story. The modern hunter-gatherer version of Nate and I was that of two people travelling to explore the film making hunting grounds of Los Angeles. In our naivety, we may have convinced ourselves that we were self-actualising from some lofty height of a creative vision. Once we pulled back the veneer of expectation, we found ourselves at the ground level basics of survival. In this arena, could we convert our skills into something that might earn a living or did the overcrowded screenwriting hunting grounds have room for more predators? If the latter were the case, then we would move on as nomads on creative landscape.

First Spark

Kicking against the norm is a natural characteristic of the creative. Doing something different is the creative's playground. Dissent from an established pattern makes way for change. Sometimes change works, other times it doesn't or at least not directly or with immediate results. Change can occur later as seeds for change take root and spread. Following the historical influence of literature, filmmakers use their medium to stimulate thought, make statements, and entertain all at once. Breaking from the formulaic is risky but necessary for creativity. Concerning film, I want to point you to a non-traditional opening sequence of a movie that tested the boundaries of the hook.

For the first ten minutes of Stanley Kubrick's *2001: A Space Odyssey*, the audience watches a story about space travel begin with semi-vertical ape creatures surviving in an arid wasteland. Not exactly what an audience would expect from a tale advertised as 'an epic drama of adventure and exploration.' Except for some strange rising beehive sound at the arrival of a mysterious black monolith on the scene, the initial ambient soundtrack is comprised of grunting, screeching, and howling primates. Released in 1968, the same year as the Charlton Heston version of *Planet of the Apes,* ape costume design had not progressed much from the Weissmuller days of Tarzan. Yet, something about the Kubrick sequence created an interest that hooked audiences. Perhaps it was a primal connection of discovery that piqued audience curiosity.

Terrance Malik's 2011 film *The Tree of Life* bested Kubrick's ten-minute evolutionary setting. With his visually stimulating fifteen-minute vision of the origins of life, Malik almost lost me a few times, but I hung on. Curiosity and an appreciation for the excellent editing kept me intrigued. Something about discovery, a unique angle of presentation, and the uncharted realms of imagination aroused my commitment. To Kubrick and author Arthur C. Clarke's credit, they never revealed the meaning of that monolith sequence in the opening scenes of 2001. Shortly after the film's release, Kubrick was interviewed for Playboy magazine and asked about the introduction. In response to the ape-monolith scene, he replied, 'You're free to speculate as you wish about the philosophical and allegorical meaning of the film—and such speculation is one indication that it has succeeded in gripping the audience at a deep level.'

2001 celebrated its fiftieth anniversary in 2018. Despite a half-century of formal and informal analysis, its widely interpretative meaning holds steadfast. Should Kubrick have explained his visual interpretation, his audience may have felt obligated to apply a specific design and then altogether missed the point. There are layers of meaning in *2001: A Space Odyssey*, but it is in those first ten minutes that the audience forms a connection. An audience member is not required to hold a degree in dramaturgy, be a film analyst, or walk the clouds with the titans of film to appreciate the obviousness of the first ten minutes.

For the ape creatures of the opening sequence, there are moment-to-moment struggles, conflict, vulnerability, barrenness, and limitations to communication. Every strand of existence is held together within a volatile social order. With the break of dawn, the scene is disrupted by change. Awakened, probably from a dream state, a single ape reacts to a strange object that appeared overnight. The questionably safe boundaries of their hollow are invaded by an object of contrast. Let's give our main ape creature the name Archie so that he feels more human to us. Archie's eyes widen as they inspect the unnatural structure. Reacting instinctively, he alerts the other apes who rally in a frenzy. The object is taller than any other stone formation on the landscape. Black, smooth and straight-edged, the monolith is a curious contrast to the surrounding red sandstone. Something is different. Archie explores the monolith with progressive advances.

Satisfied that the structure doesn't pose a threat, he touches the surface. Curiosity neutralises his fear. Other beasts follow Archie's lead with calmed interest. With a climate of safety secured, the entire troop join into the investigation by stroking and tasting the odd addition to the live diorama. The troop becomes absorbed with new sensations and watch one another in their collective discoveries. Each ape creates an experience with the monolith. To communicate their experience, perhaps they seek to form an utterance to describe what they see and feel. Early communication begins to take shape.

Using the magic of film, we skip the mundane passage of time to the next scene when Archie makes a connection between his experience and the environment. Crouched amidst a pile of sun-bleached bones, the wheels of Archie's curiosity begin to make connections. The cause-and-effect awareness of what-if grabs his attention. Bemused by the interaction of bones as they clink around to his swipes, Archie becomes aware that some bones interact differently when a collision occurs. Fully absorbed in his curiosity, Archie selects a bone to test what happens when one bone collides with other scattered bones. Within moments Archie's enthusiasm increases with force and speed, turning a jawbone into a bone-crushing tool. Archie discovered, by observation, use for something as commonplace to his environment as a sun-bleached bone.

Equipped with the tool, Archie becomes emboldened with confidence. His confidence is put to the test when a rival group challenges Archie's troop at a watering hole. The jawbone proves an effective instrument to deliver a death blow to a competing troop leader. A tool used for foraging, ploughing, or digging can also be used as a weapon. Enlightenment can be a double-edged sword, and survival is a powerful creative force. We discovered early in our evolving consciousness, the importance that necessity plays with invention.

Feeding the Nine Billion

Whether or not the first sparks of creativity were born out of a survival instinct or safety mode is anyone's guess. No one took names or conducted surveys. We will never know. In our 2001 reference, Archie held in his hand a tool for creativity or destruction. When our basic human needs are at stake, it is easy to blur the lines between survival, safety, and belonging. Our brain doesn't pause to consider which of these factors has priority. They are a tangled set of motivators that drive our actions. It's easy to look back at the traces of humanity on history and assign labels to epochs based on our contemporary perspective. For Archie and Company, we can appreciate that his progeny evolved from gatherers to hunters. The better they managed their surroundings, the more they were able to turn their creative energies toward collective activities like production — primarily in the domain of agriculture.

With the increase of safety, at least relatively, humanity gathered as communities. Those collectives required crops to maintain their hard-earned foundation of survival, safety, and a sense of belonging. Opportunities within groups to relax their vigilance against threats allowed for further exploration of creative expression. Art, production, and engineering developed from a position of comfort and security. The collective became a laboratory of social interaction wherein people observed and learned from others within the community.

Belonging is a catalyst for exploring possibilities both on an individual and communal basis. With the expansion of the community, more time can be spent contributing to the greater good. The watch-my-back mode of survival and the desperation for safety could become a secondary concern. A stronger community meant that increased numbers could contribute to the essentials of living and security. From their mutual success came increased cooperation. Prosperity is an outcome of this type of purposeful collaboration. As a result of when increased numbers of people gather under that umbrella of protection, demand for managing the population will also increase. When there is increased collaboration and growth, challenges ensue. The need for innovation becomes inevitable.

Sounds a bit utopian. An agricultural society where members work together to produce food for their community in relative safety and a universal sense of wellbeing is Utopia. In every storyline of society building, first indications of permanence begin with a group claiming territory for commerce, trade, and community. In a metaphoric sense, they are taking root in the land. Inhabitants are declaring as a symbolic overture to any witness that "We are here to stay." We here for as long as the ground produces, the environment doesn't become hostile or we are forced from the land.

All that changed in a large-scale capacity with the introduction of industrialisation. As more food was produced, more resources were needed to meet the consuming populations of urban growth. A gradual increase of movement by people to cities created sprawling metropolises across the globe. A gradual decline of the agricultural society fed the rise of the industrial, technical, service, and a plethora of other industries—including criminal and war-making. Instead of planting foodstuffs, we planted ourselves in population centres, we planted in the residential areas outside cities, and we planted in chairs or on the factory floor. We rent or purchase homes and declare, "We are here to stay." That is, until things look better on the other side of wherever.

Feeding people was humanity's core issue for millennia. Agriculture and industrialisation were the separating factors of an advanced society. Today that agrarian divide between developing and industrialised countries are narrowed due to the high demand for technology in mass food production. Nevertheless, feeding the population remains a considerable concern rather than a footnote on an agenda. Blighted by global change, armed conflict, political upheaval, or gross mismanagement of resources, many nations struggle to provide relative safety and wellbeing that appears in abundance elsewhere. Subsequently, this triggers the movement of people. It may start small and feel like a trickle, but in time sizable numbers of people will migrate from one location to another.

Historically, these and a myriad of other conditions, push people from their familiar, leading to a variety of conflicts between the Haves and Have Nots. The battle of will and resources has raged across our story. In the outcome, resources and people are reallocated and dispersed. Trails of our heritage line ancient paths marked by architecture, culture, and an engrained narrative of interaction between peoples. The double helix of our DNA is tagged with the complexity of people across a past that crisscrosses the globe. We are the evolution of the merging of peoples and cultures.

Without adversity, be that at the hand of others or the consequence of nature, we would likely remain sedentary. Adversity forces us to explore. The incentive for exploration is to find, see, or achieve something new. We want something different than what we currently have. Arguably, we look for a blend of the familiar in our seeking. The ordinary offers a sense of safety. If our destination, or the journey there, is alien to our existence, we take others along like us. Movement of people is as old as time. Only when there is an overshadowing perception of limited resources or a threat to safety—security in our current mindset—does one group restrict the integration of others. The migration of people across national borders or from rural to urban has intensified over the past century. We could easily get lost in the conversation at this point while chasing newsworthy rabbits into their burrows. We are aware of the issues. To grasp the enormity of the challenges and to find solutions demands robust creative energy.

Globalisation, politicising, exploitation and armed conflict have replaced the base conditions of safety and wellbeing. Stripped down to the foundation where people live, and apart from being an academic exercise or political debate, people move because they seek a better life. The creative energy it takes to find solutions under a steady pounding of challenges is a regular theme in the narrative of human history. Adapt or die. I don't want to trivialise the challenges one person faces in contrast to another. Ultimately, migration challenges will result in similar outcomes. A single refugee plotting a strategy to cross international borders will apply the same if not a more considerable creative effort than the collective will of people trying to keep him out. The moral question at hand regards the final tally of fatalities before we implement a workable solution.

Our global population rises at a steady pace. By 2042, there will be over nine billion people on the planet. We have evolved from a sparsely populated world of hunter-gatherers to the bustling cityscapes where artificial environments and urbanists apply their creative energy to get ahead. What we do and how we do it is generally a personal prerogative. At the close of a day, we measure our struggle relative to the challenges we face. One person's battle is another's vision of freedom. The insatiability of the human condition urges us to apply creativity to improve our safety and wellbeing—regardless of how that may be defined.

Statistically Mispresenting the Individual

One of my many quirks is a tendency to throw out an arbitrary percentage to validate a position. The coup d' grace of my argument will conclude with something like, "Given what we know, that is about 99% unlikely to happen." When I am feeling overconfident and want to punctuate my stake in reality, I will add decimal points. So that 99% certainty takes on a new depth of leverage when I nod and say "99.9%." Recognising that there are innumerable variables that can change a condition, I leave that tiny percentage to unknown influencing factors. Somewhere along the line, I picked up this habit of using this percentage additive in my daily conversation. If I had to point the finger at a specific influence for how this crept in, I'd blame the television weather presenter. For decades they have directed our attention to graphics and charts using all sorts of technology. Like eager gamblers, we sit on the edge of our seat waiting for those golden words of speculation that can shift plans to enjoy a full day of sunshine to 80% chance of showers.

Tracking and projecting weather patterns have vastly improved with satellite technology. The ability to pinpoint weather with mystical accuracy on a micro-scale has far-reaching applications. Farming, trade, and leisure are three industries that rely heavily on accurate weather projections. When the weather turns hostile, the impact on financial and insurance sectors scramble to minimise loss. Similarly, the corporate art of speculating on statistical data is fine-tuned with scientific precision. Like a farmer planting a crop based on soil conditions and projected weather patterns, companies depend on quality data for their strategies.

Data also plays a substantive role in the realm of marketing. From data collection and analysis to product development and delivery, buyer trends are sieved through data manipulation to hone finely devised campaigns. That your product preferences are culled from your purchasing and browsing history is only a small segment of the power of marketing. Another facet of marketing, often hidden from our perception because of marketing effectiveness, is the clustering of audiences into groups. We are carefully categorised into buyer groups to cultivate a sense of belonging according to how we identify with others. A fundamental human need is to feel part of something. Except for bold adventurers that reject the social constructs of belonging in favour of isolation, we all seek to belong. We also like to think that we choose how we will interact with others. We may even enjoy some success in that area on occasion. The influence of other people is a gravitational dynamic pulling us toward some measure of interaction, whether great or small.

That is just a snippet alluding to the big picture of us—the macro version. In philosophical thought, that may also be the essence of a higher consciousness. An oneness of mind that connects all thinking souls across time and space. Do you think your thoughts are your own? Whoa, hold on there cowboy. Too much to suggest this early in our relationship? The concept that we share a universal mind goes way back in philosophical history. The reason I introduce the idea of a universal mind here is to punctuate one extreme of the spectrum of consciousness. Snapped to the other end of the spectrum, the school of thought makes us out to be the product of automated neural responses, neither having nor exercising will. Consciousness in that narrow band of thinking is not even a consideration as we relate it to creativity.

Misrepresentation of the individual is an evident deficiency in the process of ad hoc—and formal—statistical associations of social behaviour. The world-gone-mad approach of categorising people in the cauldron of public discourse first fosters and then spreads a range of fallacies. Fallacies breed stereotypes, biases, prejudices, and ultimately division or worse. Replicating like a resistance mutated virus, the corrupted form of reason infects and transfers from one person to another. With the assistance of the ever-present tools of global communication literally at hand, the infected thinking spreads with pandemic impact.

To avoid drawing the ire of a particular demographic or succumb to the ideology du jour, allow me to illustrate with a fictional scenario. Our sample belongs to a much-maligned categorised group of people. Delta Sigma is an educated, middle-aged, purple-skinned person from Talitounia. Throughout history, people of this description have behaved superiorly and engaged in countless acts of dominance. As a people group, their history demonstrates advances in civilisation and acts of goodwill. However, in the public arena, the latter is perceived as a form of self-serving exploitation. Activist movements perpetuate that any person with those demographics is the root cause for all the world's woes. The fallacy goes something like this:

- Delta is a purple, middle-aged, Talitounian.
- Delta recently made a disparaging comment about the green-skinned race of Manua and has a perceived history of bending the truth.
- Therefore, it is safe to conclude that all purple, middle-aged, Talitounians are racist and liars.

Most of us know at least one purple, middle-aged Talitounian. Rho, the Talitounian that we know isn't anything like the horrible person depicted in the storm of meme-contagious thought infection we see and hear. Apart from some physical characteristics, Rho is respectful, thoughtful, and caring. From this, we know with certainty that not all purple, middle-aged Talitounians—or otherwise—are evil incarnate. Among the catalogue of consequences that comes from faulty thinking regarding people, one outcome that ranks right at the top is the impact defective thoughts have on a sense of belonging. Intuitively, we know that we belong. Somewhere, we belong. Whether we are firmly ensconced in a belonged identity or on a journey to find it, how we identify our self has a direct influence on our creative expression.

Reach out beyond the boundaries of conventional thinking, and you will find that creativity is not confined to a traditional interpretation of the arts. More than art. More than dance. More than music. Creativity is demonstrated by original thought and novelty. Original thought doesn't mean that nobody else has considered that thought. What it does mean is that your thought is unique and authentic of you. Among a broad range of experts and researchers, the definition of creativity adopts specific characteristics of the definition's source. Besides originality and novelty, another associated quality defining creativity is value. What is its worth to you? To others? Where do you place value on the process of creativity and the created?

Creativity doesn't require a canvas for expression. Where creativity resonates in your being is in the frequency of your identity. The creative is the canvas. What you create, regardless of the format, will also attract others to associate you by that expression of your creativity. A creative will influence others in more ways than you can imagine as one person's creativity can have a profound cascading impact on countless people. Measuring the scope of a viral creative action is to map a new strain of the common cold. You can see where it has been, but you can't count every person that it affects. The organic nature of creativity leaves a trace of its existence with those caught by or identify with that creative expression. With the creation nestled in your psyche, it will contribute another facet to who you are.

Smart Cities, Robotics, AI, and Eternity

We have traversed the span of human history within a few short pages. From Archie, our cave-dwelling ancestor who scratched out an existence to stay alive, to seeking a sense of belonging in a globalised world nearing a population of nine billion. Upwards of 68% per cent of the world's population will live in urban areas by 2050. Increased advances in technology attract workers to urban areas for a variety of reasons. Many migrants are drawn by conditions identified in earlier observations of this chapter, such as safety and security. The demand for creative solutions, adaptability and the will to commit are three expectations for our success. We know the answers. To achieve genuine and sustainable success, we must apply our collective creative potential to the problems we face. Creativity must be the primer for change.

The necessity to innovate comes with the concentration of people to an area. Urban infrastructures built on past foundations, as innovative as they were at the time, were not designed for the capacity of people they are experiencing. Alerted by population growth projections, and the need to secure improved positioning for trade in global markets, entire new cities are being created. These new cities are beacons of technological advancement, and models of smart city innovation. Technology can satisfy the foundational needs of its inhabitants and ensure people living in advanced urban areas thrive in relative harmony. At least that is what technology is purposed to achieve. In that kind of environment, citizens can contribute to the underlying goals of society. By doing so, the inhabitants can spend more time and energy devoted to creative thought, innovation, and value creation. As technology shifts the balance of people to the city, technology applied in the agricultural and natural resource sectors stimulate further migration to cities. An increase of city dwellers can also trigger a reduction of employment options. Could it be that innovation is both a problem and the solution?

Advances in robotics and artificial intelligence bring improved efficiency in natural resource management. Where there is a genuine collaboration among stakeholders and a will to find holistic solutions to challenges, the outcomes can lead to harmony between technology and people. The vast majority of technology is designed with the intent to improve lives. To keep us from being pulled into a debate regarding conflicts of morality, even if just momentarily, let's adopt a position that the overall intent of technology is to improve lives. In our external world, robotics should produce more efficiently, mitigate safety issues, and serve the masses.

As for our private life, robotics will enhance our leisure experiences, eliminate the mundane chores of daily duties, and perhaps augment our cure for loneliness.

We've been living with robotics as part of society, directly and indirectly, since it was introduced to manufacturing in 1962 with UNIMATE. Regardless of what some people will tell you, you can't stop progress. Along with robotics, in a somewhat symbiotic way, a robot requires a brain. Decision-making processes for the simplest robots equate to binary choices of yes-no or on-off. For manufacturing, this approach to binary decision-making speeds processes and reduces waste. Increased profitability is the result. We are not too far away when robots will have an enlarged presence in our daily life. It will happen. For now, robotic devices mostly operate quietly in the background. They keep us safe and perform countless functions out of sight. Pioneers and innovators of technology want to take that to another level.

Enter artificial intelligence or AI. By introducing artificial intelligence, robotics and the broadest imaginable spectrum of software application move from binary yes-no computations, to new levels of complexity. The concept of AI is the philosophical backbone of the Internet of Things (IoT), where the interconnectivity of technology and humans interact in tandem. Conspiracists, Luddites, techno-timids, and the wary may view the integration of AI as intrusive and a sign of the end of humanity. Technological advances only seem to affirm their predisposition that we are subjects of Big Brother. Again, we are going to take a leap here and assume a posture that AI is designed to improve our life.

Why? Why is all this technology created to enhance our experience? Can't we freeze time and remain in a state of a simple lifestyle akin to rustic communal living? Well, yes, you can. There are communities to join or create, that fit that exact ticket. Thankfully, there always will be—or at least we can hope there will be. Society needs to keep one foot squarely planted in close relation with the Earth. We must cultivate our symbiotic relationship, even if it is by just a relative handful of guardians. Hand in hand with that guardianship comes the responsibility to manage urban populations. For that task, technology is vital.

An objective of technology-assisted improved lives, or at least from a perspective of social engineering, is to facilitate people to develop to their highest potential. Everything from gene splicing to smart refrigerators has the purpose of freeing the resources of your mind. Germinating in that pool of your brain are collective thoughts, ideas, images, and experiences that may lead to alternative solutions for a problem or inspire a new creation. Technology, at its finest, should be in servitude to the user, not the user to the technology.

Meandering on this seemingly non-signposted path of thought, you may be wondering how I plan to make a connection between technology, belonging, and creativity. I've been nudging you in a direction by building up what may feel like disconnected topics. Technology is vital in this discussion because technology serves to preserve our existence. Whether that technology directly extends our life by health and medical advancements or as bytes of information lingering in cyberspace, the use of technology establishes a footnote in history that we were here. One way or another, we want to live forever.

Within the context of meaningfulness, your esteem is energised by your experience to leave a mark. Perhaps I am oversimplifying, but it may be best to speak plainly. Your self-worth or esteem is the value that you ascribe to your existence. The resulting demonstrations of creativity are inseparably linked to your self-perception. You create. In one way or another, you do create. I've had conversations with brilliant people that tell me they are not creative. Somewhere in the shades of their experience, they associated creativity within a narrow band of understanding that creativity is something that others do, but not them. Logic, reason, obligation, cultural and traditional boundaries can block an individual from demonstrating creativity in ways that satisfy their person.

Alternatively, another person, that demonstrates brilliance in the form of art may be engaged in a tumultuous battle of the mind. In that struggle, a tug of war of self-perception highs and lows may produce incredible works across multiple platforms of creative expression. History is replete with stories of people that struggle with their esteem but produce legendary work that inspires generations. Icons of art leave traces of their brilliance while their stories may be marked with tragedy. We idolise artistic remnants of genius, while at the same time, diminishing our value of creativity in the day-to-day. Creators viewed from under a cloak of idolisation, take on a mystical nature of divine favour attributed to an elect. Everybody else is just ordinary. Or so that thinking might lead you to believe.

For all its faults and failures, its use and misuse, technology improves lives. Yes, I repeated it. We use technology to make our lives better. That, in turn, makes us or should make us feel good about our self. We see evidence of the creative use of technology from those living in the abysmal conditions of waste shanties to think tank incubators calculating missions to Mars. Whereas people in developed areas may benefit from a glut of readily available and affordable new technologies, people in underdeveloped regions are forced to innovate. If only to satisfy the necessities for survival. The former group must be vigilant regarding a tendency for complacency in their pursuit of the creative. The latter group must innovate to stay alive.

What the Universal Mind Said

If you were to comment on what you consider the top issues facing humanity, what would make the top of your list? Let's set some parameters on your list. Firstly, the problem must have the potential to affect a significant portion of the global population. Looking beyond yourself nullifies the superficiality of what may be a big deal to you, but trivial in the grand scheme of broader challenges. Additionally, the issue must also have some basis in known or existing conditions. You can't include things on your list like concern for a global invasion by a hostile alien race or the Earth's destruction to make room for an intergalactic highway. Except for those two parameters, your list can include any issue facing humanity.

A once-over browse of a newsfeed should give you plenty to consider. You may even use a feed aggregator that delivers to your various devices the latest trends and developments on topics of your interest. Headlines, subject lines, or images pop up on your preferred device or Internet site announcing a 3-second flash of information to capture your attention. Even if not personalised as suggested, you will be inundated with information that is important to somebody. They will have paid for the opportunity to influence you and invade your thoughts. Influence arrives packaged in many guises to alter your thinking.

In the culmination of the final episode of *Blue Planet II*, Sir David Attenborough concluded with some alarming assertions regarding our global stewardship. The appeal to reason relating to the shocking impact of plastics in the ocean affected my thinking regarding my role as a consumer. I am much more aware, and my purchasing practises have changed. I won't say dramatically, because manufacturers make it almost impossible to eliminate the use of disposable plastics. I am, however, more actively engaged in how I spend my money concerning plastic consumption. Using my one-person buying power, I am determined to stop purchasing products packaged in non-recyclable plastic. I might only achieve reduced use. I am committed to recycling nonetheless. Anything recyclable that I use will make it into an appropriate recycling process. Religiously. I am concerned for the planet and the impact our choices have on others in that invisible-until-it-manifests cause-and-effect trail. How deep a commitment I will gain is probably growing in a matter of degrees.

For me to answer the question I posed to you, I'd have to attribute those concerns like plastic to a category I'd consider symptomatic of broader issues. Those challenges are complex and resist being categorised as solutions with a series of binary decisions. That is why my concerns tend to take on philosophical overtones. I can reduce my list of worries to three issues: The status of individuality, the perception of free will, and the external influences imposed on society to control free thought. You can barely broach the offspring of these subjects without the conversation escalating into a lively socio-political debate. Where it is possible to exchange ideas on these subjects, genuine change can occur. From an outsider listening in on the discussion, there seems to be more rhetoric than collaboration, more talk and less action. The three issues that concern me do so because they comprise the battleground of creative thought. Without applied critical thinking and creativity, legitimate change cannot be sustained.

My paths in the creative process took me across various domains before a chord struck. When that happened, my learning and experiences began to coalesce. Instead of observing life experiences as isolated instances, I started to make associations between those experiences and from them derive a sense of meaning. Creativity is the common thread that continues to weave its way through our experience. If I say to you that we adopt a survivalist mode when things are tough, you'd probably agree. You just get on. Find a solution. Move forward. You applied creativity and arrived at a conclusion. Whether in the high or low points of esteem, creative thought was present at every transition.

When I began to research creativity, it became apparent that creativity is a universal trait of cognisant humanity. I suggest cognisant humanity because there must be a spark of self-awareness for creativity to flourish. My interest in creativity leapt forward during my business administration graduate studies. The influence of creativity in business is the pulse of organisational health. One may argue that their company is not favourable toward creativity or innovation. Truth be told, creativity in business is demonstrated top to bottom, side to side. A better way to view the creative grit of an organisation may be through the internal process that fans the flames of innovation and empowers staff. A volatile business environment demands the ongoing and renewed application of creativity for survival. A stagnant environment demands the same attention.

The personalisation of my creativity research came when I read Dan Pink's book, *A Whole New Mind* (2006). Pink's observations resonated with me and triggered a stream of adaptive thinking. It felt like he was in my head, writing what I was thinking. I wanted, no, needed to act on what percolated inside. Somewhere along the line, my pursuit came to a satisfying intersection where my X qualities (dreamer) met my Y qualities (pragmatist). At that intersection, I discovered an invigorated urgency to be creative. More so, I opened untapped traits of my personality that previously laid unattended, ignored, or neglected. What may have seemed an epiphany was the culmination of a lifetime of insights and observations that reached a point of saturation. Research on brain processes, and investing in philosophical reflection, churned out a regular feast of logical argument for me to devour. Every direction I explored returned the same conclusion: at the core of humanity is a need to create. Instead of offering up answers to an endless supply of issues and problems, my objective evolved to provoke creatives to think and stimulate their awareness. Shake up existing notions. Introduce enough thought disruption to elevate creativity. Wonder. Explore.

On the journey to this point in life, I contemplated the concept of universal consciousness—or the universal mind. A simplified definition of universal consciousness could be that we don't have original thoughts. The line of thinking might continue that we share the thoughts and consciousness of the past alongside all other sentient beings. We may package our thoughts in different words, phrases, and languages—including languages of creative expression—but there is continuity of thinking among every human being. From my orientation, that proposition will evoke a collision of values. My mission includes advocating individuality, the perception of free will, and resisting those that attempt to control the two. Differences don't necessarily need to divide. They should expose unexplored pathways to new thinking. The efficient working out of disagreements demands a robust and vibrant creative process.

I am unique. You are unique. Sure, we have autonomic responses. Thankfully they keep us alive and safe. We are also conditioned to respond to conditions based on our experience. We create because we engage in that process by choice. Recently I read an article citing a study claiming everything we do is a delayed reaction predetermined by our brain. An action, measured with the latest in neuroscientific technology, can be traced to a specific neural path. Materialist thinkers are content to accept that the origin of a thought is a reaction of the brain to stimuli. My experience affirms for me otherwise. When I am in a state of flow, creativity is a series of choices culled from a singular perspective that I call "me." That journey feels like meandering at times, but I don't mind a touch of the nomadic, especially if it leads me to an oasis of personal evolutionary thought.

2

Same, but Different
(Wiring of a Creative Brain)

On 10 November 1969, the children's educational television programme Sesame Street premiered on the Public Broadcasting System (PBS) in America. The programme quickly reached the hearts and minds of millions with its positive message of pre-school learning for inner-city children. The Sesame Street setting of an urban neighbourhood represented a cross-section of cultural diversity with its cast members and muppets. Commercial-style educational spots and neighbourhood dialogue aided comprehension, retention, and relational values. I enjoyed watching episodes and repeated clips with my kids when they were young. It was fun. I still find myself humming a Sesame Street song now and then.

Among the scores of catchy jingles cleverly designed to teach, one of my children's' favourites was the *One of These Things is Not like the Other* song. A programme cast member—Bob, Maria, Big Bird, whomever—would sing the song while comparing everyday objects. Each lesson lasted less than two minutes. The song narrator set up the objective as a play activity. Feeling involved in the learning process with play, pre-school children learned to count, perform their alphabet, read words, and gain scores of other useful lessons. Not surprisingly, children around the country experienced positive affirmation from the programming. Affirmation is a necessary part of healthy development in a child's formative years.

Going back to children learning with Bob and the *One of These Things* song, while certain aspects of an object might be similar, contrasts enable us to differentiate. The act of distinguishing is essential to the creative process. The nuance between one shade to another or the depth of a margin on a written page may seem trivial to a casual observer. In the eyes of the creator, behind the shade and margin selection, difference takes on distinction. While the intent may have become rote in its implementation, the continuity of that expression remains a core characteristic of the creator's design. Evidence of this phenomena is visible in every aspect of life. Marketers depend on a smidgen of similar with a dash of different when delivering a successful combination for attracting customers. The flavour of their version of similar infuses a subtle familiarity for the observer while at the same time sprinkling enough spice to prompt us to say, "Oh, I'd like to try that." Options. We do like our power of choice even when the differences may be indistinguishable beyond the label.

Consider bottled water. The atmospheric, or perhaps earthmoving, increase of bottled water sales since the craze began will reach global sales estimates exceeding £200 billion in 2020. A website dedicated to fine drinking water lists over 4,000 brands of bottled water. Although the staff of finewaters.com probably work hard to list new brands, companies, and countries of origin, I suspect that many more bottled water brands are [1]entering the market every year than can be catalogued. Each new entrant expects to snag a slice of the market and build a brand. How they will go about that strategy is much the same way Perrier changed the way we considered bottled water from 1977 onward. Make a product look different, make it sound good, make it look refreshing, give it a hip style with an innovative, environmentally friendly packaging twist. Tell us about the magical qualities of the source, spin a tale of ancient traditions, and distribute. Your first step is to distribute your product exclusively and in trendy restaurants. Bam! You have it. Inside that bottle, the product is the same. You have the simple chemical formula of H_2O—otherwise known as water.

We are equipped with a language to communicate. So it should not be much of a surprise that our goto tool for thinking is that labeller of all things—our vocabulary. While a useful tool, it can also get in the way of creativity. Let's do a Nudge activity to throw a spanner in the language machine. In a few sentences, I will ask you to look around where you. I'd like you to either select an object or take an informal inventory of your surroundings. It doesn't matter if the subject of your attention is a manufactured object or something of nature. Do your absolute best not to label the object with any words. None. Nada. Instead, allow

---

[1] As a point of awareness, we consume over a million bottles of water a minute worldwide. Of course, that produces billions of plastic bottles of waste. Consumers in the United Kingdom use 13 billion plastic bottles a year. Of that total, only 58% of the bottles are recycled. If the world's demand for plastic bottles goes unchallenged, the estimated use of plastic bottles will increase to 318 million tonnes by 2050.

your attention to focus on how that subject makes you feel. What emotions does it evoke? Does it activate a memory? Where will your mind wander?

If you have a means of setting a timer, set it for three minutes. At my writing desk, I can ask my digital assistant to set the timer, and she will notify me when the set time lapses. We work well together, although sadly, I think she doesn't always understand what I ask. The object of my attention for this activity is a 12-input, 2-bus mixer with mic preamps, compressors, and USB/audio interface. I purchased the mixer in readiness for podcasting. My brother, a sound engineer, manages massive soundboards in his profession. My other brother is a guitarist in a band and comfortable around a mixer. Me? That flat box with sixty knobs is a mystery to be unravelled. If my brothers did this activity, they'd see that soundboard much differently. My sound engineer brother has hundreds of memories of mixing for various bands and venues. My professional musician brother may be reminded of how he arrived at the place where he took a risk to play professionally and hasn't looked back.

Give it a shot. Look around, select an object and allow yourself to be in a state of awareness. No labels. No descriptive words. Be strict with this. Don't let words crowd in. After about a minute or so, you will have hopefully cleared the clutter. Okay, do it.

If you took that small break and did the activity, you will have travelled through numerous thought processes. By not labelling objects we see, colours, contours, and all the other visual and auditory stimuli that crank our categorisation machine. Because it is such a personal activity, there is not a single person in the world that can duplicate what you just experienced. Their personal experience, vocabulary, interpretation of textures, colours, hardness, and softness is different than yours. We see things differently.

We begin the development of differentiation when we enter the world. It is what makes us unique. We share similarities in general physiology, and even our brains move us through the day with the same functionality. By force of will and demand, we adapt to compensate for exceptions. When we embrace that our differences make us who we are, we become far better equipped to succeed in a world of diversity.

Successful Networking

You may be one of those types of people that have their whole life lined out, organised, and ready to execute the next stage with absolute precision. I admire that you can do that. I am not geared that way. I stumbled through chunks of life, looking for answers to what makes me tick. Which career path was I best suited?

Should I go it alone? Do I partner with somebody? Where should I live? How do I achieve any of my loftier goals? Oh my word, the combination of life question issues is constant. To further complicate the engagement of the Q&A dilemmas of life, we are moving forward at light speed in terms of technology, communication, and accessibility. Instead of the old-fashioned approach of familial advice, we seek answers from people and sources that don't even know us. A kind of one-size-fits-all solution to living. Good ideas, fads, and trends are as easy to come by as is the next hashtag cycle.

Along the way, we will encounter a range of demands and expectations for conformity. Whether by society, culture, family, work, peers, or our interpretation of an ideal state of being, the pressure to conform is relentless. Strangely, in a world where diversity is promoted regularly, we should be able to contribute the better parts of ourselves, our differences, with purpose. Except for the persistent and risk-takers that resist the confines of conventionality, entry barriers for using our differences to contribute meaningful change are broad and high. Popular media and historical recollections of pioneers, discoverers, inventors, and leaders elevated to the rank of legend uphold that perception.

Being the audience for these celebrities of success, we apply anecdotal formulas to their story in an attempt to recreate their experiences to design our personal version of success. When all the while, the most straightforward part of the equation is overlooked. Be different. Be yourself. More, than less, of these men and women of renown earned their reputation because they chose a path of non-conformity. Sure, there are countless situations where conformity is needed. But then, I suppose, that is why robotics is such a growing industry. Code and go. Production tolerances are met with negligible failures, waste is manageable, and reject rates are virtually eliminated. The human element is neutralised. People are people. Even when full conformity is demanded, even in the worse possible totalitarian state, people will find ways to resist.

I can point to a specific period in my life when my resistance to conformity reached its peak. It wasn't a single event, but a culmination of events. That is the stealth of being nudged. Little promptings come and go mostly unnoticed. Enough of those prompts build up to critical mass, and a synergy is created. That enlivened synergy penetrates your intuition with a sense of the familiar. When enough of the familiar is present, fear gets out of the driver's seat of reaction and intuition steps into the centre of the action. Some degree of risk is predictable. Sometimes a risk is non-committal such as allowing a new thought to take up residence in your thinking. If you can keep that noisy backseat driver Fear quiet, you will do just fine.

What does this have to do with networking? More importantly, what does it have to do with being nudged, the creative process, and bearing similarities but being different? Let's look at this from two angles as a comparison: One from the brain functionality and the other from the viewpoint of business networking.

We are best able to exercise our creativity when we provide a foundation of continuity for our brain. Think of the neural pathways of your brain as a superhighway with no speed limits. In one direction of that superhighway is an eight-lane path cleared of traffic. The reason your mind is clear is that you've practised for hours. You could drive the road in your sleep. We will call that state of mind, flow. Travelling at light speed in the state of flow, you don't want to stop, slow down, or divert your attention. Since you don't have to think about functionality, your mind is free to take in the extraneous stimuli that would be otherwise hidden from view. You are free to take risks without fear of crashing. Familiarity and associations allow you to draw from whatever medium you use to explore.

Business networking, or any other people-related interaction, uses the same principles. However, the conditions are more challenging because variability is a certainty. Start with a foundation and establish the familiar to make the most of your interaction. Universal qualities that fit in every situation include values like respect, cultural sensitivity, honesty, appreciation, and the ever-needful genuine smile. The variable of cultural sensitivity is the trickiest one of that lot to navigate. However, increased awareness and open-mindedness can smooth the clunkiest situation.

When business networking found its great awakening in the 1980s, libraries of networking how-to books were written on the subject. A long list of people found their training and business niche, promoting various methods of creating quality business connections. Others have become wealthy using a range of tools from a networking success toolbox. A majority of the tools applied are simple observations and manipulation of social behaviours. Mirroring, attentiveness, active listening, and scores of other skills are promoted as keys to personal networking success. The skills are easy to implement because they are quite natural. The crucial elements of networking are that the act is social, and people tend to connect with people they trust.

Successful, long-term networking involves being genuine. By creating an open environment, you allow the other person to feel safe. As you travel down a creative pathway in the networking scenario, your mind can be unencumbered by the mental jockeying of how you are going to cinch a contract or close a deal. The exhilarating interaction of people travelling the creative superhighway enables those participating to explore possibilities that may otherwise remain uncharted.

Inside Homer's Brain

Perhaps, the dimmest person in pop media is none-other-than Homer Simpson. The number of stupid things that Homer has said and done will feed the gif and meme-making industry for years. Homer's brain has been depicted as a clacking wind-up monkey, a dancing cow, a My Little Pony, a nut-sized brain banging around in an otherwise void space of a skull, a cross-sectional display that shows regions for sleep, doughnuts, do's/dont's, beer, TV, and sex. The on-going battle with his brain can be summed up in an exchange before an exam when Homer says "All right brain, you don't like me, and I don't like you. But let's get through this, and I can get back to killing you with beer." Woe to humanity if Homer was unleashed on the public to run for office, manage nuclear power, or for a town to be dependent on his ability to find solutions when pressed between a rock and a hard place.

Fortunately, Homer and his legendary brain is a satirically conceived fictional character. Your brain is a marvel of resilience, adaptability, and operational wonder. Racing from one place to another or conducting repetitious actions may feel like you are a hamster on a treadmill, but that cannot be further from the truth. There may be times when all you can think of is that doughnut. "Shutting down" for a bit to watch television might be your tuning out solution for a day's hard work. You may very well identify yourself with Homer on some merits. Even if you surrender to your basest feeling, you are still managed by that complex organ between your ears.

We happen to live in an exciting time regarding brain science. The field of neuroscience and its various branches churn out discoveries with regularity. Like a global neural network that spans history, neuroscience builds on existing data by connecting relevant information to uncover and understand how the brain works. With each linking dendrite, scientists unlock useful data that contribute to our collective wellbeing. Health, mental health, performance, longevity, behaviour, and technology are each beneficiaries of the spillover from neural science's discoveries. Our neural processes work so well that scientists and innovators strive to mimic the human mind in the form of artificial intelligence.

Although the past several years have seen a significant increase in AI breakthroughs, we have yet to replicate precise functions of the brain. Many functions are standalone applications like those of the autonomic nervous system. Robots and AI feature coding and machinations acting out logical steps of cause-

and-effect or condition-and-reaction, dazzle us when reports are released, and videos go viral. We may not have reached the goal of replicating the brain, but we have achieved an understanding of how it functions and even mapped thought processes.

To be nudged, you don't need to know the intricacies of the human brain. We could go down that route, but for our purposes, it would be a rabbit hole that we may never find a way out. In that Wonderland, we would meet strangely named characters like Lingual Gyrus, Cingulate Cortex, and Pars Opercularis. We would travel through Pons, Neural Pathways, and be accelerated on our way by neurotransmitters. The wonders we'd experience are marvels of an ever-expanding universe.

All the aspects of how the brain works are fascinating. If not for other demands in life, I would dedicate my days to its study. Admittedly, most of the physiological details of neuroscience are over my head. Mainly because of the extensive associated vocabulary. I am not sure I need that much detail to achieve a meaningful knowledgebase. When you get into your car and drive, you don't think about your automobile's engine compression rate or whether it even has a compression rate. You get in, buckle up, turn the key, and go. If your auto gets you safely from point A to point B, that is what matters. We tend to think of our brain and body similarly. Wake up, feed the machine, dress the chassis, and go. We run all day, spend our fuel, and go to sleep.

To appreciate the processes involved in the Nudge Principle, we will find it helpful to have a basic understanding of what happens in the brain. At a basic level, a neurone is a brain cell that transmits information. Some stimulus will activate a neurone which, in effect, sends that data to another part of the brain for interpretation and action. The pathway that carries that signal along an axon from one point to another is called the neural pathway. An axon is a nerve fibre that sends electrical impulses away from a neurone to an electrified anchor called a synapse. When an impulse reaches a synapse, it releases neurotransmitters—chemicals encoded for a variety of actions. I am leaving out a lot of details and may incur the wrath of Hippocrates' Ghost with this summary. What I want to convey is how the brain works by electrical impulses that trigger actions, and responses from different parts of the brain. The more frequently that a pathway is reinforced by repetition, the faster signals can travel from point to point, or from stimulus to action.

The Human Connectome Project created a computer model of human brain connectivity to illustrate that process. The relationship viewer on their website demonstrates relationships between a source entry to a probable response lobule.

(Please prepare yourself for some physiology terms as there is hardly a way around it.) If, for instance, I select the left lingual gyrus as a starting point of the model, I discover that the most frequent connection is to the right lingual gyrus. Vision, symbols, logical order, and encoding visual memories are associated with the lingual gyrus. Equally balanced, there are connections to the lateral occipital cortex (object recognition), superior parietal cortex (spatial orientation), and pericalcarine cortex (sight). To a lesser degree, there is a connection to the right rostral middle frontal cortex (attention), and the left fusiform cortex (facial recognition). In a sentence, when you take in a visual stimulus that includes a symbol like letters and you connect those letters to a face, you have the components for a person and name. All that happens without your awareness.

On a recent trip to a Croatia, I was astonished by several people I met in the hospitality industry. Due to its incredible beauty, weather, range of activities, culture and history, Croatia draws visitors from around the world. During our stay, we overheard Croat, English, German, French, Dutch, Italian, Chinese, and several other languages I was unable to identify. On our departure, my wife and I travelled to the airport with a German couple that didn't speak English. We don't speak German. Our driver, Neno, talked to us in fluent English, answered handsfree calls in Croatian, and engaged the couple from Germany in flawless German. He repeatedly did so in the span of a few minutes. Within the industry he works, Neno is regularly exposed to multiple languages. By frequency of use, his mind switches from one language to another with ease. His neural pathways for communicating in various languages have built such robust connections, that he can seamlessly switch conversation between multiple languages.

Learning a new language is one of many neural pathway building activities a person can do to strengthen brain pliability and increase performance. Whereas I'd have to rely on an unrealistic dedication on support tools for vocabulary training, immersion brings an entirely different set of conditions to reinforce success with the language.

Priming the Pump

Activities for burning in a neural pathway are limitless. Practise, practise, practise. That is the formula. Any skill repeated enough times will lead to a state of increased proficiency. For years, I've heard or read a proposition that perpetuates a meme-state across multiple platforms of self-improvement. The proposal is the claim that a person can achieve musical phenomenon status if she practises upwards of 10,000 hours. The assertion is referred to in self-help circles as the *10,000-hour rule*. Holding to that rule is an arduous, long journey demanding extreme commitment. The source of the claim is neurologist and author David Levitin. The nugget from *This is Your Brain on Music* is that 'learning requires assimilation and consolidation of information in neural tissue. The more experiences we have with something, the stronger the memory/learning trace for that experience becomes.'

Besides music, art, and athletics, what else can you think of that might require notable expertise and benefit from 10,000 hours of practise? At the top of my list, I'd include doctors, pilots, and any other person that accepts the responsibility for another person's life. Considering a hard-line 10,000-hour rule, these experts must deliver 100% accuracy well before they reach 10,000 hours. How can they ever achieve 10,000 hours, except by applying the learned principles in other areas or in augmented environments? Perhaps where the consequence of a mistake isn't as critical as life and death?

A field of entertainment that has always baffled and astounded me is magic. As an audience member, I know I am being tricked. People can't really step through a paper-covered glass window or emerge unscathed from a razor-sharp sword riddled box. Can they? To develop their tricks or stunts, a magician must practise the art of misdirection to perfection. Ask a practitioner of magic how long it takes to master a trick, and you will get various answers. Most responses will be vague or diversionary. After all, magic is their livelihood. The craft of magic is a combination of understanding how the human brain interprets what it sees and hears based on known conventions, timing, and distraction. In just about every magic scenario, how the trick is performed is visible to your brain through tell-tale signals. Even if you consciously miss the move, it was there.

This principle is well portrayed in the 2006 film, *The Prestige*. Magician mentor and set designer John Cutter, played by Michael Caine, describes the three stages of a magic trick. First up is the pledge. That is that part of the trick when the magician affirms a commitment that everything is normal. At that moment, it feels like the laws of nature remain in motion. The second stage is called the turn when the magician turns that I'm-grounded-in-reality moment and transforms the ordinary into something you didn't expect. Then, as Cutter explains, there is a third part—the prestige. That is when the magician returns the transformed back to being ordinary. But the ordinary is no longer ordinary. During those moments of being suspended in a state of mesmerisation, the ordinary became part of something that your mind will forever view as extraordinary. "Wow, how did she do that?"

The ability to ask the question, to question reality, to challenge what you see, is due to your brain's plasticity. Neuroplasticity is that function of the brain dedicated to processing new information or in the case of brain injury, relearning to compensate for a physical loss. In early childhood development, an infant's brain has significantly less neural connections than an adult. The reason for that is that an infant doesn't have the experience or symbol associations for communication. At birth, an infant has about 2,500 synapses to the neural network of her cerebral cortex. The magic of cognition accelerates as the child begins to identify features of the ordinary. A mother's face, a favourite toy, and the comfort of a special blanket all become part of her sensory vocabulary.

Paralleling that learning development, she begins to make associations. Mother, father, sister, brother. Who is associated with a toy? What does it feel like to be covered with the special blanket? Lights out and sleep time? Neural connections spark, grow, connect, and form associations. By the age of two or three, the number of synapses per neurone will skyrocket to about 15,000. If a human brain has an estimated 100 billion neurones, we can make some estimations. If you multiply an estimated number of synapses to the number of neurones, we can conclude that the two-year-old has roughly a quadrillion synapses. Imagine if the processes of cognition were manual. Compare and contrast new sensory stimuli against an internal coding of language for each related synapsis. Just the thought of the suggestion might make a person want to take a nap.

Objects, words, and senses categorised, labelled, and reinforced on a tested neural pathway protected with a myelin sheath, and our 2-year-old is well on her way to developing her thinking processes. If it stopped there, she could live in childlike wonder forever. The suggestion makes me contemplate the implications of becoming 'like a child to enter the kingdom of heaven.' But the journey of development doesn't end there. Along the road to adulthood, something called synaptic pruning occurs. It seems that those synaptic connections are like the old oaks in a forest blocking light to the forest floor. The canopy of their influence makes those smaller, less used synapses obsolete. By the time our infant girl-grown adult reaches adulthood, the number of synapses will reduce to about half at around 7,000 synapses per neuron.

You can't lay down and give up because you reached the borderlands of adulthood. Singing by the rivers of Babylon that you only have 7,000 synapses to each of your 100 billion neurones does not signal the end of the world. On the contrary. Remember that feature of your noggin called brain neuroplasticity? That is the capacity of the brain to change physically by learning new things. Have you experienced the rush of learning something new that took an effort to secure? A sense of euphoria you may feel when you tackle a challenge is the result of physical adaptations, new connections, and the root of sustainable change in your thought processes.

Learning something new is possible at any age. That tired old saying that "you can't teach an old dog new tricks" relates to, well, dogs. People, on the other hand, can learn at any age. The challenge is to redirect those connections in the brain that resist change and modify static-oriented language (like "I can't"), toward possibilities. Any possibility. Anything new. The mere act of exploring nudges the door of possibility for you to peek through at the slightest jar. Once you see what is on the other side, the magic might carry you away to Wonderland.

10,000 Ugly Inkblots

Some of the best conversations I enjoy happen in the garden or at the front door with my neighbour. Either his or ours, it doesn't matter. The other day I told Harry, that's our neighbour, that I left my job to write this book. When asked what the book was about, I gave him a summary but peppered the conversation with words like create, creative, vision, and gotta-do-this-or-die kind of talk. To my delight, he opened up to me about his aspiration as a young man. Harry is 92 years old this year. He was telling me about how his family lived in London during World War II. Bombing raids on the city feel as fresh to him today as when the planes rumbled overhead eighty years ago. He also served two years active duty with the British Army in its post-war presence on the continent. After which, he came home, received a promised job, was let go after the obligatory six-month requirement, and then had to figure out what to do.

We didn't talk extensively about the conditions for veterans after the war, the economic hardship, or the political climate. I sensed from the undertone that it was a tough time for many, not least of all, Harry. Considering that he intimated being a bit aimless at the time, I asked: "What did you want to do?" To which our conversation took a colourful turn. "I wanted to be an artist," Harry exclaimed. He had always been good with drawing and found art to be rewarding. Post-war work as it was, and family not possibly appreciating the value of art, proved a formidable obstacle. Harry elected to follow the course of most young men and women searching for a means to live independently. He took a job. Harry went on to work diligently for decades until retirement. With about 25 years racked up in retirement, I asked if he still draws and paints. "A little here and there," he said. "But not much."

In speaking with people, reading stories, and research, I conclude, without exception, that everybody has a core element of the creative. Doesn't matter what form or medium it takes, everybody has an inner voice that seeks a means of creatively expressing itself. How many times have I heard "I am not very creative?" Making that statement is an easy thing to do when you fall into the trap of comparisons. We may be inspired by an artist, musician, author, or an extraordinary scientist. We cheapen our self-perception when we weigh the differences between self and others. Our version of self pales in significance to their brilliant star. Regardless of that negative inner voice, a creative urge beckons, calls, pleads with you to let it out.

A few years ago, while developing a workshop format for Nudge, I wrestled with some moral dilemmas surrounding the Nudge concept. In a public arena, what forms or expressions of creativity are acceptable? If it is not acceptable, why? How much prejudice do I carry in my baggage? Do I admire one style over another purely from a position of personal preference? Would I be okay if criminals used the Nudge Principle to find innovative ways of conducting business? Emotions, empathy, and feelings play a critical role in the Nudge processes. To ensure I reached a solid conclusion, the pragmatist in me had to battle with these questions. That battle lasted years. Gnawing at my mind and paralysing me off and on in its epic moral debate. Then I stepped into a solution that opened new horizons for me.

When it comes to art styles, my preference is the impressionist period with a few other artists' works included for flair. Specific genres of abstract art, however, left me puzzled with distaste. I also enjoy jazz music. Not all jazz. I do find some experimental jazz a bit hard on the ears. Discordant notes, fragmented structure, jarring instrumentalisation, and an absence of melody in experimental jazz left me reaching for headache tablets. Death metal? There is not enough time in the day to have a quality review of all genres of music. Instead, I'll start my journey of taste discovery with art. Appreciating abstract and conceptual art can be a stretch. But I learned to appreciate several degrees of abstract art. How did I make my turning point? I went page-by-page of the book *The 20th Century Art Book* and posted a sample of each artist on Pinterest. The range of styles stretched my appreciation levels and subsequent neural connections to new perspectives.

Pushing boundaries seems to be woven into the fabric of artists. Regardless of form, art has a long history of leading the revolution of thought against the Establishment. Whether subtle or loud, the revolution of creativity challenges conformity. Among the many artists that I admire is Jackson Pollock. On the first view of a Pollack piece, an observer will likely consider his work of smeared, splatted, and seemingly random paints covering a large canvas to be a mess. When you learn about the artist, you soon realise that every splotch, dash, stream, mix, or whatever medium applied to the canvas had a purpose. Pollock is attributed to have created a new art method called *action painting*. In hindsight, his radical departure of method changed the way we look at art today.

Three hundred years or so before Pollock, another painter with radical intent was creating in China. His name was Shitao. His work is famous for its departure from conventional styles of the dynasty. The piece by Shitao that caught my attention is called *10,000 Ugly Inkblots*. The painting has an allusion of an estate, but then the right panel transforms with a sense of depth that his hard to describe. Up close, standing back a bit, either way, the piece is alluring. Challenging the aesthetic norm of the day, Shitao introduced something different, yet maintained a form of the familiar.

Where we get hung up in our creativity is the interpretation that art, an innovative methodology, or a radical statement of societal change must have a monetary value. We hold to a definition of creativity that includes value as something tangible to be exchanged. Like my neighbour Harry, I wanted to be a graphic designer when I graduated high school. Living in the Greater Seattle area, I was confident about my opportunities, and there were abundant sources in the area for training. Why not go for it? Then, one well-placed seed of doubt from a person I respected was planted, and I followed the same course as Harry. I got a job. I consider myself fortunate. Over the years of dabbling in a variety of work, some of it included writing and graphics. Instead of thinking "what could have been" I learned to capitalise on the next opportunities I created. My risk-laden approach to life is well-fitted for my personality. I just had to adapt my thinking to accommodate different approaches to life challenges.

Make Room for New Thinking

Resting on the floor of the Gulf of Mexico at 30 02.555'N 87 00.397'W is the aircraft carrier USS Oriskany. Commissioned in 1950, she served through the Korean and Vietnam Wars. Decommissioned in 1976, she remained mothballed until 1995 when sold for scrap. The U.S. Navy reacquired her in 1997 due to lack of progress in the scrapping process. A new purpose for the proud ship was to make her into an artificial reef. To ensure toxic substances would not enter the ecosystem, the government conducted extensive environmental remediation. Readied for her final resting place, she was towed 22-miles south of Pensacola Florida and strategically scuttled on 17 May 2006 becoming the world's largest artificial reef.

The Oriskany Memorial Reef is one of the most popular diving locations in the United States and an international destination for divers. But the recreational value is secondary to the ship's reef status and its contribution to the Gulf's aquatic life. The nooks and crannies of the ship that nobody wanted are home to a significant population of sea creatures as the depths convert the gift into a natural habitat. At 200 feet below, the USS Oriskany is not a dive for beginners. Experienced divers are also cautioned not to venture into the interior of the ship. Exploring enclosed areas that change with time, may sound appealing to the adventurous diver, but a throw-caution-to-the-wind attitude at 200 feet below the waves can have dire consequences. There came a time when the Oriskany fulfilled her purpose. No longer a viable asset in the U.S. Navy's inventory, the ship became a liability. A costly icon of a closed chapter in its history. As it lingered in shipyards for three decades, the costs mounted. There is a price for inactivity, however nominal it may be.

We have a similar effect in our brain. Think of some skill you developed and used at an earlier point in your life. It could be anything. When you were actively using that skill, you probably did so like a well-disciplined crew of an aircraft carrier. Every action has a role in ensuring you accomplished your mission. After a few life events such as graduation, marriage, jobs, and disappointments, you stopped using that skill. Or, by some mysterious reason, it just faded away. Until one day, it was something that you "used to do." If you allow your active learning to slide into that state of inactivity, you mothball once active pathways. You can walk the decks of your mind reminiscing on the nostalgia surrounding that time, but it never feels the same. The rust and decay of non-use make you feel like you can never get "it" back.

Recalling the fact that your brain has plasticity should encourage you that you can indeed get "it" back. Perhaps your body can't quite do what you did when you were 15 years old, but there is no reason that you can't enjoy the benefits of new thinking. What stands in your way are the residual thought patterns that keep you thinking in a specific direction. Associations based on a rigid orientation of an old set of blueprints. Should you explore the interior of the Oriskany as a former crewmember, you will probably discover that nothing looks the same. Do I turn left at the crew's mess or right? Navigating that sunken ship requires sight for the way things are now, not fifty years ago. To see the way things are today, you'll need a new way of thinking, of seeing.

From a self-help or pop-psychology approach, there are libraries of data to select from to get started. I don't weigh in on other people's strategies to develop changes in thinking. I think there is plenty of room for differences. Where I will draw an invisible line is if a thinking strategy does not include an action as an outcome of the process. A seeker can listen to positive affirming podcasts, read books, go to seminars or conferences, and all sorts of other stimulating activities.

If an action does not reinforce a change of thinking, then the process is incomplete. Your brain retains new information and subsequently strengthens neural pathways when there is an affirming action involved. We can talk about building an artificial reef with all of the benefits and challenges therein. Until that old way of thinking is scuttled by an action, it remains a rust bucket taking up valuable space.

We've already discussed a few activities that may be a starting point. You can take up some form of artistic expression. Play a musical instrument. Expand your vocabulary or learn a language. The possibilities are endless. Diversify your learning as well. Introduce something that stretches your abilities and challenges your thinking. Alternatively, and is the Nudge Principle in its entirety, change the way that you do something. We tend to fall into a pattern of repetition in our day-to-day lives. I appreciate some people, and many perhaps, value that continuity. Let me encourage you that even the smallest deviations from the norm can open a pathway for change.

For the most part, we all have the same brain functionality. We need to be sensitive that the functionality of the brain can be affected by disease, injury, mental illness, and congenital brain disorders. Except for some notable conditions, the way that the brain operates is a universal feature of human physiology. When we receive stimuli, the brain initiates a similar chain of actions, that unless there are reasons for short circuits, is the same as that person seated nearby. We are indeed the same in that regard. As we mature, our circuitry can become ensconced in a pattern of repetition that feels like a perpetual loop. The solution for escaping that cycle is purposeful creative actions.

Creativity is a highly individualistic action. Personality traits, while somewhat inherited, will influence your perspective of creativity or whether it is a valid pursuit. Your thinking processes play a lead role in the play of life. Regardless of your personality, you are creative. Irrespective of the way you think, you are creative. Even if you disagree with these statements, it doesn't change the fact that you are creative. Your brain is in a 24/7 mode of receiving stimuli, processing it, making connections, and delivering something back to you. So why not be a partner in the process and make the most of the condition? Intentional creativity is the solution to fulfilment in life.

3

Converting Your Creative Capital

Where is Salvator Mundi? A renaissance-era clad Jesus Christ created by Leonardo da Vinci is one of around twenty paintings by the master to survive the centuries. Shrouded in a veil of overpainting and moved around between private collections, owners through the centuries were unaware of the treasure hidden behind the layers of paint. Then in 2006, after compelling evidence was presented to the then-present owner, a restoration project began. Imagine the delight of the workers when a renaissance blue hue was exposed in the underlying painting. More so, the thrill of watching the hidden form take shape from infrared photography. I suspect the excitement had the same suspense and reaction as the NASA/JPL mission staff landing the InSight probe on Mars. (Google it.)

Purchased at a Christie's auction in 2017 for a record £355.5 million, destined for the Louvre Abu Dhabi, the Salvator Mundi painting disappeared without a trace. While the mystery of Salvator Mundi is captivating, I am more fascinated by the money exchanged for the art. In 1958, because it was so damaged by overpainting, the unrestored masterpiece sold for a mere £1,000 in today's currency. Allowing my mind to wander to another time, I wondered what that painting sold for in the sixteenth century when Leonardo may have sold it to a collector. Mona Lisa was sold to King Francis I of France for what translates in today's market at around £1 million. Could Da Vinci fathom that somebody five hundred years in the future would pay such an astronomical price for his work? I mean, really. Christie's sale of £355.5 million would equate to something like £236 billion in the time of Leonardo. That is a lot of money in any century.

Working as the director of business development for a keenly entrepreneurial guy named Michael in the early 2000's, I learned a phrase that altered my way of looking at value. "Value is what somebody is willing to pay for a product or service," I recall hearing from Michael. I was also attending university mid-life while I worked this full-time job. My coursework was that of graduate-level business administration. Between the university courses and real-life experience, I learned pricing, cost, statistics, and other fine-tuning aspects for a competitive business edge. Our primary business was repairing obsolete and vanishing vendor electronic equipment. Michael and I worked together to submit proposals for government contracts. Where qualified to do so, we'd secure site work that promised a specific profit margin. If we were going to bid on a project, we had to find a means to make it happen and do so by ensuring value for our client. Value was measured by the contribution of the parts to the whole, regardless of whether we were insanely busy or during slow times.

How much is Salvator Mundi worth? As unique as it is, I suggest not £355.5 million. What is the value of Salvator Mundi? Any price that somebody is willing to pay. We may kick against these distinctions, but they exist. For business, the worth of an employee will have a numeric value in a ledger. As a business owner, your objective is to execute your strategy to ensure that labour costs do not chew into profits and negatively impact your balance sheet. Raises, promotions, bonuses, perks are commensurate to contracts, sales, and profit.

Yet, I have worked for, and I am aware of companies where management's bottom line doesn't demonstrate a sustainable profit-to-employee worth ratio. Instead, they have adopted a soft approach that relies on financial reserves to ensure people remain employed. An employee in that scenario may not feel valued because of a delayed cost-of-living-increase. However, their ongoing employment reflects their value as a person versus a capital haemorrhaging column on a balance sheet.

Delving into the subject of the value of creativity, we might get further along if we share a common understanding that creativity can have worth and value. For a non-hair-splitting orientation, let's make a differentiation. As it relates to creativity, not the creation, I will use the word value throughout this book. Value is what somebody is willing to pay for something, retain for personal meaning, or is created by the market. The construction paper covered storybook I made in second grade about a prince in space has no intrinsic value. Still, my Mom kept it safely put away for nearly forty years. To her, that tattered book was a treasure.

Worth is an accepted monetary value placed on a product or service. If I go to my local store to buy a £6 pepperoni pizza and I see a caviar and truffles pizza selling for £50, I am unlikely to purchase that gourmet pizza. Undoubtedly, in short order, that could-be-delicious pizza will soon be pulled from the shelf because it is not valued, despite the worth. Instead of taking the more direct approach to valuating your worth or the worth of your work, I want to spend the effort to reinforce the actual value of your creativity. The synthesis of your creative capacity in your daily living and ensuing expanding world view will enrich your life in so many more ways. If you think of your creativity as capital, where would you spend it to get the highest return on your investment? I am visibly annoyed whenever I hear the cliché "If money were no object," or its close cousin, "If you had a million pounds or won the lottery." From my experience, this line of questioning usually precedes a spiel for some money-making scheme or an invitation to a sales pitch function. Neither of which attract me.

Wouldn't it make for a much more refreshing conversation if you were asked: "Tell me, how do you creatively express yourself?" You may be thrown off at first. You may reply with that tired old standard, "Me?" You'll say. "I am not creative." But if adequately nudged into a conversation, you'll find your way down a path that leads to a creative, sustainable action with meaning and purpose. An internal compulsion pulls you along on a journey with unanticipated twists and turns. You will travel new territory. The result of that expedition, even if it is on a short diversion, will lead to more opportunities. Eventually, you will find yourself communicating creative expressions in unexpected places and moments. At some point, when you least expect, there will be a payoff. Sound like a fairy tale?

Finding Truth in Fairy Tales

The Brothers Grimm popularised many stories from old wives tales, legends, and oral history. One such story is that of a beautiful miller's daughter thrust into an avoidable scenario of spinning gold from straw. Research by anthropologists Sara Graça da Silva and Jamshid J. Tehrani assert that the Rumpelstiltskin tale may date back as far as 4,000 years[2]. The importance of that discovery is that the principles of the story tell a tale that spans human history. Let's put the time frame in perspective to things extinct. The last woolly mammoth died on Wrangel Island in what is now Alaska, give or take a few decades either side of 2000 BCE. The woolly mammoth, and the main character of *Ice Age* fame, was immortalised on cave surfaces in France and later in animated sequels. Of all the stories to repeat through time, people maintained a verbal narrative of a girl, alchemy, and magic.

By the time the Grimm's published their version of the ancient narrative, the world had dramatically changed. The story morphed to fit the times, creating critical relevancy to preserve the story principles, aka morals, while maintaining

---

[2] BBC (2016-01-20). *"Fairy tale origins thousands of years old, researchers say"*. BBC. *Retrieved 20 January 2016.*

the connection to common human themes. If you are not familiar with the story, allow me to summarise.

A miller, feeling a little too cocky in his sense of self-importance, bragged to a king that his daughter could spin gold from straw. Since millers mill grain to produce flour, who would not like to see that stunt? Naturally, the king was more than interested to see this feat performed. He called for the miller's daughter, put her in a room with a spin and straw and demanded that she, well, deliver on Dad's claim. Oh, and the caveat being that she would be executed if she didn't spin out a pile of gold by morning.

Locked away in the castle, she did what any person would do—young, old, female, male—she sat down and cried. I guess that the first thought in her mind was "Why is Dad trying to get rid of me?" Once resigned to her fate, she then started to try to figure out if the impossible task was in truth, possible. In her most dire hour of trying to figure out a solution, a person with some magical qualities appears. Let's leave out his size inference as that reinforces biases that date back millennia. We will call him the Magic Guy or better yet, the Alchemist. Also, let's give the miller's daughter a name. A story is so much more personable if we have a name. We shall call her Gladys Miller. Well, the Alchemist says to Gladys, "I can do the task for you, but you have to give me something in return."

Gladys finds herself trapped in a dungeon with a strange man who wants reciprocation. He says, "I want something in return," Gladys' thoughts go directly to one of the few things she has to offer. She offers him her necklace. Accepting the trade, the Alchemist sets to work and spins every blade of straw into shiny ribbons of gold. Relieved for her stay of execution, Gladys awaits the king in the morning. Overjoyed, the king swoops up Gladys and proposes to her. No, not really. To get where we want to go, we must expose the base human nature to the story, create a character arc, establish protagonists, antagonists, and players. For this narrative, the base quality is greed. True to form, the king leads Gladys to another, yet larger room filled with a spin, straw, and the same demand. The scenario plays out the second night when the Alchemist appears. This time, Gladys give the Alchemist her ring. He does his work, and Gladys is once again saved.

Mr Greedy King recognises that he has a goose that lays golden eggs. Wait, that is another story. The king guides Gladys to a yet a more massive storeroom of straw, but this time he changes the conditions. "If you turn this into gold," the king says, "I will make you my wife." Wow. How gracious of you, Mr Greedy King. You are the guy I'd pick out at the dance. Well, the Alchemist shows up one last time. But Gladys has surrendered the last of her items of earthly value. Is this story going to end in an impasse? Is Gladys doomed? No, because the Alchemist offers a break in negotiations. "I will spin this straw for you," as Gladys listens attentively, "but in return, I want your firstborn." Thinking she is bartering nothing immediately tangible; she agrees. The Alchemist spins, the king marries Gladys, and a year or so later a child is born.

Shortly after the child's birth, the Alchemist shows up to collect on the agreement. Not surprisingly, Gladys doesn't want to part with her firstborn. She pleads, offers alternatives, pleads, and then pleads some more. If I were to guess, I think that the Alchemist understood her angst because he too wanted a child. Given his status in the community as an outcast, he was never likely to woo a beautiful miller's daughter or perhaps position himself into a family building relationship at all. He could, by adopting a child, keep his legacy alive. Anyway, that would be a sanitised, rose-coloured glasses view of the story. Suffice to say, the Alchemist felt sorry for Gladys and suggested a compromise. He said, "I will give you three days to guess my name correctly." "If you do," he continued, "I will release you from your obligation." Not without consequence, he went on to warn, "but if you don't guess my name correctly in three days, I will come for the child."

Over the next two days, Gladys inundated the Alchemist with a name after an incorrect name. Beside herself, she again found her state of mind surrendering to powerlessness. Then, in her last-minute world of lifelines, a citizen of the kingdom came forward with information. The citizen described to Queen Gladys how he heard a man singing a song about a soon adoption of a child, all the details of the transaction, and punctuated the song by declaring his name. Equipped with a solid line for name accuracy, Queen Gladys is confident when the Alchemist appears on day three to collect on their deal. When she was allowed her third attempt, Queen Gladys didn't hesitate. She announces, "Your name is Rumpelstiltskin." Floored at being discovered, Rumpelstiltskin vanishes forever. His disappearance as a real-life interpretation probably indicated the end of a lineage. A sad end to a man capable of turning straw to gold, but as most moral stories end—the king, queen, and heir live happily ever after.

Fairy and folk tales, fables, legends, and myths are replete with metaphors for life. Whether you knew the story of Rumpelstiltskin or not, your mind will have made numerous associations, inspired a visual image, or in some way evoked an emotional response. During the process of reading, while words are leaping from the page, your mind was in the process of formulating questions, identifying contradictions, and searching for a word or phrase to which you could connect. The spoken word was the original format for communicating the human narrative. Dissecting those stories, interpreting them, applying principles contained therein, and adapting them to our narrative is essential for a story's life cycle.

Instead of giving you a 'moral of the story' spoiler, let's look at several themes in the story. We see the repeating and ascending elements of necessity, using what is available, indebtedness, discovery, and empathy.

Where is Rumpelstiltskin When You Need Him?

As noted earlier, the source of the Rumpelstiltskin fable likely dates to around 2000 BCE. Fifteen hundred years later in Athens, a legend of Greek philosophy, Plato, was building the foundations for higher learning. His circum vitae of contributions to Western thought is more than impressive. Plato immortalised a proverb about necessity, which is meaningful to our Rumpelstiltskin analogy. Recorded in *The Republic*, Plato is pressed into a dialogue about the State and individuality by his brother Adeimantus. It is the context of creating a State where we read 'the true creator is necessity, who is the mother of our invention.' Somebody translated Plato's comment into modern vernacular for smoother flow to "Necessity is the mother of invention." Gladys' issue of facing the impossible is a prime example of this axiom. We could further contemporise the adage by stating that need is the source of creativity.

On several occasions, Gladys found herself facing an impossible situation. We all know that you cannot spin straw into gold. Straw is the dry stalk residual from a grain harvest. A miller would have loads of the stuff piled around. Having milled the valuable parts of the plant, he is stuck trying to figure out what to do with the remaining chaff. There is nominal nutritional value in straw. Depending on the type of grain harvested, a farmer might augment his stock feed with straw for roughage. Back then you would use straw for bedding, mucking the stables, crafts, and as a binding source for bricks. Perhaps Mr Miller got a little too excited that his daughter was so well skilled at finding commercial value in the grain by-product of the family's primary business. He spoke out of turn, it was misinterpreted, and Gladys was thrust into an impossible state of need.

Under normal conditions, Gladys could have made a profitable little business selling straw dolls at the market or negotiating deals with brick makers. But locked away without access to her regular business connections under the weight of a literal interpretation of her skills, she was expected to create gold. If you've endured corporate austerity, this will echo a familiar ring of department cutbacks. You are required to produce the same amount or more, with fewer resources. A need is established, and a solution is demanded, which Gladys had limited experience to resolve.

Enter the Alchemist. I know what I'm about to suggest is a stretch of science but bear with me. What if the Alchemist used his expertise in mineralogy and his knowledge of local conditions to extract gold from straw? Rumpelstiltskin spun the king's straw. We can safely assume his straw is therefore harvested from specific fields. Perhaps the straw was used in a context that may have placed it in contact with gold particles. The Golden Fleece of Greek mythology may have its origin based on truth in as much as a fleece may have been used to collect gold dust from streams. Gold from straw? Eh, it could happen.

Regardless whether the straw was converted to gold or not, the critical thing for Gladys is that the Alchemist's approach to the solution was different than hers and it worked. In each instance of a solution, the Alchemist applied his knowledge to a problem for which the other person had no basis for understanding. A fundamental principle for economics is that I have something that you want or need, and you are willing to pay for it. Exchanges are made. Happy days.

Now, let's do a short recollection activity. Make a note of some situations where you had a desperate need but could not initially see how to achieve a solution. It doesn't matter how long your list is, but that you take a few minutes to write down some of those experiences. If you want, you can add elements like the conditions, situation, players, or build a narrative around it. Recall how you may have experienced, even if slightly, a sense of powerlessness. Perhaps you have a blatant example like your refrigerator-freezer dying on Christmas Eve or a car break down in a remote area. These kinds of situations typically evoke a reaction that Gladys may have felt. What would you have traded for somebody to appear with the solution to your problem? What did you pay to get out of the situation?

Although it doesn't lend itself to good storytelling, Gladys had the solution to her problems all along. She could have just been truthful and explained to the king that her Dad's spinning gold story was an exaggeration of the fact that she was just a brilliant businesswoman. The king had already played his hand that he valued money, perhaps her confidence and openness would have won him over. Her next opportunity came when she could have told the king the morning after the first miracle, "It wasn't me sire, but rather an alchemist that slipped into the chamber." That may have ended the ruse right then and there. A tangled web of deception was woven with escalating conditions and circumstances.

Truth is harder to perceive once deception takes root in the mind and is established as truth. Drama ensues, and the players commit to their respective roles. You may believe that you need a rescuer, and depending on the situation, that may be true. The easy way out is to expect a miracle. Should you follow that path, your first inclination will lean toward reliance on the miraculous for all your answers. With that course, you will also experience more than your share of disappointments. A miracle does exist, but it is much closer to home.

Your creative mettle is an immediate and reliable resource. When that moment of realisation hits you that a problem is not going to be meted by a conventional manner, you need to look for alternatives. By reinforcing your experiences with knowledge and application, you expand your capacity for more profound lateral thought. Instead of lazily thinking, "I'll just wait for the Alchemist to show up," or in a modern vernacular "Maybe I can win the lottery," you should be cognitively proactive. If you have a want or a need that requires a solution, you have at your disposal the resources to fill the demand and satisfy the want.

What Am I Going to Do with All This Straw?

Over the weekend it was beautiful and sunny on Saturday. Wanting to make the most of the weather and to steal a relaxing few hours, we took our lawn chairs over to the local cricket pitch to watch a match. As an observer, cricket is one of those sports that you don't need to know positions, what is a googly, or even how to score points. There are no raucous beer-swilling fans or massive queues to navigate. The experience is quite laid back. I brought a book to read and a box of Trivial Pursuit questions. When asked if she wants to play a board game, my wife will always decline. To play Trivial Pursuit on a team or against anybody, would not be a welcome offer—or so I thought. Once, when visiting Cornwall, we visited a café that has a box of Trivial Pursuit cards on every table. She was hooked after playing a few rounds without the board. That is why I brought the cards with me Saturday. I know she likes to test her knowledge.

Frequently, Georgina asserts that she isn't very good at "this sort of thing." Being a British version of the game, and she being British, my wife is far better at this version than me. We played for about two hours. To both our surprise, she was getting around 8 out of 10 questions correct. Even in the categories, she always claimed to be horrid. Namely, geography, science, and sport. (Neither of us is very good at sports questions.) When she responded with the answer to the middle name of MP John Powell as Enoch, I was astounded. She was getting so many obscure questions correct, that I questioned whether she had studied the deck. To which she replied that she has a "headful of useless information." Those words, as innocuous as they may sound, are incorrect. When we downplay the information we gather, we inadvertently ascribe it to the useless heaps of straw and chaff of our minds. Of course, that is so far from the truth.

Allow me to demonstrate the treasure that is Georgina's mind. She may think that knowing a bit of trivia about this or that is meaningless. Except for game shows and pub quizzes, trivia is a novelty or fodder for small talk, certainly not much in terms of monetary value. Delivered naturally and timed well, trivia can become a bridge for building relationships. Small talk, conversation, and learning about one another each strike a chord of commonality. You can use small talk trivia to add spice to an otherwise potentially dull or structured interchange intended to get a commitment. Trivia can make a conversation interesting. Not just the trivia question as a stand-alone option, but rather a launching point for learning about people.

In the people-oriented domain of work that Georgina does, building relationships and trust is vital. It comes quite naturally for her. She is also equipped with years of interesting experiences, formal and informal education, stories from conversations, and yes, trivia. She has worked in sales, interior design, event management, jewellery design, owned a couple of businesses and dabbled in art. All these qualities and her ongoing experiences add layers of depth to her people portfolio. What might be deemed useless information—straw and chaff—becomes ingrained as valued qualities of her social charm.

Gladys had at her disposal a wealth of life experiences. If she had those qualities of entrepreneurialism described earlier, we could safely assume that she had a developed capacity for lateral thinking. She could see opportunities when none otherwise appeared. She was able to navigate the emotional ladder of negotiations to gain the best deal. She was unwavering in her familial commitment, to the point of accepting what was tantamount to a death sentence to protect her father. She was not the poor daughter of a miller shoved into a bad situation and made a victim to circumstances. Faced with a new challenge, she had enough substance to reach several options and perhaps some bargaining leverage. Regardless of whether she availed herself of her choices, they were options. When the spin and straw were brought to her, she is unlikely to have just laid down and quit.

Here we can play around a bit more with the story. We can't get into trouble from copyright or purists because this is really a 4,000-year-old oral story interpreted for the twenty-first century. What resources did Gladys have available to her in the cell? Most people will look around and see the obvious. Four walls, floor, ceiling, window maybe. A spin and some straw. She wore clothes, had some jewellery, and probably some shoes of a sort. Morphing on the profile we have built of Gladys, she also had some intangible assets. Her brain. Her experience. Her savvy. What if Gladys made up the whole story of the Alchemist? What if he was her story's McGuffin? You know that part of a story that can't be corroborated and yet keeps the audience focused on it. We were not present during the spinning miracle. We only have a Chinese-whispers version of the story.

Making something out of nothing is no small effort. Success stories of Citizen Z arriving in a country with £1, only to achieve outstanding financial abundance in remarkable time, are repeated across the motivational industry landscape. How much is factual or how much is for show is only known by those intimate with the truth. We don't usually care about the incidentals. We like to think and dream that "If he or she can do it, why not me too?" What the stories often leave out is that there is a price tag for that success.

Spinning Yourself Out of a Hole

Big numbers are like a magic trick. Used in statistics, they can illustrate the magnitude or minuteness of an issue with sleight of hand. For Joe or Jane Average, reading news that India will surpass China as the highest populated country in the world by 2027 is a mere blot on the page of their attention. Toss in numbers like the projected global population will be 8.3 billion, of which, 18% per cent will be the 1.5 billion people of India, does not translate into their thinking. Give them something visual, like a sea turtle with a mesh of plastic knotted around its neck, and you secure their attention. Demonstrate how their plastic ended up in the body of a beached whale, and you have their emotions. Tell them that unless they take immediate action to reduce plastic in the environment with a clean-up beyond calculation and you will begin to lose your audience's attention. Breakdown their contribution by solving the problem with recycling, and you'll soothe their conscience. Although it is a far cry from fixing the issue, we feel better for our part.

An association with our story's character Gladys is neither about global populations nor plastic consumption. There is, however, a connection to a favourite of statisticians and economists—debt. Big numbers come into their own in this category. The numbers may change at the different times this book will be read, but today global debt hovers around £200 trillion. Further comparing with other big numbers, that is over twice the size of the global world product (GWP). Put another way; the GWP accounts for one-pound sterling for every three owed. In other words, you earn a pound, but with that, you are still two pounds in debt. Yeah, so what does that mean? "I am free and clear of debt," you might say. "Well done," I would commend. Being debt-free is a significant achievement. The category is dominated by two groups of people: the diligent and the destitute.

Debt is the direct result of risk. Perhaps we can better define risk as speculation. With each debt we incur as an individual or country, we gamble that conditions will remain favourable while marginalising potential threats. Things are going fine in our financial status, or the deal is "just too good", so we make our mark on the signature line and hope to pay later. With that signature and exchange of funds, the cogs of motion churn the machine of debt ever forward. All the while, some other person, company, or country is doing the same thing and speculating on a future that cannot be confirmed. Immediate gratification is sidelined, the prospects of consequence are ignored, until, of course, it comes time to settle.

We find Gladys in this same predicament. She bought time with her speculations that her deceit would have a satisfactory conclusion. But it escalated. She then traded all that she had of tangible value until she became void of collateral. Now, in a vulnerable condition, the stakes can be raised. "I will have your firstborn child" comes the offer. "Uh huh, you want my firstborn?" Whirring and calculating kicks off in the brain. Without a relevant association, Gladys can only speculate on what that might mean. There are many hurdles to leap over to reach the payment stage.

- The alchemist has to deliver gold again.
- The king must be satisfied and keep his word.
- We must get married.
- I need to get pregnant.
- The child must survive childbirth.
- The alchemist must recall the debt and return to collect.

Amazing feats of calculation kick in when we start the process of speculation. Fast too! For Gladys, the option was worth a gamble. "Where do I sign?" and she is in, penny for pound. Sounds so easy. But what we are addressing in this chapter is how to convert your creative capital. Otherwise, all we might pull from our story and its link to indebtedness are what not to do. Hindsight knowledge is conveniently applied when we face situations that have a similar look and feel. "I'll never do that again", we tell ourselves as we pay that last instalment for a product we bought without applying due diligence. Go into risk exercising your creative moxie. You can measure your creative capital or your Gross Creative Product (GCP) on the quality, quantity, and value that you place on it. You should carefully weigh the risks of indebtedness to achieve or improve your creative capital.

Does your creative expression require you to have an education? If so, should it be formal or informal? Do you have the necessary tools to develop the skills needed? You can ask yourself countless questions related to the cost of your creative pursuit. Your questions and answers should reflect what is important to you. What value do you put on your work? What value do you place on yourself? We see this played out all the time with apprentices, interns, and start-ups. David Newbie is offered an apprenticeship or internship in an industry that he has his eye on for a career. The placement is for a limited time, so he must get a lot out of it while he is able. The sponsoring company is stretched for staff. Holding David's hand is perceived as time-consuming and a high-risk investment because he will likely move on after the apprenticeship. (A cultural norm of a poorly applied version of the Pygmalion Effect.) To minimise the investment, David is assigned menial tasks that knock the wind from his visions of sailing to success. David's creative capital is stunted or redirected, and all parties are bereft of a positive experience.

Version two of the scenario is the start-up. Already equipped with a mature degree of competence, Davina Startup is ready to apply her skills and earn income. But she is in an awkward position. To demonstrate what she can do, she needs samples, a portfolio, a working model, anything that will prove to a prospective client that she is worth the investment. To build her portfolio, she offers to do work for a reduced price or pro bono. That works for a while, but when does it stop? Does she live like a Bohemian on opportunity crumbs that arrive from time to time? Does she search for a Rumpelstiltskin patron that will allow her to explore her creativity, spinning gold for her, patiently waiting for her success?

To these and all the other questions you will ask, there are no correct answers. There are only pathways for which each choice has a different consequence and reward. One factor will remain valid; indebtedness will be a part of that path. You may incur a debt of a financial, emotional, time, or that of a personal nature. Any or all can have an impact on your creative capital. Being able to recognise that and decide which path you can bear will have a cascading influence on your perspectives. In creative endeavours, sight not being restricted to the physical is a valuable asset.

Searching the Woods

The gift of a swaddled baby in her arms, Gladys was not thinking of the Alchemist, her debt, or anything else except the small miracle she was holding. She carried her child in her womb for about forty weeks. She felt his first wiggles, responses to her touch, and the soothing qualities of her voice brought calm when he was unsettled. Now present in the world, those same interactions are animated with coos, giggles, and eye-to-eye bonding. Funny thing when you hold a new-born baby, your mind doesn't wander off into dark places about the world he is inheriting. You aren't thinking how you will put him through university or watching him move away with his family. You are enthralled by the delicate and tiny features of the wonder before your eyes. It is as if time, with its demands and issues, is suspended. Innocence is restored.

In the era of Gladys' story, the firstborn son of nobility secured the next generation in a dynasty. There would not have been a casual response by the king to Gladys' dilemma. Perhaps she kept the secret to herself, to keep the king uninformed, or for who knows for what purpose. The story contradicts itself here. Unless he got the memo, how could a third party be aware of the queen's naming troubles? Logic concedes that the problem could not be that tightly held a secret. The word was out. The queen needs the name of a citizen fitting the following description. A reward of spun gold is on the table. Amount? Negotiable.

Having depleted her vocabulary of guy names on day two, day three puts the pressure on Gladys. Deadlines do tend to force creativity to the surface. But in this scenario, salvation again comes from an external source. We can't be clear who that person is because four thousand years have passed. Huntsman, a trader, a kid from the castle next door? Doesn't matter. The principal item of note is that Gladys expanded her resources. By recruiting others, she created a virtual network of observers to assist in her quest. One came through with the correct solution at the right time. We learn Rumpelstiltskin is so destroyed at being found out, and probably annoyed by his blunder, that he packs up and leaves the kingdom. As far as we know, he remained heirless, and his family business folded when he eventually passed.

The first nudge of the Nudge Principle is the skill of observation. Throughout the Rumpelstiltskin story, we observe how one character and the next exercise their observation skills. Some with precision results, whereas others become dependent and vulnerable. Rumpelstiltskin had his outcome nailed. Gladys was alive. She was married to an influential person. She was rich. Things were going okay for her. More than okay. Great! For Rumpelstiltskin, that Gladys would surrender her child for this positive life-changing opportunity was logical. After all, she could go on to have other children. Commenting on his behalf, this may have been his only chance for a legacy and purposeful existence.

Before the transaction completed, two powerful human emotions came into play to blindside both of our players: greed and love. I honestly don't think that Gladys or Rumpelstiltskin imagined the king's level of insatiability for wealth. The value of human life is reduced to gold by the king's behaviour. The king did not have to threaten life or imprisonment. If the claim of spinning gold were valid, he would find a tidy profit on his low investment of straw. If proven false, why punish the daughter? What would that gain the king in terms of PR equity with the locals? Once word got out, he'd be the King-who-kills-innocent-girls-because-they-can't-make-gold-from-straw. Not the kind of title that you want to make your mark on history. Instead, he played the greed card. Not only did he want gold, once proven that it was possible to spin, but twice more with escalating quantities. We can only assume by his behaviour that he wants to marry Gladys to have a ready reserve of spun straw in case his coffers become depleted.

Greed is toxic to a creative environment. It is hard to convert your creative capital when managed by somebody else's values. Modern history is full of examples of third-party representatives getting wealthy off the hard work and inspiration of others. We could easily slide off into debate on capitalism, business models, and corporate responsibility with this topic. There are plenty of stories in the news about intellectual property, copyright, and trademark battles. Besides which, I can assure you that there are loads of news items on disagreements turned into demonstrations. Google the phrase, "protests today" under the category of news, and you will receive a list of protests from around the world. If you dig deep enough into any issue, you will find somewhere on one side or the other, that greed festers at the root.

Greed is that intense, selfish desire for something that can range from things, wealth, or power. I'm not making a commentary on a specific protest, but I think you will find that greed plays a part at some level in the conflict. That is why there is less collaboration and more one-upmanship in politics. When pondering a news report, I ask, "What is their motivation for protesting?" Sometimes the answer appears obvious. Sometimes the protest is a genuine protestation of an oppressive condition. My doubts are further fuelled when I observe blatant attempts to distort or manipulate the truth. When in doubt, I assume that a protest is aimed at achieving some preferred change. How will the world be a better place if a movement wins its goals?

Although it may sound like an anthem from 1969, love is the antidote to the toxicity of greed and other corrosive qualities we emit as humans. Gladys could not have parted with her child no matter what. I find it interesting that Rumpelstiltskin didn't place an "or else" condition on this final contract. Being without a progeny and we assume a partner, Rumpelstiltskin must have yearned for love and family. He likely had a good childhood from which to base his desires. Stature, looks, a prevailing stench of chemicals may have contributed to his single status and consequent loneliness. Whatever may be the reason, having a child was his answer to the pangs of his heart. Rumpelstiltskin may have been a reasonable observer, that comes with being an alchemist, but he overlooked one make or break factor in his equation—a mother's love.

Converting your creative capital means nothing if you don't love what you do. You may as well take up an alleyway in Dafen and whip out replicas of the masters or become part of a manufacturing process that steals your identity and pays you pennies on the pound. There are undoubtedly prolific creators that leave an impressive display of their work. Art, patents, businesses, books, products, films, and thoughts are only samples of the creativity produced daily. We can't ignore the fact that some creations are implemented by greed, desperation, ambition, or ignoble virtues. We may be the benefactors of another's sordid reasons for a creation. I question if another person's motivation is something to get all excited about. We will discuss the influence of human emotions later in chapter nine. What is clear is that love, as the motivation for what you do, can give the creation and creator meaning, value, and a sense of worth.

Your Firstborn

We need to occasionally remind ourselves that our parents were probably young when we disrupted their lives. For a firstborn child, any age for a parent means that this is their first-time at the job. Photos of my Mom wrestling my cousin for a garden hose or Dad wearing goofy hats are a testament that they too were once young. Growing up in a classic parent-child relationship, it was weird to one day realise that Mom and Dad were once teens and twenty-somethings. The average age for a first child, from a global perspective, is 18 to 30. For the United Kingdom and Europe, the average age for having first-time children is the late twenties. From my perspective, Mom never looked or acted old. She was always beautiful.

More than others, perhaps, I am fortunate to have so many good memories and loads of pictures of my parents, grandparents, and extended family. As the firstborn to George Sterling and Jimmie Jean, stories of how exceptional I was as a baby were frequently told to me. All boy, I was active, exploring, independent, and demonstrably affectionate. I kept my Mom busy, but her reward was a payload in love and kisses. She was 19-years-old when I was born. Dad was twenty-one. Several years later, they separated. Mom became a single mother with Dad away working in another state. During that time, she relied heavily on my Grandmother "Meme" and Grandfather "Papa" for help. The number of times Mom must have spoken to my Meme about what to do with her boy probably lit up the switchboards at Ma Bell like a Christmas tree. One phrase Mom repeated when explaining to me one issue or another was "Remember, I haven't been down this road either," she would say. "This is my first time too." I do have to remember; she was not yet thirty.

The commitment to nurture life and bring it into being is incomprehensible. The bond between mother and child, even in nature, is legendary. What you have before you in that child is the manifested genetic soup of two people and their combined lineage. Providing for her physical, emotional, mental, and spiritual wellbeing is the environment needed for her to develop into her own. All the while she is maturing, there will be lasting characteristics that link her to your storyline. When we first meet an infant, we may attempt to attribute features resembling family members—mother or father. With some families, resemblances are so profound that it is hard not to spot similarities. For others, we may see notable features not so much in the physical realm as in behavioural. There is so much that we inherit.

Where a child will make her mark are in the choices she makes on her journey. There is already some hard wiring, as it were, in her DNA and genetic make-up. Rearing her to adolescence will contribute to her values, world view, and associations. But this wonder you call daughter will transform as you watch her develop. She will surprise you with concepts that you do not own or have ever conceived. You will smile with delight as you observe her talent blossom from which she will draw great satisfaction. Each illumination shines a spotlight of affirmation that she is her own person. Gladys had all that to experience. Her son would be her protector one day, and his success meant her success.

You may not have or ever will have a child. Nevertheless, you were a child to a mother and father. Perhaps it was a good life, with love and all the needful things to make good memories. Maybe not. You are who you are today for your DNA-gene mix and life experiences to date. What you shape from the mix is your creation. You can either take a passive approach of the victim or the active approach of the explorer. Some years ago, somebody explained to me that the word passive means having something done to you. Passive doesn't mean not doing anything. Being a creative force, you can choose to activate your creative core. Work with it. Develop its personality and style. Let it take shape and grow in directions that you may otherwise not have fathomed. Be proud of its achievements.

Rumpelstiltskin could not see everything from his vantage. The condition he offered Gladys when it was an intangible and obscure proposition had little emotional collateral. Once the theoretical materialised, that was a game-changer. Converting creative capital needs a commitment to give a creation life, to nurture, protect, and rear it to a place of independence. As a species, we are equipped to reproduce. With reproduction, we continue a lineage that has the potential of perpetuating our legacy, while the next generations make their marks on the annals of history. Creativity is a global marker of humanity. Creativity stamps its permanent presence in every age, like a DNA strand that anchors every human being to a shared past.

4

Ex Centro per Machina

Remarkable people can be easily overlooked because of their humble, if not invisible lives. One such noteworthy person that comes to mind is Indian mathematician Srinivasa Ramanujan. Why of all the remarkable people I could cite, do I choose Ramanujan? His story, first published in 1991 by Robert Kanigel and then produced as a film, is a prime example of the Nudge Principle in action. Throughout part one, I've taken you down a meandering trail of creativity. The trajectory led from our earliest ancestors to a future infused with technological wonders. I used metaphors and a variety of devices to prod you to think. Like, love, or be confused at my methods, you engaged the same processes that Ramanujan embodied. To a greater or lesser degree of realisation, you've already been Nudged.

As tempted as I am to spend the time and effort associating Nudge Principles to qualities of our Man who knew Infinity, we can't afford the luxury. Instead, allow me to summarise with a few salient Nudge related points about Srinivasa Ramanujan.

- He was able to **see** things that others could not.
- He was desperate to communicate (**tell**) what he could see to test his theories.
- He applied principles from other areas to generate a **flow** of thought to stimulate deeper thinking.
- He was challenged by an institution to verify his work, thereby forcing his success to require exploration (**play**).
- The formal education process was, to his intuitive nature, as painful as being an alien in a strange world and separated from his loved ones. The internal conflict deepened his empathetic resolve (**feel**).

- When faced with options to adapt to his environment to receive a prestigious institutional role, he yielded to his faith-based values (**be**).
- He achieved his goals because quitting was not an acceptable alternative (**do**).

The film, *The Man who knew Infinity*, primarily focused on Ramanujan's Cambridge education, and touched on highlights of the internal and external struggles he experienced. Conflicts that nearly defeated, physically destroyed, and crushed his creative spirit. Provoked on screen by his sponsor G.H. Hardy, Ramanujan is asked: "Why do you do, any of this?" Drum roll as we ready for the Eureka moment. "Because I have to," Ramanujan responds, "I see it." The strength of character and depth of his creative core is open. Everything he sees, speaks, feels, does, or is radiates from the centre of his being. There is the differentiator. Ramanujan knew it and flowed in its brilliance.

Ex Centro per Machina, the title of this chapter, is all the classic Latin, or Greek for that matter, that I plan to include in going forward with the Nudge Principle. Latin is a language used in law, medicine, and science. Using Latin by experts in these fields of study carries meaning that enables the communication between experts. For me, to speckle the following pages with references of Latin origin would be, quite honestly, artificial. Here, though, it best captures my intent. Ex centro per machina means "from the centre of the machine." There is no hidden meaning. No clever anecdote. It says what it means. For the Nudge Principle, it depicts the centrality and nature of creativity as a primary function of your person. For every person, creativity is part and parcel of their core. Your core.

The actions or nudges as they will be referred to in the Nudge Principle, that Ramanujan demonstrated above are actions we perform without thinking. Named because they can be developed purposefully with practise are the nudges of SEE, TELL, FLOW, PLAY, FEEL, BE, and DO. These verbs are presented in sequence because it is the natural flow for the activity that our brain engages. While there are aspects of each action that fall under the category of autonomic responses by the brain, the bulk of these actions involve varying degrees of cognitive dependence. At least in terms of an action influencing our brain's connectivity, plasticity, and firing power. In Part Two, we will explore the Seven Nudges, their relation to one another, and how each can be developed to complement the other while simultaneously actualising creativity.

You can train your brain with nudges to perform with scalable efficacy. Although acted out on an individual level in every circumstance, teams can also develop these competencies within businesses, employees, and across industries and institutions. Strategies implemented to cultivate the Seven Nudges will activate growth potential in terms of individual satisfaction and organisational resilience. A creative mind will challenge the status quo while searching for innovative and original ideas. Not all innovative ideas may work within the conditions of a particular corporate framework, and there are countless reasons for this situation. I'm not inferring that it is impossible. You need to be aware that an organisation in its current state may not accommodate freelance styled innovation. Yet, an environment that encourages Nudge Principle creativity empowers the individual to explore. With that kind of exploration, an organisation will benefit.

Think of it like sharing your computer's spare processing power with thousands of other computers. Your computer becomes a volunteer to help solve a problem. Some scientific communities and other interested groups need incredible computational power to crunch massive numbers or test algorithms but lack a single computer source to achieve their desired results. Many of the processor sharing groups have a curb appeal because they tackle issues like cancer, disease, astrophysics, and environmental studies. There are also playful categories like breaking Enigma messages or scouring the heavens for signs of intelligence. Using the 'brain power' of thousands of networked computers, Scientist Sally increases her rate of data collection with the potential result of a "Viola" moment of earth-shattering brilliance. Providing an environment for Nudge Principles can achieve similar results.

Not being machines, we need a lot more handling. For instance, which fuels do you put into these non-mechanised creatures that can generate such brilliance? All the while, requiring optimal conditions to function like delicate hothouse flowers? Understanding this machine of flesh and bone, you need to appreciate that while heroes and altruism are supreme examples of the human condition, there is a legitimate place and argument for self. 'There is no international formula for motivation,' writes Richard D. Lewis, author of *When Cultures Collide: Leading Across Cultures* (D.Lewis, 2006). I suggest that self may be that universal motivation. Despite any familial, cultural, financial, or other non-cited reasons for why self plays a secondary or tertiary role to our behaviours, the deference is a choice of self-preservation.

Four fuels for self-awareness relating to rewards begin with the letter I: intuition, illumination, interpretation, and imitation. Let's explore how you can top up your creative energy with these four super fuels.

Intuition

A book that had a profound influence on my pre-teen thinking was Dalton Trumbo's *Johnny Got His Gun.* Published the month and year World War II rolled into Poland, Trumbo tells the story of a young, idealistic, American serviceman named Joe Bonham. The title of the book refers to Johnny as a homage to the nameless men that left their homes to fight and die in the bloodiest conflict of American history, the Civil War. Joe's war is the First World War, dubbed the "War to end all wars" by British author H.G. Wells.

Trumbo's anti-war novel offers a glimpse into the tortured mental state of Joe as he battles reality and dreams from the confines of a hospital bed. During a battle, he was severally injured in an artillery explosion leaving him blind, deaf, first degree burns and no arms or legs. Joe has no means of communication. With limited sensory perception, he is aware of warmth from sunlight, the nibbles of vermin, and the kindness of human touch. A film version of the book was written and directed by Trumbo and released in August 1971. I read the book for a junior high literature class. The war in Vietnam had escalated at the time of the film's release. There were protests at home, daily mortality reports announced on the news, on-the-ground television news coverage most days, and the draft was in full motion. I didn't need to see the film. I was 12 years old.

My original thought for starting the Nudge Principle with intuition was prompted by the phrase "Use it or lose it." The phrase reminded me of past warnings to use the brain or biceps before they atrophy. The same principle is applied to art, writing, sports, social skills. I mean you can stick any action in the blank, and it fits. Wanting to add some weight to the concept, I set out to find statistics on atrophy produced as the result of an injury. I was keenly interested in reviewing a table that would show me global statistics for categories like injuries from land mines, diabetes, combat-related, or industrial. Hitting dead ends at every direction I turned, I thought I'd apply the thought to amputees and loss of limb statistics. I didn't want to use statistics, because that felt cold and sterile. That is when I remembered a book I read as a pre-adolescent young man and the impact it had on me.

It was not my intent to toss you into a deep end regarding intuition with the subject of war. I made the intentional switch based on a feeling evoked by a memory. I planned to ease you in with a light-hearted discussion about luck. We want to read about success and luck because it makes us feel good. Mainly when what we read teaches how to capitalise on principles that improve our chances with luck. Richard J. Wiseman Professor of the Public Understanding of Psychology at the University of Hertfordshire identifies a developed intuition as one of four principles for making successful decisions. Wiseman describes in his book, *The Luck Factor*, not how to be lucky but instead how a lucky person thinks. That luck happens more often than it does for others, puts that type of thinker in favourable positions with Destiny and the Fates. Gut feelings do indeed have a place in your decision-making.

For those of us that regularly exercise on a diet of intuition, taking risks and trusting those instincts becomes easier with practise. We get it right sometimes. We get it wrong on others. When we get it wrong, we apply the salve of Lesson Learned and try again. It is in a chaos reduced mindset of wins over losses that intuition builds its can-do muscle. Should you take a battering from life due to following your intuition, the results may feel like or perhaps result in an actual amputation. A part of you is missing—the ghost of what was remains connected in your mind. Intuition has secured a solid footing in your thinking. To build your intuition back to its better self, you need to exercise and eat right. Eating right, as a metaphor, means keep away from anything that contains fear as an ingredient. Keep fear out of your diet. It is poisonous.

I chose, instead of Lady Luck, to use the Trumbo book and simile for another group. You've stepped out in good faith and trusted your instinct. You trusted somebody else. You went wholeheartedly into a commitment trusting your gut only to have your world collapse. Destruction, disarray, confusion like a bomb went off in your lap. Your world is disrupted. You can't see the way you used to be and do. All the positive affirmations you receive from friends, family, and social media fall on your deaf ears. You don't feel like you can move forward, and you have lost a sense of purpose. You feel like Joe Bonham, trapped inside of your mind to relive mistakes and dream of what could have been. You need a nudge.

You may feel like your intuition is non-existent or has atrophied to the point where you can barely recognise that intuitiveness is even a human quality. Exercising your intuition involves taking risks. If you have developed, mature intuition, you should expand your use of intuition in different scenarios and conditions. If you are timid or have experienced trauma from trusting your intuition, resume by taking little risks. Risks in thinking, in play, in learning. Make sure the stakes are low and the consequences of "getting it wrong" are slight. Intuition, effectively developed, practised, and managed, can produce euphoric feelings of self-worth. Maintained, you can enjoy balance and an openness to new experiences.

Potential danger of overfeeding on intuition: Overconfidence and arrogance leading to the reduced discipline of responsibility to conduct due diligence. The result? Poor decisions.

Illumination

That once clear line of delineation between fake and genuine fades with an escalating range of reality-altering technological advances. Political scientists are concerned for the integrity of democracy in that the Internet has become a boon for propagating fallacies and misinformation AKA Fake News. Social media platforms, forums, and the blogosphere are a Wild West where almost anything can be presented as fact and substantiated by dubious sources. I suggest a 'once clear line of delineation' only to punctuate what I remember from where we were before on this global playground of unchecked name-calling and bullying. Maybe we have always been fooled; we just didn't realise it.

Residue from fake news, fake people, and fake realities seep into our lives from a myriad of interactive social sources. Online traffic, media, people we interact with throughout our day-to-day, and on a grander scale, the implications of high-level deception from every quarter conditioning us to be sceptical. Cynical at our worse. We can no longer feel the relative safety of the Internet as its reach far exceeds an ability for effective policing. Exceptions to the invasiveness do exist. For instance, you'll be out of touch entirely if you live on North Sentinel Island. For everybody else, we have good reason to question what we see.

Fake news is an approach to politicising newsworthy events or Internet versions of events but produced to be pawned off as reality. The power of desktop applications to edit video and audio to mimic real-time has evolved with such precision that experts can hardly tell the difference any longer. Beyond fake news, we have Deepfake where nothing can be trusted. Is that person real or computer-generated? Immersed in a digital world for hours on end, do you care? Artificial Intelligence is going to take this technology to new heights and challenges. Browse the directory of the generative adversarial network (GAN) website created by Phil Wong.[3] to see if you can spot distinguishing and original characteristics of people in the catalogue. For nothing else, see if you can select the original layer.

---

[3] www.ThisPersonDoesNotExist.com

Before the age of email, memes used to infiltrate offices from fax-to-fax, copier-to-copier. Two of the most popular memes of the time were the Project Solution and the Mushroom Analogy. The Project Solution depicted a series of illustrations of tire swing concepts designed by a typical project stakeholder. Each concept humorously demonstrated how far off the idea was transformed by different departments from what the customer originally ordered. The Mushroom Analogy, with variations, is "I must be a mushroom, all they (a management dig) do is keep me in the dark and feed me manure." The 'keep me in the dark' reference relates to not being informed or included in the communication cycle. Given the nature of deceptive practises that prey on ignorance, we may have a fine line to walk with what we perceive to be fake or genuine, real or generated. Get used to the fact that this condition ushered in with technology will become harder to separate in your mind. About the only thing you can do to ensure that you fall on the right side of events is to practise illumination. Once out of the dark through illumination, exercise intuition.

Illumination is to shed light on a subject. Institutes of higher learning, libraries, and think tanks frequently use an icon of a flame or a lighthouse to symbolise education and enlightenment. Thanks to Thomas Alva Edison, we also have the light bulb as a symbol of ideas and brightness. In ancient times these images, apart from light bulbs, were representative of the Library of Alexandria— a wonder of the ancient world. George R. R. Martin recreates similar imagery with the Citadel of Oldtown, Westeros in his *A Song of Ice and Fire* book series or the popular HBO series *Game of Thrones*. You and I could play all day and into the night passing back-and-forth quotes on the attributes of knowledge. Many people, over many years, have had plenty to say and write about the value of knowledge. The phrase "Knowledge is power" is attributed to Sir Francis Bacon, but I doubt he is the first to say it or the last to recognise its merit. When a challenge arises that makes you feel uncomfortable, get knowledge.

Flying over the Rocky Mountains of the Western United States with my nervous flyer wife, I warned her that there would be turbulence over a range of fourteeners. I likened the hot and cold air confluence to that of a fast-running stream. On rapids, a boat will travel on the surface and get tossed around a bit, but its buoyancy keeps it afloat. Rapids only last for a little while. Soon enough, we'd reach the calm. The connection seemed to work. She recalls that metaphor or one of travelling a bumpy road every time she flies now. Empowered with a basic understanding of the conditions that create turbulence, she feels safer. When the pilot announces, "We are going to make a slight adjustment to avoid some turbulence," she appreciates how the pilot is merely navigating the rapids of the sky. Fear is rendered toothless when you apply knowledge.

On the opposite end of knowledge is ignorance. As you may suspect, there are equally as many quotes about ignorance as there is for knowledge. Ignorance is like that scary movie scene when you know that some horrid person or monster is lurking in the shadows ready to pounce on a victim to make you leap from your chair. The characters in the scene fit a hundred B movie formulas to be "got" first. When the designated victim in Scene 12 wanders alone into the dark, your well-deserved comment is "Don't go in there," you cringe at the screen, "Are you stupid?" As you can also guess, that will be the exact moment the torch sputters and dies. Convenient time for bad guys and monsters. Not so much for young college students out for some fun in the country.

In tandem with intuition, illumination is a powerful ally. The fuel of learning and knowledge can keep you off the *I Should Have Known Better* list of The Fooled. With a developed intuition, you will get the occasional red flag that signals your knower that there may be danger ahead. Applying illumination by becoming informed makes you a little less vulnerable than before. You can think of this, along with the following principles, as a succession of thought: knowledge leads to understanding, understanding leads to wisdom. Wisdom is knowledge and understanding applied.

Potential danger of overfeeding on illumination: Stagnation or analysis paralysis. Feeling so safe in the mode of learning, you hold back on its application, leading to indecisiveness or delayed decisions.

Interpretation

A good prank will always bring tears to my eyes from laughing so hard. I cut my pranking teeth on Allen Funt's *Candid Camera* television programme when I was a kid. Applied to real-life, my favourite victims were my ever-affirming Mom and Grandad. I was pretty good too. The hide-in-a-box-on-the-front-porch of my Grandad's house after he came home from a late shift prank was the stuff of family legend. I loved to make my Grandma laugh. She had a great laugh that night, albeit with a warning about scaring Papa too much.

All good fun when you are a kid, but it carries a different mood when it transfers into adulthood. I gave up pranking when I once appeared to a co-worker with a gas mask on during a night shift. The look of fear that she had on her face made me hang up my pranking forever. Along with a series of grovelling apologies. I haven't done a prank since. That doesn't mean I don't appreciate a good prank. As long as people are not hurt, and it is not that bushwhacking style of humour that victimises a person's good nature of trust. I am headed down this prank trail because I recently watched a prank online that had all the classic props of a *Candid Camera* clip.

The setting is an upscale art gallery, an art student, an IKEA mass-produced piece of art, and several marks for the ruse. We are guided in the video through a series of interviews between the art student and victims who are asked to offer their interpretation of the art piece and estimate its market value. The viewer is introduced to several seemingly informed perspectives of the work that could not be further from the truth. The artwork on display purchased at IKEA for £7 was assessed a staggering £1.7 million by one deeply philosophical patron. Each mark looked at the same object but incorrectly interpreted the work.

I've also read stories of incorrectly interpreted works by authors, poets, filmmakers, sculptors, and designers. We get into a muddle when we set out to explain the work of other people. As an exercise of exploration, interpretation has value and merit. Some do so as a profession, paid for their perceptions of work produced by others. We may even align with the opinions of those professionals and escalate them to celebrity status. The reasons why a creative make something in a style or manner that is unique to their signature belongs to the creator. If asked, they may not even know why they like or dislike their work. Let alone what was the nature of their motivation. It may sound like I am mixing the two qualities of interpretation and motivation. I am not. I am making a case that you will find yourself on a slippery slope when you try to attribute motive behind what other people do or create. I think it goes together with the truism that you can observe a person's behaviour, but you can't genuinely know their motive.

Developing interpretation muscle can be likened to becoming fluent in another language. Earlier, I mentioned Neno and his multilingual talent. Multilingual speakers can move between languages with increasing comfortably the more they use their skills to communicate. Stopping to interpret a language from one to another taxes the brain, but at the same time builds new associative patterns. Interpreting in this sense is a literal interpretation. We are under a regular barrage of symbols that demand fixed interpretation. Blue lights flashing in the rear-view mirror of our car indicates an emergency vehicle is approaching from behind. We don't need to interpret that symbol with an "I wonder what that is?" kind of question. Flashing lights of any colour while driving intends to grab your attention. Different countries may have variations of emergency vehicle symbolism, but they are designed to achieve the same results.

Hard interpretations also apply in law, sciences, and medicine. Where a literal translation of a difficult topic is required, consensus can be a problem to achieve. We frequently observe this acted out across legislative and media platforms on issues associated with constitutional law. Conditions have changed, but society demands compliance. When that happens, we then have look to the spirit of the law and precedents. Among the annals of legal libraries, old mindsets collide with an enlightened public. Look around. There are volumes of examples.

Bending the rules, laws, and structure to fit an interpretation can open the door to all sorts of problems. Take on bad rules, regulations, laws, and structure if you are committed to a cause. Just be aware that your battle may be against prejudice, ignorance, and traditionalism—and perhaps culture and faith. Where you can experience robust growth in your interpretive skills without the commitment of an activist is in the arena of soft interpretations. Getting it "just right" with a soft definition isn't as crucial when playing around with possibilities. You can build your interpretive muscle for big issues by starting with less weighty activities.

Let's do another activity. You need to suspend judgement for this one; otherwise, it will corrupt the process. To build your interpretive muscle—people watch. Go someplace where you can watch people. Pick a person from a crowd and create a narrative about him or her. Think about where they may be from, where they are going, what problems they may be experiencing, what successes they have enjoyed. Add to your narrative what you think they may be thinking, feeling, or what may be their concerns. If you can suppress labelling, judging, or bias, you can have fun with these narratives. It doesn't matter whether you are right or wrong. Nobody will know what you think. Unless of course, you play the narrative people-watching game with a friend or partner. Now that can be an eye-opener.

Potential danger of overfeeding on interpretation: Wrong interpretation and self-centric prejudice. The deepest concern of wrongful interpretation is that you may eventually believe what you interpret is the truth.

Imitation

"Paradox though it may seem—and paradoxes are always dangerous things," Vivian responds to Cyril. "It is none the less true that Life imitates art far more than Art imitates life."

The classical which-came-first argument in Oscar Wilde's essay *The Decay of Lying* is a paradox of an anti-establishment perspective. Our orientation of art is that it reflects what we perceive of the world around us. We are comfortable believing that 'Art imitates life'—not the other way around. Art should imitate—or reflect—what we identify with as being familiar. The result of that art may not reflect your orientation, but you can appreciate it as a representation of another person's orientation. Wilde's character, Vivian, makes a great argument. Her premise is more compelling in the twenty-first century than it was when Wilde penned the essay in the nineteenth century.

The revolutionary power of art is visible in all forms of art and creative processes. The mere act of creation is to create something new—a perception, concept, form, style, or technology. A creative will produce a work that blends her life experiences with innumerable other factors. Something new is created. What therefore happens with that new thing? On the casual side, it becomes such a regular aspect of daily living that we feel it has always been there. Technology is a widespread example of that. Technology's creative influence is everywhere we turn. We adopt memes based on the exposure of meme pollination passed from person to person. In many places, I can lift my arm toward the side of my head, extend pinkie finger and thumb, give my hand a waggle, and my gesture sends a message. That being "call me" or "I'll call you." In that exchange, the meme is propagated through imitation. An oversimplified example, but valid.

A more extensive and much deeper range of life imitating art is visible in the music industry. Artists experiment with sound, lyrical content, branding, and style. Their contributions to a culture influence their fandom to adopt the artist's persona and the created—or manufactured— version of the artist takes on a life of its own. The intonation of language, a swagger or strut, and emotive style reinforced with aggressive merchandising all blend together to create a compelling visual and audio profile. The result is that we end up sounding, acting, and in many cases thinking like the creator of the meme. Unless of course, you are a parent of a pre-teen or teen. Then you are about a decade behind the imitation game. You can find that out when you take your teen shopping or say "Yo yo yo" only to be told, "Dad, that is so old."

Much of our imitation is deliberate. We see or hear something we like, and we take it on board. For those instances the adage "Imitation is the sincerest form of flattery" may be better suited than Wilde's paradox. Have you ever asked yourself "Where did I pick that up?" referring to a behaviour or phrase? I am an American. My wife is British. Even though we speak a common language which makes communicating easier to manage, there are a lot of words that are different in their use. Frequently she is caught out by a friend or family member that notices her distinctly American application of a word. On the flip side, I've lived in the United Kingdom on this second time around for eight years. My accent is most often guessed correctly but sometimes perceived as Irish or Canadian. When I am asked whether I think I will ever lose my accent, I reply "Which English accent should I adopt?" Out of respect to my new home, I try to use the appropriate British words and pronunciation. I leave off any attempt at an English accent except the occasional playful Mrs Doubtfire greeting. Otherwise, I end up sounding like so many Americans that learned English accents from old films from which I am told "Nobody speaks like that."

Few things give us a more profound sense of personal satisfaction than when somebody adopts a behaviour, idea, word, or phrase that we use. In a way, it imbues us with a sense of validation. On the other extreme, you may experience mockery. You may have seen, been a perpetrator or victim of the sibling battle of copycat. For the sheer delight of annoyance, a sibling starts a row with a sibling by copying what the other says. Verbatim. As the success of that annoyance accelerates, the copycat will introduce copying gestures and posture. The scenario crescendos to an intervention. Those behaviours are usually associated with childhood development, not adult behaviour — playground antics, not boardrooms.

Imitation has to do with collaboration, cooperation, and community. Demonstrated naturally in body language, we see it in the mirroring effect. People working together or in a social setting will begin to mirror each other unconsciously. Group behaviours expose subtle affirmations that participants are connecting, or they are not. Imitation, while it can be practised as a standalone action, is best nurtured in the natural flow of human interaction.

Should you want to be more proactive in the process and explore the productive interactions of genuine imitation, ensure that you apply the other muscles of your core. Read the room and people (intuition), ask questions that give you insight into a personality (illuminate), try to read between the lines of conversation and appearance (interpret), and then seek commonality (imitation). You may surprise yourself with the quality of the interactions you attain.

Potential danger of overfeeding on imitation: Stereotyping and marginalising people or their values. If practised in an ingenuine manner, imitation may be perceived as mockery. Once crossed into that perception, you find yourself in a deep hole to dig out.

Introducing Seven Nudges for Creative Success

I've laid the groundwork for how the brain processes data, how the creative process is relevant and presented an overview of the core from which creativity thrives. Your core is that quality of you that stamps its identity on all that you do. Where I want to take you now is on a trip of discovery for how you can fine-tune your thinking and maximise your creative core. Instead of viewing creativity as a passive process bestowed by Divine intervention, we are going to activate those creative functions that are pre-wired in your brain. Since we use these nudges all the time—to greater or lesser degrees—what we need to do to activate more neural connections is to be nudged. By aligning these nudges into logical stages, you can better follow a path to a goal.

The outcome of any creative process must include an action. For the most part, the creative process is internalised. Evidence of creativity will be expressed in a medium that is transferrable. I began to study creativity and the brain in 2006. There are some well-established authors and scientists that have weighed in on the topic. Although well-read on the subject, I have not read everything. The study of creativity and the brain is an ever-evolving field of study. New technology, maturing brain mapping research, and the unshakeable interest in creativity regularly crack open discoveries. I won't be replicating that research with quotes and references. The science is solid. I present this to you with the assurance that there is enough data to support the Nudge Principle and the Seven Nudges for an understanding of creative success.

A challenge of identifying the Seven Nudges was crafting the stages with short, memorable, and relevant words. Each nudge had to be action oriented. My aim is for those practising Nudge to engage in the process rather than theorising its applicability. Plus, it is more fun. Part Two will cover the Seven Nudges.

SEE

Every introduction to the creative process comes by way of seeing. To see, of course, has numerous meanings. The apparent association is the seeing with your eyes. But not every person has eyes to see or for that case ears to hear. To SEE, then must adopt a broader orientation. You need to include the five senses: sight, hearing, taste, smell, and touch. Purely on a physical level, you have more senses than just five. Beyond the physical, you also have understanding, comprehension, imagination, intuition, and a gaggle of cognitive knower types of observation nudges.

TELL

Communication is the next stage of the Nudge Principle. Once an idea is conceived, it must at some point be communicated. Communicating creates form for a concept to be transmitted. The feedback loop of communications enables you to toss out ideas, receive feedback, evaluate that feedback based on your observations (SEE), and attribute value. You can engage in the TELL process with others or dialogue in the back-and-forth of your mind. An idea spoken aloud or formulated in your head tends to sound different than when first conceived.

FLOW

To break from the SEE-TELL cycle, you need to synergise your aggregate information and concepts into a hybrid concept. The confluence of ideas morphs into something integrating bits from this idea or that with a dose of influence from here or there. From this point on, your creation begins to take on a unique shape. You'll apply principles that work in your domain. Where those principles work with the synergised concept, you move on to the next stage or reinter the SEE-TELL cycle to shake out the problems.

PLAY

The act of play is fundamental for discovering new vistas but is often misunderstood as a frivolous time-wasting activity for children. To play is to explore. You test boundaries, abilities, social skills, and new territories. You challenge the status quo mindsets of possibilities. All the while, you build and strengthen your neural networks for speed, capacity, and plasticity. Play evokes emotions and has the innate ability to expose areas of emotional maturity that could benefit from a maturing catalyst. Play can be fun. Play can also be serious. Regardless of how it is applied, PLAY is the accelerator for creativity.

FEEL

Creativity, in a broad sense, contains primers for emotional investment. For the creator, a sense of real or perceived ownership can stir up all sorts of emotions and their associated feelings. The host of potential feelings experienced by a creator is a catalogue of the human emotional experience. Pick any feeling between ambivalent to zealous, and you'll touch a root emotion sensed by a creator. However, a creation doesn't end with the creator's emotional investment. Those that share or are exposed to a creation also have an emotional investment.

BE

Being is a profoundly personal quality you own. From a sense of being you judge and measure your and other peoples place in the creative process. You assign merit for your creation based on a set of values. In turn, your values contribute to the fabric of who you are. To act contrary to that set of values can have a considerable impact on the sustainability of a creative endeavour. The same can be said for organisations and institutions. A values statement will articulate an espoused value under which an organisation is intended to operate. Whereas, demonstrated values will determine the degrees of internal and external trust.

DO

Actions. Outcomes. Results. Every trace of the creative process has a perceivable appearance that expresses the concept of the creator. A creation must move through the creative stages to a conclusion. Businesses measure the value of a creation by profitability, market lead, or influence. Institutions may measure the value of creativity by organisational efficiency and cultural change. You, the individual creator, may measure your creation by the revenue it generates or the reward of satisfaction in completing a creation.

Working through the Seven Nudges, by intent or nature, stimulates all the right kind of brain activity leading to success. A proactive approach can be replicated for creative projects by individuals, innovation in business, or cultural change in institutions. Building personal nudges is rewarding. Building a future depends on it.

Two

Seven Nudges for Creative Success

5

SEE

The late actor Noriyuki "Pat" Morita endeared film viewers with his portrayal of a wise sensei in the 1984 version of *The Karate Kid* as Mr Miyagi. His protegee, Daniel LaRusso played by Ralph Maccio is a recent transplant from Newark, New Jersey. Reseda, California is located in the San Fernando valley or what is referred to as "The Valley." Characterised as a small suburban town, Reseda was a town where you'd go to raise your kids. The Valley was the backdrop for the most iconic coming of age films of the 1980s and a swath of associated slang, sounds, and styles.

Daniel, being from New Jersey, might as well have been from an alien planet for the reception he received by locals. A formulaic but entertaining story, Daniel has several run-ins with some school bullies, received training from Mr Miyagi, and learned about himself on the way. A classic sequence is Daniel's initial martial arts education by Miyagi. Tasked to perform a series of chores on Miyagi's property, Daniel must complete the tasks as instructed to satisfy their agreement. The duties include waxing a lot full of cars using a "wax on, wax off" pattern, sanding the raised wooden paths of a Japanese garden with "right circle, left circle," and painting a fence with full length "up, down" strokes.

Frustrated that he feels used by Miyagi to do work for no pay, Daniel has a teenaged hissy fit and threatens to quit. But there is more to the tasking than Daniel can see. Driving his point home, Myagi surprises Daniel with a series of Kiai leading attacks. His automatic responses activated, Daniel realised how the work-based repetitive tasks helped him gain strength and the habituation of various defensive techniques. The key to Daniel's education was not a show-me approach. Miyagi wanted Daniel to understand. He needed to know as much about himself as technique, competitiveness, fair play, and the intent of the art form he was learning. To see beyond what was before him, he needed insight.

The Miyagi-LaRusso relationship is a vivid example of the Nudge Principle in practise. Alienated and out-of-place, Daniel must discover a way to overcome in his new environment. He needs to be creative. Miyagi a seasoned observer, and practitioner of Nudge oriented principles, guides Daniel with appropriate nudges toward self-discovery. Without understanding, self-discovery cannot occur.

Consider a repeat offender. I've chosen the example of a criminal because it is low hanging fruit. You can apply the principle to any repeated unproductive behaviour despite there being an awareness of the consequences. Time after time, a repeat offender is caught and convicted for a crime. That person will know there are consequences of getting caught. When asked, they may even give mental assent to that awareness. Should you ask, "Don't you see what this is doing to you and the people that love you?" you may get a hesitation as they search for an answer. While they may see it as a concept, they don't understand the ramifications of their questionable behaviour. The cycle continues with its associated outcomes. The adage that they 'have eyes, but do not see, who have ears but do not hear,' reinforces reality.

To SEE is the first stage of the Nudge Principle and the cornerstone of the Seven Nudges. Regardless of which stage of the creative process a creator may be engaged, what they see will always be the anchor or point of reference. No matter how many times you replay a vision in your consciousness, you will have the symbolism and an array of associated images linked to what you saw. Adaptations to what is seen will be made as you navigate your creativity and what you see will morph accordingly. A new vision of what you see will take root and establish another anchor as a reference. What you see provides stability for understanding and a pool of resources for creativity.

The pool of experience and knowledge we accumulate with SEE is an instantly accessible resource. For as long as we have our recall capacity, we can draw from that pool with relative ease. Understanding, on the other hand, requires cognition. A massive amount of what we take in through our senses as SEE is passively received. Sight formed in your understanding, on the other hand, is a playground to a vast world of possibilities. Understanding is the receptacle, a holy grail, for creativity. Healing and power are the contents. No matter which medium that you demonstrate your creativity; understanding is the goal. Understanding empowers you to open doors closed by ignorance and to enter the richness of illumination. For the value understanding brings, the ability to achieve that goal is diverse and not equally distributed.

You can never assume that another person will see in the same way you do. Another's limited capacity in one area, doesn't mean that they can't see. They just see differently. For example, you are reading this on print or a screen. Those that are blind cannot read in this format. Perhaps braille. Short of a braille version, the best I can offer is to produce an audio version. Understanding that need, I've already prepared to meet that need with an audiobook and a steady offering of complimenting podcasts. Audiobooks also help where literacy may be limited. I'll have to figure out something for multiple languages. To see, and understand, cannot be dependent on a single approach if you are to reach a broad audience.

What if I am a person that can see, but cannot hear? What if I have chromesthesia and listen to sounds in colours? Those with dyslexia, in its varied forms, also affects the way some process information. So many physiological and mental conditions can influence your creativity. Dementia patients may have diminished recall capacity, but activating their creative core keeps the person connected. I mainly want you to see that your own set of circumstances does not bind creativity. The basic idea is that you are aware that there are options outside of your understanding or experience that can be applied for reaching understanding. You need to be able to see it. On a positive note, the volumes of stories of creatives that have overcome what may appear as physical disadvantages are inspiring. Creatives dedicated to their medium will find a way to create.

We are going to explore those abilities that pave the way to understanding. With a broadened approach, we will combine the traditional five senses into a category called the visible and physical world. Following that, we'll touch the invisible of intuition and imagination. Your senses don't end with sight, hearing, feeling, taste, and smell. We are also going to investigate linear, spatial, and connection awareness.

Visible and the Physical

For awareness of your body's surroundings, a vast system of nerves is networked to send signals to and from the brain. Of the 100 trillion cells that make up your body, some of those cells are allocated as neurones and exist as part of the brain and nervous system. As the traditional five senses go, each sensory function has corresponding receptors that react in conjunction with an associated neurotransmitter. You can confirm that information in Human Biology 101. To cultivate an understanding of consciousness, we need to step up to another level.

As amazing as our brain is, it cannot consciously process all the data that it receives. How cool would it be if we could access increased levels of brainpower?

For now, we have science fiction to spin narratives for us through movie characters like Lucy, Eddie Morra, or Neo. These and others demonstrate worlds where anything is possible. Tor Nørrentranders puts the consciousness-sensory connection in perspective as The Bandwidth of Consciousness in his book *The User Illusion*. Nørrentranders theorises that the amount of data transmitted to the brain from our sensory receptors can be measured by the number of receptors attributed to a sensory function. Data transfer between the respective receptors, according to Nørrentranders, can be quantified in bits per second (bps) either megabits per second (Mpbs) or kilobits per second (Kbps). The five senses are measured to process the following speeds to the brain:

- Eyes at least 10 Mbps
- Skin 1 Mbps
- Ear 100 Kbps
- Smell 100 Kbps
- Taste 1 Kbps

A likely volume of 11 megabits of information is being fed to your brain every second. Put in context for sight, a recommended Internet download speed for streaming video is 5 Mbps. Your eyes capture data at a 2-to-1 ratio faster than what is needed to stream high-definition television. Ultra-high-definition (UHD) streaming flashes through at a recommended speed of 25 Mbps which is at least two and a half times the speed your eyes can process data. Your brain marginalises anything above or beyond the scope of your receptors. Filtered content is discarded in favour of consciousness associated triggers. Data that surges in through the five senses is just data. Complex data, but data, nonetheless. There is no meaning to that information until it is ascribed value by your brain. That is why images process so much faster than other data. A study by neuroscientists at MIT reported that your eyes move three or four times a second[4]. Rapid scanning within your visual range can identify images as fast as 13 milliseconds. Your data collecting ability is not a problem—even if it must compensate for imbalances.

What about your other four physical senses? Although not the data collection powerhouse of sight, the combined remaining four senses bring in an additional megabit per second to your inbound data. All of it barges into your brain with sensory abandon. While I am writing, it is daylight. Sunny. Bright. The

---

[4] http://news.mit.edu/2014/in-the-blink-of-an-eye-0116

temperature is an ambient 21°C. Classical piano music plays in the background. Automobiles of all sorts pass outside the window. By the sound of the road noise and rattling cargo, I can tell which vehicles are cars, motorcycles, lorries, or buses. Across the road at the pond, chattering school children in bright yellow hi-vis vests congregate to be amused by the ducklings. A burning eucalyptus candle fills the air of my studio with a soothing fragrance. Lingering in my mouth is the potent taste of peanut butter from a wrap I ate three hours ago. Meanwhile, my fingers clatter on a keyboard trying to keep up with my mind as it lays down words—one on top of the other. Each sequence rolls over to the next piling up of experiences.

The complementary pairing of your sensory inflow is a buffet for consciousness to sort. A colour stands out in a ray of light. "I'll have some of that." A chord resonates, triggering a sense of elation. "That sounds good." Taste, feel, and smell yourself through the buffet until your metaphorical plate is full of all that you want to consume. For the creator, these are the tools for building the foundation for a creation. Before a pen is selected, brush, medium, instrument, or canvas of conversation is stroked, your palette is readied with what you bring to the table. Do we want to create a mouth-watering rich flavour that comforts while wooing the senses to a deeper place of reflection? Shall we introduce a zesty citrus sound that mirrors your inspired moment?

Your five senses encompass an environmental array for gathering information. Information that, in turn, ignites a chain reaction of associations. Feeding your consciousness with the broadest range of physical stimuli cannot satisfy its insatiable demand for more. Every new connection fractalises with organic dynamism. Studies on the psychological effect of sensory awareness are well documented. As with any viable scientific method, a challenging counterbalance of a theorem is the basis for affirming or disproving a thesis. Sensory deprivation, which is a reduction or absence of sensory receptivity, is a methodology for testing sensory perceptions. Short term sensory deprivation can heighten sensory appreciation and deepen awareness, such as that produced during meditation. On the flip side, long-term sensory deprivation can result in mental health issues such as depression, anxiety, and psychosis-like symptoms. Your brain functions well in a sensory world.

What can we do to enhance your SEE Nudge in the physical? Be more proactive in its development. Daniel J. Siegel, author of *The Mindful Brain: Reflections and Attunement in the Cultivation of Wellbeing,* encourages mindfulness. Seigel writes 'Mindfulness, in its most general sense, is about waking up from a life on automatic, and being sensitive to novelty in our everyday experiences.' In many definitions of creativity, novelty is central. Being mindful or aware of novelty means that you are allowing yourself to see, hear, feel, taste, and smell to the broadest experience but also attentive to the change. Expect and create opportunities where you can respond with "I never saw it like that before." You'll be well on your way to activating the connections that will change the way you SEE.

Invisible and the Hidden

Alan Hakman is the fictitious protagonist in the science-fiction film thriller *The Final Cut*. Hakman works for EYE Tech, a futuristic technology company with a patented algorithm that converts memories into images and sound. The device for capturing memory data is called a Zoe Implant. Typically inserted at birth, the Zoe Implant records everything that the visual and aural senses process over a lifetime. At the end of life, the implant is removed, and a *cutter* like Alan assembles a visual presentation of the deceased's life. Hakman, a rather obvious name correlation to a hacker, edits the data to present the best possible depiction of the deceased over their lifetime. Naturally, cutters are paid well for their work. A pleased customer expects the omission of the more disreputable segments of the deceased's memories.

Back in the real world of our present-day AI and nanotechnology, companies race against each other to realise EYE Tech inspired technology. Those first to market with the ability to convert brain activity into images have the power to dominate a high demand product. If you could replicate the complexity of memory, imagination, dreams, or thought processes, you'd hold the keys to empowering AI with near-human qualities. Research with deep neural networks brings the world closer to this reality. Your life condensed into bytes and bits. Even though the technology exists in *The Final Cut*, one aspect of humanity befuddles tech science. Hakman asserts that an implant with a flaw makes data collection unreliable in that it "can't see the difference between what the eye sees and what the mind sees." How does the brain differentiate visible perception versus an internally generated impression? Dream or reality?

What of those images and thoughts that fire in your head and ricochet down pathways allocated to slower traffic? Do they end up in some mass storage room of unused 90% brain we've been fabled with through pop culture? A massive file storage area from which you can call up data by triggers that bring a memory and all its associated links to the front of your consciousness? Are they intricate networks that amass bits of information from multiple locations until a whole is manifest? If you were to sever a dendrite or extract a neurone, would you find it coded with information? Can we create a new Enigma machine to break the code of our brain signalling that forms a thought? We certainly are trying. The matter safely encased in your skull, by itself, has not been unlocked that way. Nevertheless, the activity of thought and creativity is, without question, measurable.

Have you ever attempted to describe something to somebody who has no point of reference to what you are describing? Say, for instance, you want to describe a giant sequoia tree to a person that has lived their life in a place like Alert, Nunavut, Canada. Deep in the Arctic Circle, Alert is the northernmost permanently inhabited location in the world. Assuming your interviewee has never seen pictures of any area beyond 50 miles of Alert or browsed the Internet, how would you describe a giant sequoia? A tree that rises to a phenomenal 300 feet with a base circumference of 115 feet. A forest of these trees, that when you stand under the canopy, blocks out sunlight. Words alone could not get the point across well enough. You might have some success if you drew picture contrasts for your friend to see. All the while you are describing this magnificent living thing, the mind of the person you are trying to convince is whirring with activity. In auto-response, their brain has engaged in a familiarity search trying to relate to your description.

Once that person has played out their matching associations, their brain activates the realm of imagination. To provide a contrast, I propose that my friend is the size of a gnat standing at the base of a stalk of Arctic cotton. That might give a glimpse of perspective, but my imagining friend would still struggle to formulate an image in his head. Now suppose I shared the vision of the giant sequoia day after day for weeks. I described how some trees are cored at the base for cars to pass through. I show him what a similar texture of the bark is like and keep drawing pictures. Eventually, the consciously assimilated images, form a point of reference. The capacity to imagine what a giant sequoia is like percolates in his mind. Depending on the other activities of his day, the images he sees and his imagination pour over into his sleep state. He dreams of the giant sequoia. In awe of its size and presence, he wakes to proclaim, "I can see it now" — even though he has never seen a sequoia.

The capacity to envision something that has not been seen or heard is to imagine. Later in the nudges of FLOW and PLAY, imagination assumes the centre stage where it can facilitate your exploration of possibilities. I've heard the woeful cries and accusations from some that they "Have no imagination." A dedicated dreamer and admirer of imagination, I gently guide with "That is only because you don't allow it to grow." The invisible and hidden parts of your thinking process can become dormant. Withering and brittle from lack of use. You may hear claims that imagination is for children and artists or "I gave that up long ago when I grew up." Maybe the imaginative holdback claims came as the less-inclined creative ditched imagination "When I became responsible." It is not that you grew up, became responsible, or your imagination became unimportant to you. You forgot how to do it.

Plasticity in a child's development is essential for exploring self and the world around them. Imagination is the magic carpet that lets them see things that they cannot see. To be and do things they may be currently limited to achieve. Imagination is a state of "what if" that has not been tainted with "…but." The same conditions that children face—unable to see what they cannot see, be or do—also trouble adults. The solution is the same; to SEE a creative solution through the eyes of wonder.

The Linear Nature of Cause-and-effect

We were out for a nice meal at an Asian style restaurant near where we live. Thinking back, I believe we were the only customers as it was early in the evening. Service seemed exceptionally slow, so of course, my mind wandered to the point of distraction. A server brought a foot-long metal slab to the table and placed it in the centre of the table between my wife and me. The steely, apparently cold, surface caught my interest. What was this nifty thing they brought to us? What did it do? Before my brain had a chance to say "No," I reached out and touched the surface with the tips of the four fingers of my right hand. Albeit just a slight touch, I quickly learned that the slab of metal was, in fact, a hotplate. My hand's retraction was immediate.

At first, I thought I'd be okay. "I didn't touch it for long," I told myself. When the redness started to show, I asked for ice. When the throbbing started, I knew I was going to blister. My self-talk at that moment followed a line that included words like "stupid" and "dumb." At the same time, I wondered what happened to the courteous caution of "Please be careful, this is hot" from the server. Pondering my bandaged fingertips, I understood how my Mom once fell prey to the firecracker temptation of simultaneously lighting multiple Black Cats in her hand. Same results. Daring as she was, I don't think she tried that manoeuvre again. I know I learned my lesson about touching shiny flat silver slabs of metal at restaurants. My brain let me down. I didn't see what should have been obvious.

From your early childhood development, you were immersed in the education of boundaries. Based on the relational environment in which you were reared, learning points were a mix of safety, value, and inherited boundaries. "Don't touch that, it's hot," being a relevant example of a safety boundary. A defined cause-and-effect alertness is established. Theoretically, when a child encounters the conditions on her own, she will apply the rules of that situation — thereby avoiding the potentially harmful consequences of non-compliance. The ability to carry over the learning pattern obtained in the safety boundary climate provides the foundation for our adult safety mechanisms.

Values and inherited boundaries, while somewhat subject to cause-and-effect, fit into a different category. At least as it relates to our illustration. Value boundaries are those constraints stamped on our childhood psyche by intentional or cultural conditioning. We will look at this more in chapter ten with the BE Nudge. But to set the stage, let's use the example of a father reinforcing a value with his son. In the 1995 Disney film *Tall Tale: The Unbelievable Adventures of Pecos Bill*, farmer Jonas Hackett stands alone in his fight against a resource-consuming corporate machine lead by J.P. Stiles. Hackett's son, Daniel, is less enthusiastic about fighting for the land that yields such a small return.

When Daniel expresses his misgivings for not accepting Stiles' offer to buy the farm at a fraction of its worth, his father reminds Daniel of the family's core values. "You do know the Code of the West, don't you?" Jonas asks his son. He continues in a solemn tone, "Respect the land, defend the defenceless, and don't you never spit in front of women or children." You have your codes of passed down values that form a central ingredient to how you view the world. And also an unwritten rule of consequences for breaking from that value set.

Insidious when evoking a negative reaction, liberating when fear is marginalised, inherited boundaries are those cautionary mental checks that appear in our observed behaviours instead of intentional conditioning. Again, you will have your own. One of my inherited boundaries still catches me off guard on occasion. My mother had an inordinate fear of snakes. I remember two events when her fear caused her to become temporarily paralysed. Once on a picnic, she sat, feet up on the seat of the car, and would not step out into the long grass. A fear of snakes, even the garden variety, created a scenario in her mind that the six-inch-deep grass of the field was unsafe. I began to understand the depth of her ophidiophobia when she turned away in fear as a snake appeared on the television screen in a programme. I remember saying to her "But, Mom, it's only TV." That meant nothing in her mind. For years, and still today, I scan the edge of trails and open fields for snakes. By reasoning, I have overcome that specific inherited boundary. I don't think I am frightened of snakes as much as I was when I was younger. I just don't like to be startled by them.

Being aware of boundary factors that influence your behaviours and thinking opens your ability to see with greater clarity. Perceiving, rightly or wrongly, the cause-and-effect of a condition stretches your capacity for lateral thinking. You understand that if A happens, B or perhaps C will occur as a result. This way of processing cause-and-effect is also central to your understanding of time. On its own, our brain has no concept of time. Should you float blissfully in a sensory deprivation tank, you'd be unaware of the length of time that passes. Time is a linear measurement of events in the past, present, and future. For deadlines and remembering a partner's anniversary, awareness of that linear measurement helps us succeed in a time-conscious society.

Harnessing cause-and-effect into a SEE orientation empowers you to test boundaries. When you can SEE underlying reasons for why such-and-such occurs, you may elect to pursue a different course. Rules and boundaries, whether subject to physical laws or inculturation, should be tested.

An associative image that comes to mind is the 2017 collapse of the Ponte Morandi bridge in Genoa, Italy. Bridges are supposed to be regularly checked for safety under governmental regulations. When standing, Ponte Morandi was the busiest bridge in Italy. The bridge required regular inspection and remediation to remain safe under load and a deteriorating infrastructure. That did not happen in association with the bridge's rate of decline and use. When the bridge collapsed, 43 people died. Challenging your boundaries and adapting where necessary, ensures stability in a changing world. Quoting a philosophical sage of pop-culture in referring to rules, "Some [rules] can be bent, others can be broken." You will never know which rules and boundaries can and cannot be bent, broken, or should be unless you test them.

Space is Not the Final Frontier

From the use of my illustrations and examples, you probably have sussed a profile of me, my generation, preferences, and writing style. Introducing the SEE concept as it relates to spatial reasoning, it wouldn't be surprising that I'd associate space with *Star Trek*. Three years following the date that time lord Dr Who arrived on British television in 1963, intrepid space explorers of the starship Enterprise debuted on American television. The voice of Captain James T. Kirk opens each episode with the iconic phrase "Space, a final frontier." Space to which Kirk refers, of course, is the vastness of the universe. Since that first episode, the Star Trek franchise has taken fans on a journey across galaxies and dimensions. We've been introduced to humanoid and non-humanoid life forms that challenge our views of morality, justice, and relationships. The universe and multiverses we discover are more easily conceptualised when considered in the context of our human orientation. Space doesn't seem so big when you are travelling with others and the familiar.

Space used in that setting is the free, available, or unoccupied expanse of a defined area. Space is an unexplored and a vast frontier for discovery. While fun to play in and measure, that is not space of which I refer. We go places to occupy a space, like a restaurant or a seat on a plane. Our physical art or creative work will take up space someplace as will the materials and tools required to create. I suppose we could stretch the boundaries and say that audible or sensory experiences can consume space. The thing is, these all fit in the SEE category of visible as described earlier. Where I want to nudge you along is in your understanding of the other noun definition for space. That being, 'the dimensions of height, depth, width within which all things exist and move.'

Self-centric, spatial reasoning is your ability to see dimensionality—specifically in 3D. As a component of the SEE Nudge, spatial reasoning adds depth, height and width to a concept or perspective. A tech example of what I am talking about is the 3D printers on the market. The price of 3D printers has dropped to affordable levels for hobbyists. Now you can create 3D versions of your creations at home. I am wildly keen on this idea as I want to create some game pieces. With a design in mind, I can enter the data for the 3D printer to produce my concept. Before I do that, I need to convert my idea from its one-dimensional prison on a sheet of paper.

Fortunately, there is software to create 3D images. You must still conceptualise in 3D, but the software will assist in the calculations and rendering. I like the idea of crafting 3D in traditional ways. Sculpting gives me a chance to use my hands to create. I could design my game piece with modelling clay, make a latex mould, and then use coloured resin to create my master. With that, I'd have a low-cost version of the game piece to show to prospective investors, manufacturers, and game testers. To reach my goals for the mass marketing of the game, I will need a 3D digital version complete with dimensions, weight, density, colour, and a solid handle on price per unit impact on the project. Making that game piece, in whichever phase of development, demands a 3D orientation.

Not only is spatial reasoning essential for literal 3D productions, but it also opens your mind to lateral thinking. I once took an art course for drawing where the textbook was Betty Edwards' *Drawing on the Right Side of the Brain.* Besides thoroughly enjoying the course, I was introduced to the concept of the brain's left-right hemisphere orientation. Edwards' book was first published in 1979. My course instructor was fast on Edwards' work in 1980 when she introduced the concepts to her students. Of the many exercises we completed in our effort to unlock hidden artistic talent, one activity was to work with negative space. According to Edwards, the left hemisphere centre of logic doesn't deal well with empty spaces. To prime the less linear oriented right hemisphere of the brain, we had to draw the empty spaces in and around an object. In so doing, you were able to see the form of the object without the hindrances of labels and prejudice.

I readily admit that the drawing course that I took in 1980 was a seminal event for my interest in creativity and the brain. My study pieces reside in a storage container in Colorado, where they remain with other treasures collected over the years. Understanding of left-right brain hemisphere functionality has matured since Edwards published. Advanced neuroimaging techniques exposed flaws in the left-right brain hemisphere proposition called hemispheric lateralisation. The science of Edwards' *Drawing on the Right Side of the Brain* may not stand up to existing scientific research, but that doesn't alter the results. Conducting activities that stimulate lateralisation, especially with spatial reasoning, does have a positive cascading effect on the way you see. I often revisit the exercises in Edwards' book. If for nothing else, to add a refreshed perspective on the way I see.

Bridging the Social Gap

Musician Joe Jackson tells the story in song of a young man struggling in a confused state of mind. At the centre of his turmoil is his sense of value with the opposite sex. Jackson refers to other men walking down his street with pretty women. The story's character expresses his confusion when he blurts out in the chorus, "Is she really going out with him?" He further punctuates his angst by stating "cause if my eyes don't deceive me, there's something going wrong around here." Listening to the song again, forty-one years later, I wonder if there wasn't a bit more behind the struggle than a young man's issues of acceptance. Regardless of Jackson's inspiration for the lyrics, the chorus catalyses another aspect of SEE of which we do well to be aware—interpersonal relations.

In this chapter, I've promoted the connection between seeing and understanding. We are aware that a wide range of conditions, influences like memes, capacity, personal history, and other factors affect the way we view events. Seeing is a uniquely individual experience. What we see and how we interpret, apart from that conditioning thing, is ours to own. When it comes to understanding interpersonal relations, we step into the realm of "My word, why did I go there?" Interpersonal relationships, good or bad, must be a consideration for creativity. Nestled snuggly in a crevice like a viper ready to strike, this topic has the potential for misunderstanding and offence. A single word can divert your attention from a positive, creative flow to divisive, hypersensitive levels. It happens all the time.

A few pages back, when we were covering cause-and-effect, we discussed values and inherited boundaries. Connections we make in our brain from specific cause-and-effect experiences shape the way we view other people. That orientation will invariably influence your creative expression. Subtle or in-your-face, biases and prejudices will eventually surface. The societal climate of today, especially online, is postured to strike at the smallest semblance of an -ism. From our perspective, we might aim to promote diversity, seek inclusion, and assimilate understanding to counter our ignorance about others. I think that is what some factions of the global community want to realise by imposition. At the other end of the spectrum, are those that demand segregation, resist inclusion, and embrace their ignorance in the name of personal rights. The polarisation, in some cases, is beyond extreme.

Adjusting the limits to someplace closer to the centre is not my goal. I don't know where you stand with your worldview of diversity and inclusion. Do your views rise and fall to an extreme, or do they hover softly in the middle? The challenge is posed to you not to change your mind, but for you to check biases. Preferences if you think bias is too harsh. Understand how that predisposition impacts your creative processes, and how it affects your relationship with other people.

History abounds with stories of the reclusive creator type. Cranky, abrasive, isolated, totally lacking social graces. Fictional author Melvin Udall played masterfully by Jack Nicholson, from the film *As Good as it Gets* comes to mind. Udall says so many offensive things in the movie that it is hard to pick a single quote that best represents his character. Each offending remark plays through his ensconced stereotype, regardless of his target. You'd expect that he would have some degree of appreciation for fans, but that is not the case. When asked by a fan named Jackie "How do you write women so well?" Melvin replies with Udall sharpness: "I think of a man. And I take away reason and accountability." Not exactly the kind of response he would have learned from *How to Win Friends and Influence People.*

We are all the more aware today that numerous mental conditions may affect a person's abilities in social situations. People-oriented phobias, degrees of autism, dementia, depression, and psychosis are some of the more well-known conditions and disorders. There are also personality types that cause a person to lean more in one behavioural direction than another. Unless you are a trained professional, you may never realise that a person you are with battles with or is unaware of their state. Functioning in a state of awareness that a person's behaviour may be affected by unseen conditions in the brain can help you to develop a sense of empathy. We will discuss this further in chapter nine when I introduce the FEEL Nudge and its relation to emotions.

From the vantage of the SEE Nudge, perhaps the most valuable position you can assume is that of knowing your strengths and limitations regarding interpersonal relations. I am, for instance, an introvert. I don't register on the high end of the introvert scale, but closer to extrovert. Knowing the difference between the two helped me to understand myself better. An introvert may be shy, but being shy does not make an introvert. The difference between an introvert and an extrovert is how they recharge their mental and emotional state. An introvert prefers a self-contained or controlled environment. An extrovert gets energised by being around other people. These are relatively safe generalisations if we keep in mind that there are variables in degrees of each person.

I think that it should be noted that developing the SEE Nudge as it relates to creativity has an incredibly broad assortment of manifestations. Brilliance is not restricted to whether a person can get along with others. I can quickly whip out a list of well-documented artists, scientists, authors, and other creators that made history despite their lack of social skills. Neither is it mandatory that a creator is even aware of their state or that of another person. I aim to provoke your awareness (SEE) that interpersonal relations play a role in the scope of your creative success.

Blind but Now I See

Born with a medical condition that contributed to a lifetime of blindness, 68-year old Canadian Pierre-Paul Thomas.[5] had a stumble down some stairs in 2011. The facial damage that Thomas incurred in the fall required plastic surgery around his eyes. Dr Lucie Lessard, renowned for her innovative techniques in plastic surgery, asked Thomas if he wanted his eyes fixed as well. Was that possible? He was functionally blind since birth. His visual world was restricted to transitions of grey, black, and white. For sixty-six years, he saw objects through touch. Throughout his story, the notion that he could receive his sight was outside of his consideration. What kept Thomas from seeing was not a congenital condition, but that cataracts had formed. Removal of those cataracts and Pierre-Paul Thomas should be able to see.

After the cataracts were removed and a short period of recovery, Thomas saw with his eyes for the first time. He had previously resigned to a life of blindness where he attributed his lack of sight to "How I was made." No longer was he restricted to the dullness of a grey, black, and white world but a spectrum of colour opened in the blink of an eye. Faces and objects, long perceived through contact, took on previously unrealised depth, contour, and tone. Decades of training his brain to see through touch jump-started a rush of new connections in his brain. To compensate for the overwhelming sensory input, Thomas found himself reverting to touch to see or perhaps confirm, the associations created in his mind.

Opening your mind by actively developing your SEE Nudge will induce moments of pleasure as if you see something for the first time. There will be those discoveries beyond entrenched thought patterns that demand hard work and diligence. You may find yourself frequently returning to a familiar point of reference to stabilise your perspective. Deciding to be proactive in your pursuit to SEE will lead to understanding. That is if you are willing to evaluate what you see in an open-minded environment. Seeing, by itself, does not produce understanding. Standing alone, seeing exposes you to sensory, intuitive, imaginative, sequential, spatial, and interpersonal observations. To understand demands, a higher level of cognitive engagement.

The curiosity factor must be very high for those that see for the first time following the restoration of sight from blindness. Perhaps in equal measure, those

---

[5] Man sees for the first time in old age: 'It s like I m a child all over again'. 29 July 2013, https://o.canada.com/news/pierre-paul-thomas-blind-cataracts

that are involved in the life of a person gifted with receiving sight must be curious. The wraps are pulled away from the eyes. The dark glasses are placed to the side. The on switch is flipped with new technology. The first question on everybody's mind is "What do you see?" To SEE is the first Nudge because it establishes a base. To measure what we see, to see if it has merit or value, we need to communicate that vision. Regardless of which expression of sight it applies.

6

TELL

Professional poker playing attracts millions of players worldwide with a get rich, strategy laced appeal, and big win enticements. From friendly home games and online giants to world champions, legends of the game lure more to the table every year. The mechanics of poker are quite simple. You need to know the basic rules of the game along with how and when to bet. The how and when to bet is where the money is made and lost. Players follow wildly diverse approaches on how they play the game. Winners win because they adhere to a set of confirmable rules. Play by those rules, don't deviate, and you will win most of the time. Even if winning means you walk away with your maximum loss cap.

The game is full of colourful characters with a style and strategy they are confident will get them to the final table. Nine will make it. One will win the prize. There are the actors, the bullies, the mathematicians, online addicts, inebriated and stone-cold sober, alongside the man or woman next door. They wear hoodies, sunglasses, hats, colourful clothes to distract or they may look like the "kid" working down at the corner shop. Besides the fact that they all play poker, they have other common attributes. Each has their giveaways called tells, and they have seen astronomically more poker hands than a newbie. Over an hour of the average live game, a player will see twenty-five to thirty hands. Online, you can double or triple that amount. Crunch the numbers to multiply how many hours, days, and years a person plays. Also, factor in those games played in a tournament environment.

A difference between a live and online game is that tells are not exposed online. Not really. In a live session, with an opponent seated nearby, a tell can be the difference between winning and losing. Good players work on minimising their tell. It throws the opposition off guard. A tell is an unconscious physical action that can potentially expose a player's intent on a hand. They are there, even if ever so slight. You may have seen a painting by C.M. Coolidge of dogs playing poker. Around the year 1900, Coolidge painted a series on the commission of Brown & Bigelow to advertise cigars. Imagine if a dog could play poker and held a good poker hand. To keep that tail from wagging, not so much as a twitch, would be an unrealistic challenge. On the other end, if he had a bad hand, he'd find it difficult not to utter a subdued growl or keep his ears from lowering. Without realising, we can demonstrate, tell, signal, or otherwise communicate our thought processes for others to pick up.

Of course, when we are intentional in that communication process, we stand a far more improved prospect for understanding to occur. The elementary parts of the communication model are the sender, a message, and a receiver. In a closed-loop model, the communication process includes feedback from the receiver to the sender. An open-loop model is one-way. Feedback, in that case, requires a different method to evaluate a receiver source, measure the clarity of the message, and assess the message value. A closed-loop communication model has a higher probability of a message's meaning to be immediately perceived for comprehension (understanding) by the receiver. As the Nudge Principle goes, we want to develop a closed-loop communication model because that is where you can see that your message is appropriately received. Think of the open-loop model as a message still rattling around in your head or you've allocated it to a shelf called 'In Development.' Allow me to note that great ideas die there.

Your goal with TELL is to do everything within your power and influence to ensure your message is received and clearly understood. What the receiver does with that message is up to them. What about that message? Of what does it consist? Your message is the formulation of what has occurred in the SEE Nudge. Your message is what you want to communicate and adapted into your medium of choice. You can look at the SEE-TELL cycle as a single microburst of creative thought or part of a project campaign where interlacing parts fit together. TELL is the testing grounds for what you SEE. By communicating the thoughts in your head, in whichever format you use, you are enabled to see from a different perspective. That may come in the form of writing, drawing, speaking, forming, crafting in 3D, whatever. TELL translates the invisible into the visible and measurable realm of observation.

We have more outlets for communicating our TELL than ever before. We are saturated with words, images, sounds, and what seems a relentless stream of variables. Since we are working to validate our SEE Nudge observations, let's limit our conversation to a manageable range of topics. In this chapter, we will look at our internal and external messages, expressions, symbology, and the closed-loop communication model or feedback loop to improve understanding. The fun of this part of the Nudge Principle is discovering ways to communicate in various settings with diverse communication styles or methods. The people factor, always being the wild card.

Self-Talk

An entire industry and countless acolytes follow the personal development gurus of self-talk. It is a safe suggestion that any personal development programme probably includes an element of self-talk as a core contribution to personal success. My entry point to the topic of self-talk came in 1990 when I read Shad Helmstetter's classic *What to Say When You Talk to Your Self.* Since its first edition, the book has sold millions of copies. I hadn't read the book in years, so I ordered a copy to replace my lost one. I also checked Helmstetter's website to see what has been doing since *What to Say* was published. He has been very busy with more books, twenty-four according to his website. He has a training institute and has spoken to millions through radio, television, live audiences, and audio.

Scientific understanding is an accumulation of work on which others lay a foundation. Self-talk was not new information, but Helmstetter conveyed the concepts in easy to understand and applicable language. Any reader could theoretically read the book, apply the principles, and achieve a modicum of success. The proposition is that you can change a behaviour by regulating the dialogue that occurs in your brain or, as presented in chapter two, modify and expand brain connections. Negative or toxic thinking can be mitigated by applying techniques that increase the volume of positive self-talk. The application of positive self-talk heavily influences the global self-help industry and some psychology techniques like cognitive behavioural therapy.

What we gain from the body of this subject is the knowledge that it is not so much what you think as it is how you think. At the core of any self-talk strategy, are steps to condition the brain. The outcome of the conditioning expectantly leads to positive behaviours. Put another way, a mind that seeks and reinforces the practise of alternatives increases its capacity for creating options. An internal feedback loop engages a message-receiver connection to test concepts for validation. Possibilities are scanned from the catalogue of our experience, associations are made, and our mind accepts or rejects the results. If kept, the association will eventually be revealed as an action. As noted earlier, this all happens at superfast speeds. Even cognisant of the process, you can't keep up with the steps that occur.

That your brain moves faster than you can think, doesn't mean that you can't participate. At this point, I am not promoting any form of self-talk over the other. I am not promoting self-talk as a personal development technique at all. In the Nudge Principle, self-talk is simply the internal chatter that you engage in to test what you SEE. It is an open-loop process that leaves the perpetual door open to possibilities. An observed event changes the conditions of a premise, so you must find an alternative. Variables are weighed, the internal checks that influence your thinking crowd in to play their part, and a solution pops into consciousness like a behind-a-door mystery is revealed. You might go through this process with so many iterations that you lose sight of the original premise. Thoughts evolve, morphing with each successive generation of change.

SEE and TELL, especially related to self-talk, are like your left and right hand, shaping a thought like clay in the hands of a master sculptor. Investigate what it feels like to visualise your thoughts. Listen to what you are thinking by speaking it out —by an utterance, by reading a written account, or ad hoc speaking out loud. For no other reason, do this so that you can hear the sound of your idea. I regularly use this technique when I am preparing to speak to an audience. Most of the time, I will envision my topic, collate supportive parts, organise the components into a sequence, and play with how I want to say it. All that happens in my head. Rarely do I apply those thoughts to an external source like an outline or slide deck until I have matured the ideas in my head. Once my presentation has a structure, I apply an order sequence and appropriate mnemonic devices.

Now, how do I improve the quality of my speaking from this all-in-my-head internalisation? I repeat the main points, subpoints, supporting data, and anecdotes in my head as if presenting to my audience. Doing something in your mind can satisfy the brain's need to engage in the doing of an action. Athletes use this technique across a spectrum of disciplines. Envision crossing the finishing line or pushing past a challenging stage of a routine. Although practising in your mind doesn't override the need for physical activity, it does establish a mental orientation for the steps and stages involved. When I speak, by the time I step in front of an audience, I am so comfortable with the material that it flows. Instead of losing momentum on the content, I can focus on and engage the audience.

When you ponder the partnership between observation skills and self-talk, think of the process as your drawing board. You may have heard the phrase "Go back to the drawing board." The drawing board is the traditional table used by engineers, architects, and drafting technicians. A concept was developed, modelled, and did not work according to the expected outcome of the plans. Going back meant investigating what went wrong. Now we use computer models that run algorithms. For our mind's health, back to the drawing board moments don't represent failures or mistakes. Instead, they add a wealth of experience that can and will be, used someplace else.

You are Your Own Narrator

You've reached the saturation point in your thinking, and now you want to spill it out. Depending on your personality type and specific conditions, the way you introduce your private thoughts to an awaiting audience will vary. Your singular goal is for the audience, be it one or a thousand, to understand your concepts as you do. The value of that thought is about to be weighed and considered by another person's thought processes. In a way, your task is to sell your idea to somebody else. The currency of that transaction is an investment of trust; the return on that investment is understanding. For that, you need to build your TELL Nudge for converting your thoughts into demonstrable actions. There you stand a better chance of being understood.

Converting your thoughts into demonstrable actions is not as difficult as you may think. You do it all the time and have done so since birth. You've advanced the process considerably, but it is a never-ending activity of development. An infant will cry due to five underlying conditions or a combination thereof: she is hungry, uncomfortable, in pain, tired, or wants attention. The parent's job is to figure out which condition is the most urgent, satisfy that need, and restore peace to the cosmos. Older now, and matured in your communication skills, you can better craft complex communications to express what you want or need.

A recurring theme in your life will have involved reciting to another person about events. Maturity in communications and interpersonal relationships are evidenced in your message about that sequence. The teen, when asked "How was school today?" is set up to answer with a stereotypical short vocabulary of four-letter adjectives. Top favourite one-word responses for teenaged boys are "Okay," "Good," "Fine." There is also the infamous growl that expresses anything from "Please don't talk to me now" to "I am going to have a bowl of cereal and go to bed." We can laugh about the atypical teen behaviour as with many of our parenting experiences. We can take it in as part of their development and apply some empathy as they mature physically, mentally, and emotionally. The same scenario may play out again a decade later when that teen is an adult and in a partner-partner relationship. The messages will change to "How was work today?" Top automatic answers are "Okay," "Good," "Fine," or the infamous growl that expresses anything from "You don't want to know" to "Let's just have dinner and watch television."

Sure, these are stereotypes and cartoonish depictions of communication. In situations like this, when we reduce our messages to simple forms, I think it is due to a level of familiarity we have with the receiver. We expect the receiver to understand our message, even when it is reduced to four-letter adjectives, growls, or silence. We hope that our message will be understood, but we leave an awful lot of wiggle room for interpretation.

Understanding is your goal for a compelling message. You are aiming for clarity in the mind of your receiver. The message is that vehicle. For a moment, let's look at it another way. Turn it around. Harry Beckwith and Christine Clifford propose in their book *You, Inc.* that communicating to be understood may need an adjustment as the first rule of communication. Instead, they suggest, 'Communicate so that you cannot be misunderstood.' I like that. I can apply that principle to so many situations. However, if I adhere to it in every case, I may not ever verbalise my thoughts. I could follow the line of thinking in the proverb 'A person is considered wise until they speak and remove all doubt.' But that also won't get me to where I want to be. I want to be understood. You want to be understood. That is why we work so hard at communication.

Allow me to be bold. There are no hard or set rules for how you communicate. Honestly, there are just too many variations and variables to consider. If you are a person that likes lists and convenient factoids on which you can hang a memory jogger, I can't do that for you. We can borrow from Beckwith and Clifford again. What are the answers to tricks and shortcuts in planning and preparing to communicate? There are none. You must do the work. What I'd like to offer is a suggested approach to communication that you might find useful in most scenarios: the narrative.

What is being played out in your mind, apart from facts and figures, is a manner of story. It has an entry point where you begin, the body of what you want to say, and a point where you close. Crafting and practising a narrative style of communicating also applies to a wide range of mediums. Not restricted to words, either oral or written, you can tell a story from your unique perspective in a variety of ways. A narrative is, simply put, a story. A story can be short "Doris walked to the corner store", or it can be epic. You also use story in work. A project is essentially a story outline with milestones marking events. Relationships are a story in progress with drama, humour, love, pain, and a journey. Ledgers are a story of a company's business history, marked by anecdotes of sales and losses, successes and failures.

You are the narrator of your story and an observer of the stories that surround. What you see is indelibly etched in your person. As an external communication, that narrative is the extension of your creative person. The two are inseparable. What you communicate is your passport into the domain of another's thinking. To build upon the SEE and TELL Nudges is to become a better communicator and participant in life. A key to making the most of your experiences is to find ways to communicate that fulfil you as a person and best enable understanding.

Express Yourself

Words are my favourite tools of a creative toolbox. Whether conducting a workshop, developing training material, or endeavouring to write a book, words hold a prominent attraction for me as a creative expression. Rich with colour and history, words are my building materials for communicating my thoughts. This book is the culmination of about fifteen years of study, reading, intentional employment selections, and hundreds of hours of reflection. I wrote it to synthesise my ideas. The creative momentum can't stop with words on a page. To practise what I preach, I need to branch out from my comfort zone and work at other expressions.

My studio is loosely divided into four creative parts: the hub of my writing, graphic design and recording desk, stacks of books read and to be read, an art corner, and a sofa to practise my guitar. How good I am at any of the expressions is not essential to me. I want to experience as much as I can in as many mediums within the shortest amount of time as is reasonable. Words will always be my primary expression, but I want to expand my base of exploration. I am not so good at dividing up my time for my interests. Usually, one project will dominate my time more than another. But I am working on it.

You could argue a case that you want to be expert in one discipline. Say you want to be the best possible software engineer you can be. Muddling up your life with extraneous activities would get in the way of your focus. I am not suggesting that you should become a life experience pack rat at the expense of your ambitions. On the contrary, I recommend that you explore a diversity of expressions to enhance your focus and enthusiasm. Somewhere in my stack of books and notes is a bit I read about the creative vibe of Austin, Texas. The tech boom in Austin attracts start-ups and relocating tech companies to the Austin area to capitalise on what author Richard Florida calls the "creative class." It is worthwhile to reference Florida directly.

> *The distinguishing characteristic of the creative class is that its members engage in work whose function is to "create meaningful new forms." The super-creative core of this new class includes scientists and engineers, university professors, poets and novelists, artists, entertainers, actors, designers, and architects, as well as the "thought leadership" of modern society: non-fiction writers, editors, cultural figures, think-tank researchers, analysts, and other opinion-makers. Members of this super-creative core produce new forms or designs that are readily transferable and broadly useful, such as designing a product that can be widely made, sold, and used; coming up with a theorem or strategy that can be applied in many cases; or composing music that can be performed again and again..[6]*

Back to that article to which I referred. The premise was that creatives seek expanded expressions of creativity outside of their work orientation. The examples of creative exploration by executives, engineers, and people across disciplines highlight a mindset toward creativity. Among the office-bound leaders of corporate innovation, you have guitar players, artists, writers, photographers, and numerous other forms of creative expression. I am lead to wonder if the traditional work-until-you-drop stereotype of success still holds true. How long can a person go full tilt without proper recharging? The diversion of a creative outlet allows you to see things differently and fire those neurons down neglected pathways. Who wouldn't want to diversify their creative portfolio with an investment of quality creativity?

Perhaps I am overselling the concept. I may be missing that hook that enables the idea to sell itself. I don't want you to lose the intentional goal of this section. That being, naturally, to understand the value of diversifying the way you express yourself. You may be nodding your head with complete identification. You already find ways to express yourself outside of the parameters of your work mindset. Shifting from a work mindset to an open-minded, creative expression can be a thrill ride, especially if your work is demanding or riddled with

---

[6] Florida, Richard. *Cities and the Creative Class.* Carnegie Mellon University. 2003 https://creativeclass.com/rfcgdb/articles/4%20Cities%20and%20the%20Creative%20Clas s.pdf

interpersonal challenges. You may already be aware that your creative machine is working all the time. It doesn't have to be turned on like an augmented category to your life. Whether at work, in between, or post-work, you actively integrate creative expressions into your daily routines. You get it. Doing so has become part and parcel to who you are. Anything less is unusual.

Another lot of folks will view expanding creative expression as a waste of time. Satisfied with life as it is, they neither have intention or aspiration for adding creativity to their life. They could be of that demographic that had the notion they are not creative burned into their brain years ago. To now think any differently is an obstacle unworthy of attention. Sure, you can get by like that and never notice a difference or change. On the odd chance that you want more and to develop your influence, then expanding your horizons to appreciate the creative process is going to be a part of that journey. Not exploring ways of upping your expression is not a deal-breaker in the Nudge Principle, nor is it critical for the TELL Nudge. Think of it as a diversion on a road trip that allows you to see things that you could not see from a motorway. It may take you longer to get to your destination, but you will enjoy the scenery.

Po Bronson published *What Should I Do With My Life?* in 2002. I read the book as part of an optional reading assignment during my mid-life return to university. Bronson interviewed 900 people about their lives and settled on the stories of 70 from that near thousand. The stories encompass people from all walks of life and economic status. Reading about people with whom I could identify, made the stories more compelling. Although I enjoyed the stories, I struggled with the tone of the economic divide. A financially successful person with a hefty nest egg could self-finance a life-changing path. Whereas, a person locked into unfulfilling, demanding, and underpaid employment was unlikely to have the resources to make a daring leap into chance. Regardless of their pre-existing statuses, they each found a path leading to life satisfaction.

Over the past few years, I've met an increasing number of people that fit both categories. Some are underpaid, and others are doing well financially but burdened with a lifestyle that traps them no differently than a person trying to make ends meet. When I am asked in casual conversation what I do, I tell them my vision for Nudge. If they want a narrative, I tell them what it has taken to get this far. Lawyers, accountants, engineers, and bankers with decades in their industry all say the same thing "I wish I could do that." My answer is always the same "What do you like to do? Watching the creative sparks ignite their eyes is one of life's greatest pleasures for me. Put a smile on your face. Express yourself.

Imagery, Allegories, and Metaphors

Charades is a popular parlour game from eighteenth-century France. Originally it was played by throwing out verbal hints for syllables that when strung together would create a word or phrase. That game was called literary charades. By the nineteenth century, the game evolved to include performing the hints. That is the version mainly played today at parties and family gatherings. The charade presenter, or charader, is given the word or phrase to mimic. Players must correctly guess the word or phrase within an agreed time to win the coveted role of being the next charader. Centerstage, the charader acts out a representation of a movie, book, television show, or person. While in play, the charade presenter may gesture wildly with syllable counting fingers slashing, entertaining antics acted with vigour, and a tap on the nose to indicate a correct response to the puzzle.

To win at charades, a player doesn't need to be a quiz night champion. The game is not set up to test knowledge. What you need for playing are your observational skills and to participate in the guessing (TELL) part. You also need the ability to draw from your observations and translate your mimics into an action. To win, you'll need to understand what the charader is trying to communicate. What? Yes. Understand. Acting out *A Tale of Two Cities* or *Les Misérables* with "How many words?" and a portrayal of a bummed-out person are the depictions of your understanding that you hope others will understand

For as long as we have walked upright as a species, we've used imagery to tell stories. Bison on cave walls, a collage of handprints, etchings from a vision quest, or pictograms that became the basis for written language our history of communicating for posterity includes images. Where a word may require a specialised understanding of a language or etymology, a picture has the potential of achieving understanding across a broader audience.

You don't need to know the details if you can appreciate that the context of images—in the iconography of symbols—can carry significant meaning to an observer. Those symbols can evoke emotions from assurance to rage. The swastika, for instance, is a widely known ancient symbol that indicated wellbeing and good fortune. Then came the twentieth century when the symbol became synonymous with fascism and a traumatic period of human history. What once was painted or etched into art to evoke a sense of good fortune, now elicits quite a different emotional response.

The use of images in your TELL Nudge adds colour and interest to your narrative. As the adage goes "A picture is worth a thousand words." Whether the phrase should be attributed to journalism or marketing, both industries rely heavily on the impact that an image can have on their target audience. We buy, with our purchasing power or emotional investment, mainly by what we see. Intuitively we know this to be true because images play a significant part of who we are and how we represent ourselves. What we wear, how we write our names, the doodles we scribble on paper, hairstyle, cosmetics, and so much more are the representational imagery that permeates our being. We use it to craft how we want to be seen.

Perhaps not as comprehensive in the application as images, we also use allusions to entice a sense of commonality. A bond based on a shared experience can reduce barriers more quickly between two people than extended social play. I use pop culture references a lot in my writing and speaking, knowing full well that some references demand an explanation. In the context of writing that is not as big of an issue as it is when speaking. If speaking to a diverse audience, a pop culture reference that misses the mark might leave a sole receiver or the whole group panning their mind to make a connection. Meanwhile, I will be of course, unaware that I've left some members of the audience behind. It can be a tricky business in the understanding cycle.

Fortunately, we have the right stock of material in our repertoire to help us out when we need to achieve understanding from verbal illustrations. Elevating our communication to comparisons, from which we hope to gain a common understanding, may require the use of allegories and metaphors. Perhaps the most famous collection of parables is *Aesop's fables*. Children are introduced to the role of allegory from a young age. Allegory teaches a moral or can convey multifaceted social conditions. When my children were younger, I used to read to them most nights before bed. Their favourite stories came from an early edition of *Uncle Wiggily* and William J. Bennett's *The Book of Virtues*. Unsavoury types like the Pipsisewah or the rude little boy named Dick contrasted issues like bullying and courtesy. I think if you gave it some thought, you'd quickly see the influence allegory has had on you over the years. And it remains a valuable tool for conveying a message.

Close in style, but shorter in delivery is the metaphor. Whereas an allegory trusts understanding from a position of contrasts, metaphors hinge on similarities. That is why you will often hear the word "like" in a metaphor. I think a metaphor is more flexible and agile than an allegory. It can be delivered and adapted for the receiver's orientation on the fly. By activating a purposeful measure of observation skills, you can pick out images and cultural icons of your receiver's orientation. Then, you can apply those similarities to a metaphor that works in your cultural orientation. Metaphors can be a delightful diversion in the communication loop. Testing one idea, bouncing another, bantering and exploring until that moment of realisation when similarity is apprehended. That can be so much fun. Life relationships can develop in those interactions.

Treasure in the Feedback Loop

My cousin lives in Central Oregon on the west coast of the United States. With the passing of the senior members of our families, he is now the oldest—the patriarch in old-timey kind of speech. I can call him that because I think he would prefer to have been born in a different era. He built a cabin in the woods and pans for gold in his spare time. Panning for gold is labour intensive, and the rewards are minuscule if anything. A prospector's dream is to discover that prized nugget that surfaces during agitation. If gold is present, it will mostly show up in trace evidence of gold dust remaining in the pan as the alluvial deposits are swished away. As a hobbyist, my cousin pans for relaxation. Gold sign remains an exciting discovery, but it is not an all-in-all goal.

Panning has a deeper satisfaction than just brushing a sample of gold dust into a one-dram glass vial. Gold discovered in a creek bed might signpost a prospector to a vein that leads to a mother lode and riches beyond description. Dialogue, in whichever form it assumes, is like panning for gold. You scoop up a sample of the subject, pour some life into the pan of your mind, and agitate it. If you are fortunate, the conversation will expose sparkling fragments of commonality. Scoop up an additional sample, swish the material, and check for more sign. Convinced that there might be more than superficial signs of gold, you set up to mine for your Eldorado.

What we hope to achieve in a feedback loop is not just the attainment of our understanding, but mutual understanding. That is where the richness of creativity abides. The illumination of our observations (SEE) make sense and are comprehended. Understanding may be self-centralised where the echoes of "Eureka" sound off with peals of jubilation from within your head. You may even get that elation when group understanding forms. That would be the instance when your team recognises a problematic condition and mutually grasps the fullness of the issue. Moreover, the paths of corrective actions suddenly come into view like fog lifting to the brightness of midday. The road is made clear and safe to travel.

A feedback loop in a TELL Nudge can deliver that invaluable piece of missing information that fits in with a broader picture. A piece may not fit, but it can stir up your thinking to pursue connecting information to form value. Persistence, like panning for gold, will pay off. Either your stamina will expose further possibilities or mark the time for you to move on. Recalling the parts of closed-loop communication, you first have your sender. Embarking from a stage that starts with self, the sender will always be you.

If you want to wax philosophically, you might argue that your person is a dichotomy of the conscious and unconscious. Appreciating that you have an autonomic response system to consider, your argument has validity. An intentional act of communication, when a message is purposefully manipulated and packaged for a receiver, is a conscious act. Where you are in control of the message that is the position you want to assume.

As the bridge between sender and receiver, the message is everything. With the nuances of message style and delivery factored into the structure, a clear message facilitates a short path between people. A convoluted message forces the communication process into a belaboured state where interest is threatened, the intent is subject to interpretation, and progress toward understanding is slowed. Instead of fording the chasms of ignorance by the shortest points of navigation, you must look for another way around. Perhaps find a superficial ground where crossing allows you to meet in the middle. That is if you can convince the receiver to go on that adventure with you.

Part of the journey I've followed in my Nudge Principle development is to work in various industries. What you can learn about people, organisations, and business by diversifying your work experience may well be a top-rated masterclass for developing understanding. Life experience of this type may be a heavy investment, but it is well worth the results. One of the organisations I worked with was a public institution with around 8,000 staff. A challenge for any large organisation is disseminating essential messages to the broadest range of receivers and achieve the highest level of assimilation. You want your staff from top-to-bottom, side-to-side, to understand the message. Apart from applying Orwellian methods of compliance, 100% receptivity to a message is a stringent standard to achieve. That, however, doesn't mean that it is an impossible goal.

If you have a message that you need to get out to 8,000 staff members and ensure they receive and understand the message, you can't look at the group as a single receiver. Falling into that trap is easy because the group list is formed or used by an individual sender. Instead of thinking of my audience as a group, I need to view my recipients as 8,000 receivers. That means I must find a way to establish commonality of purpose on which we can build a foundation. My single receiver in the pool of 8,000 must want to receive my message. An unsolicited periodic email in her inbox falls into the category of dismissible noise. Should that happen, I've already lost as the sender. My message lies dead in a recycle-bin, spam folder, or forever unopened to clutter her inbox. For her to open, read, and respond to my message, she must want to do so. To get 8,000 receivers to wish to do so requires a culture that fosters that receptivity.

An organisational culture capable of sustaining the value of communication is one that respects the mutual pursuit of understanding. The value that an organisation can receive in return for the staff's investment of trust is feedback. Quality feedback is sifted from the gangue and refined for analysis. The refined data becomes the premise for developing stratagems for innovation, early identification of issues, cultural change, staff wellbeing, and organisational development. I should include compliance as well but will do so as a separate aspect. Compliance as a stand-alone condition means adherence to production standards that are critical in many industries. Compliance can also shape behavioural expectations of interpersonal relationships and be vulnerable to personal interpretation.

Completing the feedback loop with a message returned from the receiver, you gain new information for your knowledge base. You can now integrate that information to your understanding for affirmation of a premise or development of a hybrid version. You've taken a risk to test the receptivity of a message by a receiver. With the success of that message being understood, you can evaluate and adapt.

Danger of the Ouroboros

The symbol of the ouroboros can illustrate the condition of a Nudge stalemating. The iconography dates to ancient Egypt, with the depiction of a snake or dragon that consumes itself by eating its tail. The word ouroboros means 'tail food' or 'I eat my tail.' Symbolically it can mean infinity, wholeness, or an endless cycle. The Nudge Principle promotes the progression of the core nudges that lead to a creation or an action. The creative process without action, as noted before and not last, is a theory. Nobody else can appreciate a creation until it is created. You can move between nudges in the creative process as long as there is a forward movement toward action. Make no mistake; there must be an action.

What I've witnessed time and again is the creative or creative collective getting stuck in a perpetual cycle of SEE and TELL. There are many reasons for this behaviour and uncovering those reasons makes for a meaningful group activity. The creative might be caught in the eddy of analysis paralysis, research redundancy, or ignorance. Struggling to escape the current, calls for help and reaching out only works temporarily as the victim of the cycle falls back into the eddy's pull. Inaction or a poorly executed action is the natural result of being trapped in this cycle. Fortified with enough data to justify an action, the creative will also abort the nudges between TELL and DO going straight to the action stage of DO. Your urgency demands action, so an action is delivered. With each successive lurch forward, the ouroboros gulps down another segment of itself.

Self-consumption is destructive. It is neither good for your creative energy or mental state. Surrendered to that state, voices from the shadows of your consciousness whisper accusations, blame, and procrastination. The glass ceiling in your mind allows you to see, but not participate in the possibilities available around you. You talk yourself into a place where you become satisfied with your observation skills and ability to communicate but are unwilling to take that next step to achieve creative fulfilment. You can break free from that cycle. You can follow a natural creative path and convert the investments of SEE and TELL.

What you need to do is activate another nudge.

7

FLOW

The hoo-hah that brewed following the installation of a traffic roundabout on the Douglas Island side of the Juneau-Douglas bridge was the buzz of Juneauites on Facebook. In 2001, the first roundabout in Alaska was completed in Juneau at Marine Way and Franklin Street. Besides fishing and bear encounter stories, a roundabout grumble might still be the fuel of campfire conversation. Population growth of the Alaskan capital city meant that the original two-lane bridge built in 1935 was unable to meet the demand of a growing population. A new four-lane bridge was built beside the old bridge and opened to the public in 1980. A year later, the first bridge was demolished. Twenty-five years later, the State Department of Transportation engineered and installed a roundabout.

Considering a twenty-five-year gap between 1987 and 2011, I've lived in the United Kingdom approaching fifteen years. Navigating roundabouts is second nature for me now. Travelling around England in the 1980s and navigating roundabouts during my first stay was, for the most part, uneventful. The population of England in 1986, when I left, was 47 million. When I returned in 2011, the population had only grown by 6 million. I am sure the additional 6 million all drive cars.

I boast that I get along well with roundabouts. A notable exception to that is a roundabout that rattled me back in the 1980s—the Plough Roundabout in Hemel Hempstead. The traffic management layout of the Plough consists of six-mini roundabouts around a larger roundabout. A similar roundabout exists in Swindon, and it is called the Magic Roundabout. The way to survive a complex roundabout system like the Plough or the Magic is simple.

- Avoid collisions.
- Follow the lines and directional arrows.
- Give way to vehicles in the roundabout.
- Proceed toward your exit from the roundabout.

Even though these two infamous roundabouts may cause mental anguish for the unprepared, their intent is the same. With any road travel scenario, a basic knowledge of road conditions, signage, and a cautious approach to driver behaviour should help you arrive safely at your destination. Traffic engineering is purposed to move people from one location to another with a nominal impact on drivers. Public safety and removal of impediments to the flow of trade are the engineers' primary considerations. More than ever, environmental impact also plays a major role in planning. Where that engineering works well, there are fewer accidents, a reduction of congestion and gridlock, prosperity, and happier drivers. Okay, maybe I am stretching for that last one, but either way, good intentions are calculated to achieve flow.

Creatively speaking, we have three definitions of flow that apply to the Nudge Principle. The first follows the pattern described above. Whereby, the objects for movement progress at a steady pace according to the rhythm of the mass. Urban planners study people movement and their modes of transportation when designing cities and the infrastructures that enable movement. Psychology, neuroscience, anthropology, statistical analysis, and computer modelling make up a part of the whole in urban planning with new fields steadily being introduced. Smart cities are opening incredible possibilities for flow innovation. Flow, as it relates to moving people toward the future, is a creative process and quite exciting to observe.

Another aspect of flow refers to a state of mind coined by psychologist Mihaly Csikszentmihályi. During periods of optimal performance, a creative may undergo a sense of timelessness while swept up in their creative activity. To be in a flow or "in the zone" is to achieve optimal experience. That also happens to be the title of Csikszentmihályi's book on the subject—*Flow: The Psychology of Optimal Experience*. In an earlier publication, *Beyond Boredom and Anxiety*, Csikszentmihályi defines flow as the 'satisfying, exhilarating feeling of creative accomplishment and heightened functioning.' We have all felt that feeling and the energising residual that comes from the momentary lapse of time consciousness while in a creative mental place. Once you've experienced it and are mindful of that experience, you will likely seek to find ways to repeat the experience. Exhilarating and productive, flow might even be viewed as transcendental. My expectation for you, as you apply the Nudge Principle, is to experience this type of flow often and with life-changing affect.

The third version of flow, which is the basis of the FLOW Nudge, is the combining of thoughts to synthesise a new thought. Our observations are what we see, feel, hear, imagine, et al. We can develop our SEE Nudge to improve our observation skills. Progressing from SEE to TELL, we convert what we observe into internal or external forms of communication to test our perceptions of an observation. We may experience flow in either state. Flow, in the latter context, is a state of mind rather than a nudge to be activated by our cognisance. As a stage or element of the creative process, we want to develop our FLOW Nudge to benefit our creative activity.

To break from the SEE-TELL cycle and adventure into new areas of creative development, we need to test combinations from our existing knowledge and experience bases. Once again, there are likely to be an ever-expanding combination of possibilities you can pursue to develop a FLOW Nudge. We are going to look at four activities to set the stage for our next Nudge. The four actions for FLOW are confluence, divergence, alliance, and synthesis.

Confluence

The largest gathering of people for a festival occurred in early 2019 over fifty-five days in Prayagraj, Uttar Pradesh, India. There, the sacred rivers of the Ganges and Yamuna that flow from the Himalayas converge into one. A third river, the mythical Saraswati of the Rigveda, is a heavenly river that flows with immortality. At the convergence of the Ganges and Yamuna is the Triveni Sangam, and one of the most sacred locations in India for Hindu devotees. As representative of the rivers' importance, India granted legal status to the two rivers. Essentially this meant bestowing the same legal rights as a human on the rivers. The Kumbh Mela is the largest religious gathering in the world. One of its cyclic locations is the confluence of the Ganges and Yamuna Rivers. For the 2019 Kumbh Mela, upwards of 133 million pilgrims and tourists descended on Prayagraj for that instalment of the 12-year cycle of celebration.

Pilgrims bathe in the water of the confluence in a purification ritual whereby a devotee's sins are purged. According to the faith, Lord Vishnu spilt from a pot (Kumbh) a drink of immortality called Amrita in four locations. One of those locations, where the nectar of life spilt, and the most visited site of the Kumbh Mela cycle, is the confluence of the Ganges, Yamuna, and Saraswati rivers. This place where three rivers come together illustrates the concept of divergent bodies merging into one. Although the Yamuna ceases as a separate body of water once it merges with the Ganges, the two remain inescapably connected with its flow, washing away wrongs and giving hope for new.

From the heights of your thinking, like that of a river's mountain source, streams of your experience percolate to develop a thought. Surfaced, that stream of thought will meander its way along as a pattern of thought collecting and gaining volume by adding other ideas. Simultaneous streams of thought are developing under different patterns of thinking. The composition of that thought can formulate any outcome. The choice of outcome is dependent on the direction you want to go. The diverse nature of a pattern of thinking demonstrates that it carries with it unique connectivity. When two of those patterns of thinking converge at a new connection point, you have a confluence—two streams of thought blended into one new.

Developing the FLOW Nudge merges the best of multiple streams and creates a distinctive flowing pattern of thought. A purposeful confluence is created when two thoughts are brought together that would not naturally occur. A classic example of a mental confluence is the origin of the hook-and-loop fastener. Swiss engineer George de Mestral came up with the concept of the hook-and-loop fastener, popularised by the brand Velcro, after hunting with his dog. The ritual of removing burdock burs from his clothing and his dog's fur must have been acted out on numerous previous occasions. On one such time, de Mestral saw something that made him think differently. Instead of the typical recurring frustration of removing burs, his curiosity was piqued. Expanding on that inquisitiveness, de Mestral investigated the composition of the burs under a microscope. There, the concept of applicability took shape. An observation of a natural phenomenon combined with an engineering pattern of thinking converted into a business concept. A flow of ideas created something new.

Not to be restricted to our thinking and the observations stored in our head, we can also use the confluence of a team environment to create flow. That is where the Nudge Principle can get quite exciting. We've already established that different people can provide different perspectives. Life experiences, education, motivation, and everything that we are as an individual add a quality of understanding to problem-solving to which a team would otherwise not have access. Using the confluence metaphor of two rivers, imagine a graphic depiction of merging thoughts. We will refer to that as a creative confluence model. Both streams of thought are bound for the same destination. For a natural river, its destination would be an ocean, sea, or a larger body of water. Also, both river and thought have an origin. In our flow of creative thinking, the source is that state of original thought and the destination is a creative action.

Let's do an activity together that may help graphically catalyse the concept. Draw a horizontal line and label the left-hand end Original Thought or A. Next label the right-hand end Creative Action or B. If you can identify and name the Original Thought and Creative Action, swap the generic for specific labels. Unless you are working on a project that defines your creative action, I'd leave that open. You may find that by the time you work through this activity, the creative action will have changed.

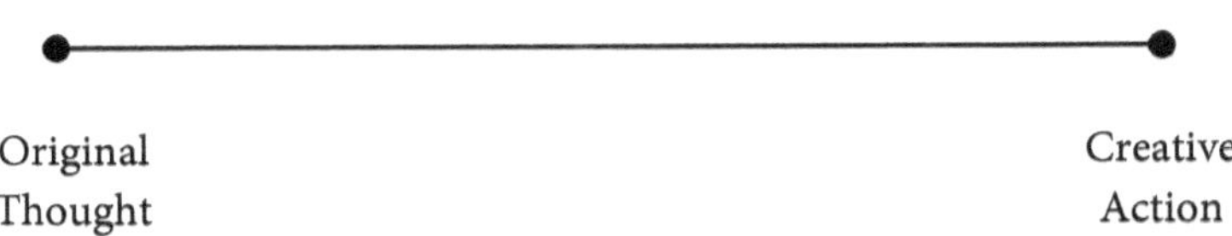

Original   Creative
Thought   Action

Next, draw a vertical or angled line near the A end of the line and stop at the horizontal line. The vertical line represents a diverse thought. Where the vertical line stops at the horizontal line is the confluence. Each confluence represents the introduction of a new thought to be merged to the original thought. Successive confluences will have a direct influence on the shape of the original thought. The concluding creative action will be something that aligns with your evolved original thought but will have integrated aspects that you may not have considered. Let me illustrate with an example currently in the works.

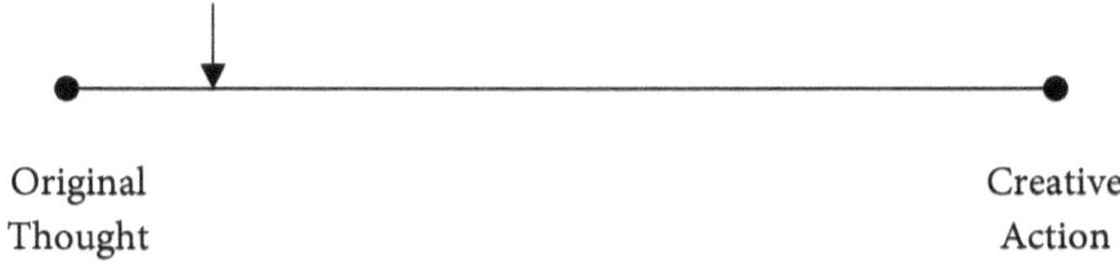

Original   Creative
Thought   Action

I am designing a board game to complement the Nudge Principle and workshops called Nudge Creative Labs. My expertise in designing, manufacturing, and distributing games is limited. The original thought of a board game will require multiple infusions of diverse thought to achieve success. Therefore, I'll use several versions of the creative confluence model to achieve my creative action. One version will focus on game pieces. I've toyed with several concepts from traditional pawn shaped game pieces to more elaborate models similar to *Gogo's Crazy Bones*. I like the non-standardised version of the Crazy Bones concept. The cost, price per unit impact on the game, collaboration, and contractual negotiations are some obvious manufacturing hurdles.

Using the creative confluence model, I will take that original Gogo style idea and work with team members and manufacturers to find alternatives. Along that path, we will probably come across ideas like game players creating their own pieces for each game, using tokens of their preference—thereby saving on price per unit costs—and digital versions. By using the creative confluence model, the potential for uncovering different ways to deliver a creative action grows with ever-expanding possibilities.

Divergence and Separation

Once the fourth-largest body of inland water, the Aral Sea is a ghostly landscape of 26,000 square miles speckled with abandoned equipment, desert conditions, and impoverished communities. The dry lakebed is a stark reminder of what happens when an environment is poorly managed. During Soviet administration, rivers that once fed the Aral Sea were diverted to irrigate agricultural land. Mostly to irrigate water-hungry crops contributing to disastrous inefficiencies in irrigation processes. Efforts to restore the Aral and undo some of the damage done on the people and environment is being conducted. Recovery will be a long process that may never restore the region to its once flourishing state.

The second aspect of FLOW involves the consequences of divergence and separation. Where efficiently managed, a divergence from an original thought can produce exciting results. Flow can continue, relatively unimpeded, in that trough of thinking. We will explore that concept more with the PLAY Nudge. Evaluated by the creative confluence model, divergence from the path of an original thought may require a new criterion. For instance, an original thought intended for application in hydroponics may find a different value in eco-friendly packing materials. Intersections with divergence mark the history of invention and innovation. To wander off in this direction is to get lost in possibilities. However, there are incredible opportunities for an intrepid creative.

Keep in mind that we always want to strive for understanding, regardless of the nudge we are highlighting. A divergent approach to an original thought excites potential avenues to examine the surrounding area for new prospects. We can look at divergence in flow as an aggregator for different thinking. Flow brings in new thought as the primary filter, and divergence prompts alternatives. Separation removes impediments to flow.

Think of separation as a traditional brainstorming session. An idea generation session is meant to be a free-flowing of ideas where judgement is suspended, and no idea or contribution is rejected. From my experience, brainstorming sessions can deteriorate into a guided session whereby dominant personalities validate their opinion. Deviating from the path in that style of controlled environment will sequester contrary ideas to an A1 sized sheet labelled 'To Be Considered' where ideas stagnate. Separation in that sense is not conducive to flow.

The actual value of separation is realised when used to sift irrelevant or excessive information. Every morning I walk to a country park. A stream trickles through the park feeding three small lakes. There, by the stream, is an area cleared of underbrush where kids build stick huts against trees. I've walked past that area several times when an outing of school children is busily working together constructing their woodland shelters. The forest floor has plenty of sticks to cull for shelter building. After the buzz of activity diminishes and quiet is restored, a bundle of sticks always makes its way into the stream bed. Useful for fort building, those sticks piled in the tricking stream choke the water flow from reaching the rightful destination. The obstructions must be cleared.

Children find separating items into categories to be an engaging activity. I think it is one of the ways they affirm that their perception aligns with the view of another. I recall how my grandson once lined up several small toy cars on my arm and asked me to rank them. "Grandad," he said, "Which one is the best?" Being me, I had to respond with "Well, best is relative. Which do you think is best?" He was toying with me. I toyed back. What I think he wanted to know was which one of his car models I thought to be fastest in the real world. We then proceeded to right the miniature car question by ranking his cars, still on my arm, from slowest to fastest. He grinned rather proudly when I ultimately agreed that his favourite was fastest.

Recognising what to keep, put in reserve, and discard is an invaluable skill in the FLOW Nudge. The talent is played out in business meetings as well as on the forest floor where little wildings run amok. A board room gathering may apply separation as a FLOW Nudge to identify and correct cash flow problems. Where is the company haemorrhaging capital? Is our fixed asset depreciation worth an extension on long-term credit? What can I automate to reduce labour costs? At your next business meeting, discretely tally each instance where an action can lead to some form of separation. An organisation's profitability is decided on degrees of separation. On the forest floor, it is measured by which stick will hold the most weight and whether it is the right length. Uncovering the hidden obstacles of flow to facilitate separation, can be a challenge. If you know which issue is at the root of a problem, then you might be better positioned to deal with it. Might, in that there are likely to be hidden interdependencies that restrict direct action without triggering counteractions. The principle of cause-and-effect flags the naïve with a warning that a single action can have multiple reactions. Let's consider the premise of environmental concerns in the context of FLOW's divergence and separation.

We are our own worst enemies when it comes to environmental ignorance or, let's be frank, where greed drives decisions over habitat. Widespread deforestation and plastic in the ocean are two critical concerns given the chain reaction impact these conditions have on micro and macro ecosystems. Examples, where human negligence introduces an invasive species to a non-native environment, is a modern plight. Abandoned Burmese pythons spreading in Florida grow large enough to eat competitive predators like alligators. Non-native brown tree snakes decimated the native bird population of Guam in just a few decades. Corrective measures to reduce the brown rat population introduced to Hawaii by sailing ships was to introduce the mongoose—a species that prefer birds and eggs over rat meat. Also introduced to Hawaii, for managing sugar cane beetles, was the cane toad. Whose diet is by no means restricted to cane beetles. Australian cane growers made the same mistake in 1935 when they introduced 3,000 cane toads— now numbered in the millions.

Our complex world demands that we sift issues into categories. Without a separation process in our thinking and actions, we might live in a perpetual state of paralysis. We may not always get it right, but we have the responsibility to try. Applying the FLOW Nudge comes at an early stage of the creative process. There are four more stages to ensure that a creative does not become bogged down in the mire of separation. FLOW is meant to keep thoughts and actions moving forward. Keep that in mind when you need to build strength for a creative endeavour.

Alliance

Typically, we think of an alliance as being between two or more affirming, non-aggressor parties. In an alliance, differences are put to one side to focus on the source of an obstacle. The antagonist of a story being that obstacle. The protagonist is the hero. The word alliance, by itself, carries with it no implied value, which means that you can have alliances comprised of aggressors. Standing alone against a more powerful force may sound heroic, but most of the time that kind of heroism ends badly for the hero. Forging an alignment with another that shares a mutual benefit for an alliance is a preferred approach. Building on strengths can bind people, companies, and nations together as formidable allies against obstacles. The Japanese proverb "A single arrow can be easily broken, but not in a bundle of ten arrows" illustrates the concept.

History offers a steady feed of successful and failed alliances. You may have heard that "the victors write history." That said, the perception of any win-loss among partnerships may be a matter of which side you favour. Looking for historical examples, I browsed Herodotus' *The Histories*. Between the pages of that source alone, there are numerous examples. Modern and ancient history is rife with stories of the noble hero standing against all the odds. Instead, let me turn to pop culture again. The film industry produces a steady stream of overcoming underdog films. Modern storytelling through film spotlights the hero as the star attraction.

A classic example of a movie where this is not the case is the 1954 film *Seven Samurai* directed by Akira Kurosawa. Seven masterless samurai (rōnin) are hired by a village of poor farmers to protect them from a marauding, well-organised gang of thieves. With little to offer in remuneration, the samurai accept the task as if under a banner of former nobility. Outnumbered by the marauders, but not out skilled, the samurai prepare the farmers to participate in the inevitable battle. Traps set, assets deployed, and each with a samurai leading a defensive position, the villagers wait for the bandits to attack. Although the samurai prevail, they do so at a deadly cost to their cadre.

If the potential of failure exists, despite an alliance, what might be the value of trying? I've heard that argument against alliances in so many words. Usually, it comes under the guise of "What do you have to offer that I need?" A tone of arrogance may frame the question so that it puts you on your back foot. What that person may not recognise is that there is an opportunity for failure with or without an alliance. A partnership doesn't just happen. It takes work and requires collaboration and negotiation. I wrestled with the idea of whether to make this section about collaboration instead of alliance. While collaboration is necessary for an alliance, it alone does not create a bond. What it does do is create the foundation for bonding and working together. But it is an alliance that breaks through the obstacles.

Let's discuss collaboration while it is in our sights. Collaboration is an aspect of the FLOW Nudge for which we will assume a role in some situations. One is when a creative collaborates on a primarily art-based project. Musicians do this all the time. Besides with other members of their band, they have a necessary alliance, among many others, with sound engineers to ensure sound quality. Installation artists also require collaboration to complete a project. Bulgarian-born artist Christo spent twenty years forging alliances, collaborating, negotiating, and reengineering his *Over the River* project in Colorado USA. The proposed six-mile section of the Arkansas River in Colorado was to be draped with a material creating a translucent umbrella effect over the river. The project was abandoned in 2017 due to ongoing legal battles with environmentalists and the government — a nonetheless powerful example of the demand for alliances and collaboration.

Where alliances are demonstrated daily, with ongoing collaboration, are in business settings. The necessity to work together to achieve a common objective is what makes or breaks a company. Without a trustworthy alliance with suppliers, distribution channels, employees, and the most valuable group—customers—a company doesn't have much of a future. Intricate alliances are knit on a local level with networks that extend globally and with reciprocity. The infrastructures of nations are also built on similar condition regarding alliances of trade and commerce. Successful organisations use the power of alliance to accomplish their goals, knowing that the balance of a profit margin is one of the interdependencies. Management of those alliances is what gives the edge to one organisation over another. Succeeding with the internal and external collaborations required to maintain that edge is commentary for tales of business success.

However, that assumption is based on a traditional business model where company-customer relations are paramount. An alternative business model might be characterised by a blitz style marketing strategy, quick return on investment, and move on. We can call this an opportunist business model. Strike fast, make money, get out. The notion of building a relationship that cares for the customer any more than he or she as a cash cow is contrary to the opportunist. We tend to be suspicious of the opportunist in the fast-paced, technology-driven, generationally segmented world of the Internet. Some provide quality goods and services; others peddle a modern version of snake oil.

While considering the different roles of an alliance as a FLOW Nudge, I spent considerable time working through the likelihood of mental unions. Can we have alliances in our head? Can the same kind of alliance forged with another person exist between two independent streams of thought? Are we able to be of "two minds" in this regard? If possible, a mental amalgamation would be prone to duplicity. The brain would need to allocate equal portions of resources to maintain balance. Remove the governors that keep thoughts separate, blur the lines of consciousness, and it is possible. But I think that may produce a mental state the resembles schizophrenia rather than an optimised capacity for distinguishing allied thoughts. To achieve that goal, we want to synthesise our thoughts.

Synthesise

Where two rivers meet at a point and become one is called a confluence. The FLOW Nudge for that action brings together similar ideas. Filtering thoughts to make way for clearer thinking are FLOW Nudge actions of divergence or separation. Allying with two or more contributors to a project engages the FLOW Nudge in the form of an alliance. Bringing together two or more unique elements to create a new element is to synthesise using a FLOW Nudge. The actions of confluence, divergence, separation, and alliance may assist in your pursuit of a new idea, but a synthesised thought is a super seed for a creativity hybrid. Until the creative rumblings in your head reach the point of synthesis, you are just moving around containers in the warehouse of your mind.

Creating is to bring into existence something that formerly only existed in theory. Until there is a manifestation of a creation, it doesn't exist. We might want to test that theory on the playground of philosophy, where we are allowed to challenge the very nature of the universe. "If a tree falls in the forest and no one is around to hear it, does it make a sound?" is a classic thought experiment. Does the Moon exist if you are not looking at it? Or is Invisible Boy from *Mystery Men* invisible or just naked? Ultimately, can a creation exist before it is created? A sheet of paper is nothing more than a sheet of paper until a creator allows a creative thought to transform that sheet of paper with a medium — pen, ink, paint, whatever. Before a medium was applied, a creative thought was a series of electric impulses firing in a brain. Once manifest, then, the creation sprung into existence.

The synthesis of those thoughts can be the result of millions of separate neural interactions. We are not conscious of where it comes from or how it arrived knocking at the door of our prefrontal cortex. But it knocks loudly and demands an audience. Synthesised on arrival, you can reverse engineer the thought to explore its building materials and design or take it on face value. The FLOW Nudge's hard work has already been done for you. Somewhere in the slumber of your unconsciousness, existing patterns of thought have been working together to synthesise something new. You need to allow it to flow together and give that creative thought life. Unfettered from the shackles of the will, you, as creator, can manifest that creative thought into reality.

As a FLOW Nudge, the synthesis I just described is an autonomic overspill of neural activity. The flash of inspiration could even show up in your dreams during REM sleep. Excitingly, we can also participate in the process of synthesis as a FLOW Nudge. Start with two disparate entities—thoughts, items, actions—and work them together until they fit. For a simple activity to test this concept, think of some words that are a mix of two to form a new word. For instance, a motel is a motor hotel. Glamping is glamorous camping. The word to describe this type of word is portmanteau. Have some fun with the activity. Think of existing portmanteaus. Create new words from two words and give it a definition. Make the exercise a game with friends and family. It won't be very long into the activity when you become aware of the speed that synthesis occurs. Like playing flashcards, you'll pop off a word, add another, blend them, laugh, give a definition, laugh some more. Erupt creative fountains like a thought geyser.

A pleasant side effect of the synthesis activity is the sense of personal reward that comes with creating. The unmistakable experience of anticipation that spills over in emotion when the creation is manifest. Something as simple as crafting a portmanteau and sharing it can produce enjoyment. Another impromptu synthesising activity I used to do with my kids was to make up lyrics for songs playing on the radio. I know I am not the only one who does it. Could be a Dad thing, but I'd guess that the silliness is acted out all over the world by people of all ages and gender. The act of creation can be bold, defiant, energetic, or subtly personal. An inspiration that unfolds takes on as many expressions of personality as there are people on the planet. And that makes living even more interesting.

When working out a synthesis, we can't expect that all combinations will work. Perhaps they work but only last for a while. Ben Cohen and Jerry Greenfield came up with a great idea for ice cream in 1978. From its humble beginnings in a renovated petrol station in Burlington, Vermont Ben & Jerry's ice cream has become renowned the world over. My personal favourite is Cherry Garcia. Sadly, I have yet to see it in a freezer case in England Daring to try out non-traditional combinations, Ben & Jerry have churned out some classic successes, failures, and short-lived flavour combinations. Retired flavours are given a ceremonious final resting place. Among the 'dearly de-pinted' flavours gracing the *Ded & Buried Flavour Graveyard* in Waterbury, Vermont are Schweddy Balls, Turtle Soup, and Miz Jelena's Sweet Potato Pie. Don't feel too sad if your favourite Ben & Jerry's ice cream is resting in the flavour graveyard. Ben & Jerry's company ethos is that of 'Celebrating our failures since 1978.' Your failed flavour was given the respect it deserved. Be thankful for failures. They are the trying ground for success.

Integration

Emboldened with a creative idea and ready to try out their newly formed creation, the creative will be tempted to jump straight to the last of the Seven Nudges—DO. In fairness, jumping around in the nudges is fine. I encourage you to do so. An episode of creativity with a mix-up approach can yield a wide range of different results. While there is a strong case for a linear development of creativity with the nudges, there are no hard rules. Will jumping to an action (DO) from TELL work? Yes. Can you regress from FEEL to SEE? I hope so. That is one way that you can mature in empathy. Creativity is an organic experience that happens through intentionality and inspiration. The path you take to achieve your creative aspiration can be a direct approach or a meandering wander.

An eager creative will be tempted to select a Chance card and skip nudges in the hope of landing that Advance to Go Collect £200 prize. If you've arrived at the FLOW stage in creative development, you've surpassed many that remain in that SEE-TELL cycle that I cited earlier. Why not work the process through to gain the most from the experience? Having worked through FLOW, you have moved to the point of integration. You are left with an integrated concept after you've converged like-for-like ideas, culled redundant elements, strengthened your alliances, and synthesised the results of your new creation. Now ready to be tested, you want to see what it looks like, feels like, and does what it was designed to do. You want to climb on to the riser where your creation is strapped down and bellow "Give my creation life!"

Honestly, I've practised the core nudges of creativity with such regularity that the process is almost automatic and became my foundation for decision-making. I started my research for the Nudge Principle in 2006 while studying for a master's degree. Besides study and practising each nudge, I apply these principles to the development of my creative aspirations. This book, while hopeful as a business asset, is my creation. Observations, feedback, the flow of ideas, exploring branches of application, working through how Nudge affects others as well as my own emotional wellbeing, what are my core beliefs, and what are the hindrances to action are realised with each word I commit to these pages. What you are reading is the integration of a lifetime of experience and over a decade of commitment to the creation.

The most exciting prospect of the Nudge Principle and applying nudges regards what will happen next. With the FLOW Nudge of the creative foundation laid, we'll focus our attention on creating a design to deploy our concepts. From a business sense, navigating the start-up process includes structure by which a company, a creation, is to be governed. Who the audience is and what service or products to offer are questions that will also demand a creative approach. If you or I were to jump from FLOW to DO at this time, we'd likely miss essential, yet unseen, opportunities. From this strong position of an integrated creative concept, we can explore possibilities with increased confidence. Phrased another way, I want to have a play with my creation.

8

PLAY

Summer holidays run their course at different times of the year depending on where you live. Your location, relative to north or south of the equator, is a significant factor. I grew up in the northern hemisphere in the United States. My summer holidays as a kid spanned from dates in late May through August. That range on the calendar covers most of North America, Europe, Russia, and China. Southern hemisphere schools have a summer holiday range that generally spans the months between December and March. Regardless when it happens, children look forward to the break with anticipation. "No more pencils, no more books, no more teacher's dirty looks," is the tone of Vincent Furnier's immortal anthem to the summer break.

The other day a person asked me a question; "For which period of your life do you have the fondest summertime memories—childhood or adulthood?" That was an easy one to answer—childhood. I was more fortunate than many, I suppose. I had that stereotypical American youth like that depicted on the television series *The Wonder Years*. The show's main character, Kevin Arnold, would have been my senior by only three years. Watching reruns of *Wonder Years* episodes is like a time capsule of when I was a boy. The setting was designed to reflect any town in the United States. My Anytown, USA, was Bellevue, Washington. There, as a boy, summer was a glorious adventure.

Imagine Kevin Arnold on his Schwinn Stingray bicycle cruising the streets of Anytown. Summer vacation is on, and there is a world to explore. My Stingray was a steed of two wheels designed to carry me to places whispered between boys who explored secret destinations. "Have you ever been to the rope swing over that gully where a teenager died?" one might be asked. Curiosity kicks in with the mystery, "No, I haven't…where is it?" With only scraps of information, my best friend and I set out to find "The Gully." Along the way to Who-Knows-Where, we'd stop to slide down piles of dirt, fall into a creek, rip our jeans on a fence while being chased by teenagers, and eat our fill of wild blackberries. When the sunlight started to fade, we'd return to our respective homes.

Upon arrival home, I'd dump my bike in the front yard. Invariably I'd be late for dinner. After pouring copious amounts of dirt and sand from my PF Flyers into the driveway, I'd go inside. My Mom would be waiting with the oft-repeated question teetering on her lips "Where have you been?" Before I can answer, the next question is fired "What have you done to your jeans?" I think my Mom was convinced that I walked the Earth on my knees, given my propensity to wear holes in my rugged denim trousers. Even the rigid iron-on patches she applied in the hope of extending the life of my denim trousers suffered from my wanderlust. Cleaned up and ready for dinner, the conversation would continue. "So, what did you do today?" Mom would ask again. "Gary and I played all day." To "play" was synonymous with "explore" in the mind of that ten-year-old boy. Where I played, while important to my Mom, was just a series of settings for adventure.

Childhood summer play was always quite magical for me. I am aware, with hindsight, that I may tend to skew my perception of the past. The nostalgia of a precious period of youth lingers and reminds me of what was good and bad. Perhaps that is why, being far removed from that time, I chose childhood summer memories as my favourite holidays over adulthood memories. Adulthood summer memories also carry nostalgic value. Raising a family and contributing to their childhood memories was also rewarding and memorable. Exploring the world as an adult also enriches life. I am in constant awe of those that squeeze as much as they can into living. Not restricted to the summer months, they make the most of life year-round. Life is an exploration of experiences. Life for them is a playground.

Spread throughout motivational and leadership development circles is the story of an assembly line worker at an early Ford production plant fired for smiling. Perhaps he was laughing. Who knows since the story changes with the retelling. George Goethals mentions the infamous Ford Rogue River Plant incident in his 2004 *Encyclopaedia of Leadership*. Goethals notes how plant managers in the 1930s and 1940s 'prohibited workers from talking and fired some employees for smiling and laughing with colleagues.' Early manufacture assembly lines depended heavily on cheap labour. The work was repetitious and, most likely, mind-numbingly dull. During the first decades of mass manufacturing, it was a common practice to apply an authoritarian management style to secure employee compliance. Getting the best from an employee meant them delivering a quota with little consideration for the worker's wellbeing. Imagine pitching to a plant manager in 1935 how they can implement a strategy to generate more profit, increase staff wellbeing, and maintain market dominance using play as a methodology. The amount of laughter from the manager's office would make each person present a subject for dismissal.

Fortunately, much of the production today does not adhere to a 1935 style of authoritarian management. Play, as a synonym for explore, has found a welcome place in organisational culture. Although it may still require some pitch finesse and supporting metrics to win over the stoic heart, play has earned a place in business. If we were having this conversation solely among artists and musicians, the debate would be unnecessary. Their livelihood depends on play. What you will discover with the PLAY Nudge is that play applies to every aspect of life. When we use the word PLAY as a nudge, think, explore. In this chapter, we are going to explore the applications of PLAY in its function, fun, fact, and fiction.

Function

Los Angeles Police Department Homicide Division Captain Amos Burke was enjoying a pleasant evening meal out with his date when a house phone was brought to his table. "Phone call for you, Captain Burke," the concierge announced. On answering the call, Burke commented to the caller "Why that is just around the corner," he said, "I will be right there." Captain Amos Burke was a millionaire detective on the 1960's television programme *Burke's Law*. Sleuthing was more of a hobby for Burke than work. He certainly didn't need the income. Travelling in style whether to a crime scene or a high society event in his 1962 Rolls Royce Silver Cloud II, Burke was not the typical lawman of television.

Regarding that call at dinner, it was to inform Burke that a shady businessman named Buddy Jack Cook was found murdered in a lift at a nearby hotel. Burke and team would meet on-site to start their investigation by interviewing witnesses. Early in the *Who Killed 711?* episode, Captain Burke and Detectives Tilson and Hart arrive to interview the victim's neighbour in the apartment below the victim's residence. The now-former accountant for Cook, Harold Harold is interrupted by the team of detectives while tinkering with a machine. According to some sources, an infamous line was broadcast for the first time in television or film history. As Harold's machine whirs to a stop, Detective Tilson asks Harold "What does it do?" "Do?" Harold responds, incredulously. "What's it for?" Tilson responds.

I find it unlikely that "What does it do?" was uttered for the first time by a fictitious police detective on a television programme. Countless times in every language, somebody will have asked a similar question regarding the functionality of a creation. Perhaps the creation does little more than exist or provide some aesthetic pleasure to the creator. Play, as a form of creative engagement, also has its share of rational doubters. Play? What is it? What does it do? What is it for? Where does that fit into my business plan? How do I measure the results where a play-oriented strategy relates to the marriage of staff wellbeing and productivity? We want a better reply to "What's it for?" than Harold Harold's, "Well, nothing — nothing. I mean, that's the beauty of it. Every machine in the world does something, but not mine." Let's answer the pragmatists first so that they can have some fun with the other elements of PLAY.

For Harold Harold, whose mother had no imagination and was the named Myrtle Myrtle, tinkering on a machine that served no purpose was therapy. Pressed every so lightly, Harold exclaims that his machine is "a rebellion against efficiency." Whirring, plopping, and bell ringing with synchronistic precision, even Harold's rebellion against efficiency proved to be efficient. Play functionality may be harder to measure than a machine's productivity, but it is possible. Getting an accurate metric depends on what is being measured. Like creativity, defining play garners several expert opinions. Some of those definitions of play are age or activity-specific. Common themes of play include development as the outcome. To develop intimates that there is a starting point, milestones, and some form of conclusion. The finale could be a sample closure in a research study or an endpoint for a stage of development. If there is development or progression, measurement is attainable.

Among the available definitions, I dismiss any label that minimises play as frivolity or play is the opposite of work. By applying traditionalist perceptions to a word that carries such depth that it permeates every aspect of our lives, is to deny a commonness that we share with all other humans. Regardless of age, gender, national origin, ethnicity, cultural identity or any other categorisation, play is a fundamental element of our existence. Also, PLAY is a nudge that needs to be developed. Therefore, the broadest range definition for play defined in terms of a verb is to explore. The functionality of play can be written as an objective. What does play do? To play is to explore artistic skills. To play is to explore interpersonal relationships. To play is to explore divergent or lateral thinking.

How do you measure PLAY? Again, what do you want to measure? Let's use the example of exploring artistic skills. First, let's create an objective. For an objective, you need a condition, a behaviour, and a change for measuring the outcome. For my condition, I may choose my medium and other factors like a time frame for delivery. As a behaviour, I may not shoot for the Moon at first. We will keep the bar attainable and say, 'with pencil and paper' and 'in one hour' are my conditions. My behaviour is 'draw a human face', and my degree is to do so 'that the image resembles the subject.' Altogether my objective will be 'With pencil and paper, draw a human face that resembles the subject within one hour.' Equipped with my objective, I can now measure my play outcome.

From their particular frame of reference, some might say "I can't draw. This is not going to be fun. That is going to be work." That is where misconceptions of play, creativity, and function are born. Many tend to equate play solely as fun. As a result, the perception of play is skewed to encompass a single orientation for a play related behaviour. Even though the activity is that of exploring, the attribution of associated tasks and the mental intensity it may require are categorised as work. When the mind makes that switch, from play to work, a different dynamic fires neural connection to accommodate that orientation. While in a state of play, you are poised for discovery and lateral thinking. Whereas with a mindset of work, you may slip into a linear thinking orientation.

Consider a machinist. While working a lathe or universal grinder, the machinist's mind must be in work mode. Safety steps, processes, and alertness must have top billing in the theatre of the mind to ensure accuracy of production—and to minimise the potential loss of digits. What might happen if the machinist allowed her mind to meander off into an exploring state to answer, "How are we going to get the car fixed?" That could precipitate her distractions leading to failures in safety and production problems. However, if she shelved those thoughts for a more appropriate time, she would have the mental resources to focus on the task at hand. Perhaps during a break, a playful colleague makes her laugh. The momentary play can refresh her for when she returns to her tedium. For our machinist, chalking up another eight hours on the 'No Accidents for 217 Days' board is measured with pride.

Fun

I've long held the position that fun is a relative word. One person's view of fun may vastly differ from that of another. Fun, rather than beauty alone, is in the eyes of the beholder. We usually make our own fun. We've been making fun since we first discovered our toes while lying prone in a bassinet. Each of us knows what fun is. As we mature, our preferences shape our views of fun. Auguring post holes for 836 feet of fencing does not carry the same degree of fun as a three-year-old digging in the dirt. Conduct a test. With a friend or workmate, not a family member, ask him to write down a list of things he finds fun. You do the same. Then compare lists. To better understand, ask your friend why he finds such-and-such fun. You will discover what I mean how fun is a relative term.

Fun, by definition, should be about enjoyment, entertainment, or light-hearted pleasure. Fun activities will most often rouse a laugh, giggle, or guffaw when you are surprised by a reaction to a condition or circumstance. You are less guarded when you are having fun or engage in fun activities. Children are usually oblivious to their surroundings while they play and have fun. That is why we must keep a close eye on them when we are parenting. They don't see the dangers that we observe from our position of vigilance.

As teens, my best friend and I once won a load of arcade prizes at the Seattle Center in Seattle, Washington. While hauling around our winnings, we came across a basketball arcade game that caught our attention. The game had a bubble top, and the table was set with a series of colourised and labelled pockets. A ball was released to roll into a depression. A press of a button and the ball would shoot out of the pocket toward the opponent's hoop. We placed our hard-earned treasures on a table no less than three feet away, plopped coins in the game slot and began to play. It was a lot of fun and demanded our concentration. Once exhausted from our playing, we stopped and had a good laugh. Our laughter turned to dismay when we discovered that our stack of stuffed animals was stolen from under our noses. Our in-the-flow mode got the better of us.

Maturity doesn't necessarily exempt people from freeing their inhibitions during play. Despite efforts for self-restraint, when people of any age become overwhelmed in fun gameplay, their brain becomes more active in the prefrontal cortex. Observe adults involved in gameplay as a source of fun. When fun liberates inhibitions, discovery fuels all manner of emotional, performance, and relational dynamics. Reserved wallflowers can become the most animated, boisterous and competitive in the room when it comes to gameplay. From what I've observed that is the failure of most work-related brainstorming sessions. There is far too much work involved and not much play. Imagine if you could turn a project for innovation and change into a game? Like any game, you'd have rules of play, but the results gained would be far more diverse and perhaps productive.

Professional activities where work is defined as play can blur the lines between work and play, making it difficult to separate one from the other. Even professional athletes are engaged in play as a form of exploration. In their pursuit of performance improvements, professional athletes must find and exploit methods to better their game. Winning pays for the roof over their head and lifestyle. Awareness that playing does not necessarily equate to fun is an essential distinction for pros. A game face can say it all. When your favourite team is down by bad odds at the half, their faces are not likely mirroring how much fun they're having getting trounced. No, instead they have that game face the exposes their internalised pep rally. "Find a way to block 23!" "You can do this, but you are going to have to try something else." What they won't be saying is "Give up now and go home."

I probably don't need to explain the benefits of developing the PLAY Nudge, especially in the context of fun. So why do it? A lot of readers, perhaps yourself, engage in fun, play games, and the like as part of their daily living. You may tell jokes, play a sport, have fun collecting coupons, or get a thrill describing the time you spotted a nightjar on the common. Another lot consider fun and play to be a frivolous time-wasting activity.

"All work and no play make Jack a dull boy" is a description few want to earn among their peers. A person's seriousness and purposeful disengagement can be interpreted as an unsociable attitude. For Jack, loosening up by having fun will expose a trait that should otherwise be kept in check. Some of that attitude can be attributed to generational values. The root of a person's attitude may be more profound than we probably credit during a casual conversation. Don't assume that Jack is incapable of fun. He may not want to have fun with you, because he can't be free to be himself. Fun, after all, can lead to those walls of inhibition being breached.

Banging away at my keyboard, my appreciation for the depth and breadth of the PLAY Nudge grows, especially in context to fun. Inside the brain, the rapid-fire connections that occur when you have fun, fire salvo after salvo through your limbic system. Your emotions become charged, the way you see things is altered, you may change the way you that usually speak, and your prefrontal cortex is bombarded with waves of emotion that demand a response.

What you'll observe from yourself and others in a state of fun is a glimpse into their genuine character. Apply rules to that fun to achieve the best of a person in a safe environment and watch the transformation. The exploration of us, others, and the conditions we face may be heavy at times. True. Sometimes a smear of fun balm on an ache can make the pain go away—or at least give you a refreshing respite for a moment.

Fact

Applied sciences and mathematics work well for illustrating this section. I contemplated including an Einstein, Feynman, or Hawkings anecdote and capping off the section with a pithy quote. Chess grandmaster Judit Polgar also came to mind. As a professional chess player, her take on play, and the factual aspects of strategy made her a perfect candidate to illustrate factual play. In terms of narratives, the category of people with high IQs that engage in systematical exploration exemplifies play. For the non-factual person trying to make a connection between fact and play, the narrative of a genius may not flick a switch. Instead, how about I present some generalisations for this category? That way, we all get to enjoy the prospect of play and facts.

I am going to suggest that we set aside the bias of a small sample for a moment. We are going to look at two classes of thinking. From a purely scientific approach, the first question a scientist of any discipline will likely ask is "Why?" We could change the word for "How?" in that the core of the question is to reveal the dynamics of the subject of curiosity. Archimedes' likely pondered the reason why water dispersed when he stepped into a water-filled bath with, "Where is all that extra water coming from?" Da Vinci worked on the concept of human flight by first seeking to understand how a bird's form makes it possible to fly. "How do bird wings keep it aloft with such agility and ease?" likely came across Leonardo's mind more than a few times. Every field of study across the board, asks "why" or "how" as part of their SEE Nudge. We are the beneficiaries of those discoveries.

The second class of thinking converts the why and how of observation into action. Asking "why" is one way that we learn and orient our self to new experiences. Age is inconsequential in that wonder begins before we can form words or a coherent thought. Curiosity is the foundation for learning. Take that wondering "why" stage another step forward in development and turn it into a fact-finding adventure in uncharted territory. Ask, "what if?" The curious toddler that discovers an open toilet may ponder, in his pre-linguistic state, "What if I drop in here that thing Momma always carries around?" Only to find out that a mobile phone sinks to the bottom. As does a hairbrush, a set of keys, and a full sippy cup. The scientist running an experiment with the CERN Large Hadron Collider (LHC) will ask a more complex "What if?" condition, but the wonder element remains valid. "What if we collide two charm quarks and one up quark?"

Every human-made creation or discovery can be traced to a root query of "what if?" Our innate propensity to be curious furthers our adventure into the unknown. We have a lot to be thankful from the people that went before us, and today work, in a playful environment of scientific discovery. Starting from a premise of the known, the curious creator ventures into a state of the unknown. "What if" ploughs a path of courage for risk-taking, realisation, and reward. You've already exercised the "What if" thinking when you worked through the FLOW Nudge. With one thought in mind, you sought to combine a second thought with the bridge of "What if?" The power of curiosity is the source of all discovery—and it applies to everything. No aspect of humanity is exempt from the influence of curiosity. The action is an essence in creativity.

Does that mean that wonder and curiosity are creativity? No, that would be an affirming the consequent fallacy. More likely, we can state that wonder and curiosity trigger creativity. To create fire, you need a combustible material, oxygen, and a source of heat. Any fire prevention training uses that triad for explaining fire basics. Similarly, you need conditions or triggers for creativity. I've mentioned a few already. Curiosity would have to be in the triad for starting a creativity fire. Making a parallel to fire, I'd say that would equate to oxygen. Take away curiosity and creativity will die. Combustible material for our fire comes from your observations (SEE). Run out of ideas, observations converted into thoughts, and the fire goes out. The source of heat? I'm going to stick with action or the DO Nudge, which we will discuss in Chapter Eleven.

The scientific community is expert at play. Especially fact-oriented play. Pushing the boundaries of possibility, probability, and certainty, scientists must seek a state of play to open new avenues for exploration. Their activities include research of chemicals, elements of the universe, and realities we could easily take for granted. Scientists may best demonstrate play as a form of creativity. Given the wild things people want to build today, engineers may also have to carry the creativity trait. Playing with facts is an undeniable nudge of creativity. We should not devalue the importance of fact building in a PLAY environment.

Fact-finding, or discovery, might better be called fact gameplay. If we were sitting with one another over a cup of coffee, I'd ask you to describe how discovery plays out in your work. Where an accountant or an analyst is required to uncover challenges for a client, they may rely on playing with possibilities of how a condition occurred. That will set the analyst on a path to explore. That new path can open previously unseen avenues of investigation. All the while, the fact-finding element of PLAY leans heavily on observation discovered in the first nudge—SEE.

By applying the SEE Nudge to gather information, communicating what we SEE through TELL, furthering our concept by combining possibilities in FLOW, and then PLAY with new possibilities, the creative is empowered to create. This process is the way new things are brought into existence. What the mind can envision, or imagine, can be done.

Fiction

I mentioned this earlier that science-fiction has long been of interest to me. I suppose being a second-generation child of the space race fuelled the fascination.

First-generation people being those born in the nineteen-forties and early nineteen-fifties, they were the first Baby Boomers. My entry point was closer to the end of the Boomer generation, but I benefited from their wonder. I was toddling unaware when Yuri Gagarin left Earth's atmosphere to view the blue planet from space. What a total rush that must have been for Yuri. The space race was the source of one of the most prolific periods of innovation in human history. Play was in absolute full-on mode. Those born a decade before me were inspired by their imaginations and realised the possibilities of space and space travel. To lead the way by employing indirect propaganda, Hollywood produced and distributed scores of B-list movies in the 1950s with all their black and white glory. The fad of space found good soil in the minds of young people.

Themes in those B movies included aliens, the effect of radioactivity, and space exploration. In those movies, Earth was plagued by giant ants, killer shrews, massive spiders, a 200-foot-tall praying mantis, and a diabolical gelatinous creature that consumed everything and everybody in its path. Further threats to humanity also included a fire breathing dragon that terrorised Asia, giant women, little men, an invading alien race susceptible to the common cold, and a gesture from a superior culture that offered citizens of Earth a future of peace. A message of humanity's vulnerability to the unknown and a philosophical tone of warning marked each film with a capstone quotable line in the script. It was the age of space exploration. The prospect of travelling beyond the Earth's atmosphere to our nearest neighbour galvanised the imagination of the world. Nations invested millions, billions, into their space programmes in the race to achieve the title of being the first of numerous firsts. First, to make it out of the Earth's atmosphere. The first to get a live creature into space. First to get that live creature back from space. First to get a man on the Moon…and to bring him back.

Captivating our imagination, probably since the beginning of time, is that bright orb in the night sky. There are libraries of literature on space found in the catalogues of science fiction anthology. I could fill a book on reviews for authors and sci-fi works that I enjoy. Two of my favourites are C.S. Lewis' *Space Trilogy* and Italo Calvino's *Cosmicomics*. Calvino describes one person's relationship to the Moon's in his short story *The Distance from the Moon*. In Calvino's story, the distance of the Moon to the Earth was much closer than today. So close that the expanse could be bridged without leaving the atmosphere. To traverse the gap between the Moon and Earth, one had to first be at the apex of the Earth's relationship to the Moon. At that point, a ladder would suffice to cross between the two orbiting surfaces. On the Moon, visitors could harvest Moon-milk and enjoy the other benefits of the lunar surface. Early filmmaker Georges Méliès, created the first moving visual descriptions of man interacting with the Moon in his film short *A Trip to the Moon* (1902). We have come far in film making since Méliès thrilled moviegoers with his turn of the century technology.

We imagine ourselves in various roles. We envision a life ahead of us. We imagine a life yet materialised. Success being dependent upon our actions or the limitations of our thinking. We imagine ourselves in relationships. We imagine ourselves in environments for which we may not be accustomed. We imagine ourselves travelling or adventuring into areas that don't currently exist. By this vehicle of imaginary transport, we can experience life without limitations and boundaries. Imagination inspires the fictional narrative for which we alone own the rights and outcome.

Fiction is something that is not real. While it may parallel aspects to life, fiction is a story. We enjoy reading fiction because it inspires us as it relates to our commonality or because the stories are so different from our personal experience. Fiction transports the traveller of imagination from the mundane of a 9-to-5 work existence to places where the mind is refreshed and changed. Words absorbed and corroborated by visualisation are a treatment for mental complacency. No act of reading can occur without building on neural connectivity that previously didn't exist.

Although I've placed a lot of emphasis on reading and writing fiction, I don't want you to lose focus on the imagination machine that drives the PLAY Nudge. There are as many ways to demonstrate play via imagination as there is the collective mental energy of all human life. With the current world population, and a conservative estimate of 50,000 thoughts a day per person, humanity generates over 385 trillion thoughts per day. How many of those thoughts are imaginations and "what ifs?" is anybody's guess. We can be confident of several realisations regarding our imagination and its role in PLAY:

- we all have an imagination,
- imagination is essential to the creative process, and
- imagination can be used to contribute to the betterment of society or its destruction.

The battle between good and evil is rampant in our collective history. The actors change, but every day the stage is set to test which influence will mark up the most points. I genuinely wish I could promote the Nudge Principle so that only good outcomes are produced. In 2006, a phrase kept me moving the Nudge vision forward: 'Let us think of ways to motivate one another to acts of love and good works.' Despite my vigilance to see it otherwise, I could not factor out the destructive power of imagination in the mind of somebody that neither values love or good works. For as much as is possible, my mandate is to keep the scales tipped in favour of the good to minimise the bad that encroaches through 'evil imaginations.'

Playing Nice

We've explored the function of play. Why is function so crucial to the creative process? In many ways, function is what sells. We've looked at the fun aspect of play. If we are honest with ourselves, that is the most often adopted perspective of play when we consider play as part of the creative process. We looked at facts and the importance that play has in the role of curiosity, wonder, and its place with exploration. Finally, imagination and the fictional aspect of play. All of these attributes of play can and do lead to creation. From out of fragments of our mind, something new is created in play. Fiction is that story you create to narrate the creative process until it is materialised. Creativity and the act of creation is your opportunity to make a mark for your existence because what you create lives on.

Should you aspire to fame, then you must be prolific in your creative expression. If you are a politician who aspires to higher government roles, then your circum vitae must include accomplishments. Your accomplishments are the culmination of your creative processes. Your portfolio must consist of evidence of your ability to lead others that help make the creation real. The same goes for literally any creative process. Artists, musicians, poets and authors can have the one-off masterpiece or a one-hit-wonder. Looking into the collection of another creative's life from the outside, we may only see the pieces that made it to the public. Behind the curtain of that life, was significant work conducted on which the visible was built.

Louis Daniel Armstrong was an undeniable major influence of the twentieth-century jazz movement. His influence continues to echo in our consciousness. Growing up in New Orleans around the turn of the last century, he experienced poverty, prejudice, and discrimination. The names of locales where Louis lived as a child reflect his surroundings. Places like The Battlefield and Storyville, where he eked out an impoverished life, seemed the destiny of men of African descent in the early 1900s American south. A turn of fortune occurred when a family of Lithuanian Jews surnamed Karnofsky took kindly to Satch and employed him to do odd jobs. The music he was exposed to during this time of his life was a mix of African roots, spirituals, and the echoes of slavery. We know this connection of musical influences as blues and jazz.

Last week we had the privilege to attend a Sir Tom Jones concert. For his encore song, he described how he knew Louis Armstrong and asked the audience if he could finish the concert with a song by Pops. The song he sang, *What a Wonderful World*, is a testimonial to how a person can change the way he sees the world. A person that experienced discrimination and hate could somehow write lyrics of such beauty that they will last forever. The following day I was listening to an Armstrong playlist when I heard the song *Black and Blue*. I listened carefully to the lyrics and found myself tearfully moved by the contrast from *Wonderful World*.

> Cold empty bed, springs hard as lead
> Pains in my head, feel like old Ned
> What did I do to be so black and blue?
> No joys for me, no company
> Even the mouse ran from my house
> All my life through I've been so black and blue
> I'm white inside, but that don't help my case
> Cause I can't hide what is on my face
> I'm so forlorn. Life's just a thorn
> My heart is torn. Why was I born?
> What did I do to be so black and blue?
> I'm hurt inside, but that don't help my case
> Cause I can't hide what is on my face
> How will it end? Ain't got a friend
> My only sin is in my skin
> What did I do to be so black and blue?

Behind his disarming smile and charm, Louis Daniel Armstrong had a lifetime of emotional investments and losses that contributed to his legendary status. You may or may not have endured discrimination, prejudice, or hate. I think it is safe to say that you have experienced some level of ignorance. People do and say things to which they don't give much thought beforehand. The pain it causes can scar a person for a lifetime. We all want to be remembered in some way. Our life is a monument to our experiences and all that we have become.

By the time we reach the PLAY Nudge of the creative process, we should be ready to answer ethical questions regarding the content and form of our creation. How does my envisioned creation make me feel? What is my emotional investment? How will what I create affect others?

9

FEEL

Had you known me when I was transitioning from teen to twenty, you'd never suspect that I concealed an abiding appreciation for art and classical music. I credit two primary factors for the seeds of culture that found good soil in my being—my Mom and growing up in Seattle. Although I can't point to a specific instance when Mom guided me toward cultural awareness, she had a certain way about her that exuded class. Perhaps it was the music of Ferrante and Teicher, Wes Montgomery, and Herb Alpert that she played on the HiFi console Saturday afternoons while doing weekend cleaning. Doesn't really matter what, when, or how she influenced me. Among many other memories, I have this emotional attachment to her in my thoughts of childhood.

Growing up in the eastside suburb of Bellevue, we had the benefits of Seattle's cultural appetite on our doorstep. School field trips included an introduction to classical music at the Seattle Opera House (now McCaw Hall), Bach compositions played on the Flentop pipe organ of St. Mark's Cathedral, scientific discovery at a 1962 World's Fair landmark called the Pacific Science Center and Asian art at the very cool Art Deco style Seattle Asian Art Museum in Volunteer Park. Our family also made trips to other surrounding museums. Exposure to culture may not make a person culturally intelligent, but it can till the ground for seeds of culture to be sown. Nurtured by curiosity, the culturally stimulated mind of a child can produce incredible results. Along with reading, exposure to culture can lead to an awakening.

During my later teen years, I had a gap in my practice of reading for pleasure. Let's say I was distracted for about four years. Coming out of that phase, I took up reading again. I started out easy with 200 – 300 paged books. I enjoyed history and the human drama. In fiction, I was attracted to books from authors like Steinbeck, Hemmingway, Hesse, and Solzhenitsyn. For some inexplicable reason, the first long novel I chose to read was *The Agony and the Ecstasy* by Irving Stone. The story is that of a battle of wills between Pope Julius II and Michelangelo di Lodovico Buonarroti Simoni. At the core of their disagreements was the Pope's insistence that Michelangelo, an established sculptor, paint the ceiling of the Sistine Chapel. Michelangelo contending to the Pope that his medium was marble not paint. If he were to paint the famous frescoes, he would do so as he saw fit. I trudged through that book with a determination to get through it no matter what it took. Sometime afterwards, I watched the film of the same title. Movies, CliffsNotes, video blogs with spoilers, reviews, and Wiki summaries are a fast track to the last page.

The film version is perhaps the best reference for my purposes as it visually portrays the emotional intensity of the story's two main characters. Both are strong-willed, determined, and skilled in their different roles. Emotional outbursts between the two characters are frequent and penetrating. As the Sistine Chapel project extends and word of Michelangelo's work spreads among the Vatican cardinals. Opposition increases until emotions collide. The nude portrayal of Michelangelo's subjects on the ceiling of the Chapel draws the ire of a group of cardinals. Accusing Michelangelo of blasphemy, heresy, and sinfulness the cardinals demand that the panels depicting nudity be over painted or removed. Defending his work, the artist bellows "Who are you to judge my work?" Throughout the project's four-year saga, a frequent question and response between Julius and Michelangelo punctuate their feelings of frustration.

Pope Julius II: "When will you make an end?"
Michelangelo: "When I am finished."

Covered by decades of analysis, film critics assail Charlton Heston's portrayal of Michelangelo as overacting. Lay aside for a moment the film style of epic films typically cast with Heston such as *The Ten Commandments, El Cid,* and *Ben Hur.* For each performance, Heston conveys raw and intense emotional energy. A viewer won't have any doubt of the emotional state of a Heston character. I suspect that is a primary reason he was cast in the roles he played is his ability to convey the intensity of emotion.

Set during the period of the Italian Wars, Stone used the backdrop of physical war as an analogy of the internal conflict in humankind. The agony is that internal battle Michelangelo fought to be true to himself despite internal and external pressure. The ecstasy comes as Michelangelo channels his emotions into feelings that he can master. For all the conflicts that marked the commissioned project, the physical demands on his body, relational strains exacted, stretching himself in a new medium, Michelangelo did finish. A collection of work by Michelangelo, including the frescoes at the Sistine Chapel, remains for us to enjoy. Looking up in awe at the Creation of Adam or marvelling at the beauty of The Pietà is a privilege. For the emotion an observer may experience, we can thank the agony and ecstasy of Michelangelo. What we feel from an encounter like that is deeply personal and ours alone.

We tend to confuse the words emotion and feeling. We seek entertainment in all its form because of the emotions it arouses. Emotion is a physiological reaction to stimuli. Our face softens or hardens according to the emotion evoked. Our words become gentle or brutal. Our physicality retreats or advances. A feeling is the conscious response to an emotion. Emotions are ingrained in our autonomous nervous system. Tucked in between these two states is the condition of mood. As emotions go, the best example to illustrate emotion is fear. The fear-and-flight effect is a universal autonomic reaction to a fear-induced situation. How you feel about that fear-induced condition is quite a different matter.

Consider the fascination with being purposefully frightened. Box Office Mojo lists nine categories for the horror genre. If I include sci-fi horror, werewolves, vampires, zombies, and assorted terror-related films, the total revenue for the genres listed is £34.8 billion. The three categories for superhero films have grossed £27.4 billion. Apparently, filmgoers prefer to be more scared than inspired by caped crusaders et al. I think the attraction comes from the uncontrolled or anticipated rush of emotion that surfaces with the surprisingly powerful physiological reaction to fear.

Emotion, mood, and feeling are intricately woven into the fabric of the creative process. Like an overlay, each state lays comfortably on top of each of the core nudges. A creative cannot isolate these powerful internal forces from the other nudges, as each is filtered for action through the interpretive influence of feeling.

E-I, E-A, Oh

On my first visit to a county library in Essex a few years ago, I arrived during story hour. Besides listening to a children's story, pre-school aged children are entertained with sing songs and nursery rhymes. I recall that most of the songs sung were familiar as those sung by my children when they were young. Some of the songs had slight differences from the familiar American way my kids learned, but each was clearly distinguishable. Old favourites for the age group of knee-highs included *Head, Shoulders, Knees, and Toes, If You're Happy and You Know It*, and *London Bridge is Falling Down*. Many of the songs and nursery rhymes are sung by children in America have their origins in England. What surprised me was the cross over of the song *Old MacDonald*. I know the tune is sung around the world and certain farm animal sounds are expressed with regional vocalisations. We know the song, regardless of language, and can deduce the animal sound from context. The subject of mood and feelings is a bit like that. We all know the song, but some variations depend on who is singing.

Psychologists, neuroscientists, and researchers continue to build on the foundations of previous emotion studies in search of the exactness of how the brain manages emotion. A casual researcher will soon discover that there is significant information available on the subject. Although researchers may have a slightly different take than another, as heirs of that work, we can glean something valuable from context. The Nudge Principle was conceived to stimulate you to think, conceptualise, wonder, and act on your creative core. Each proposal's premise in the Nudge Principle and core nudges are grounded in peer-reviewed research and presented so that you don't get bogged down with data. We are in the chase for creativity—not the scientific study thereof.

When I collated the essentials of creativity into the core nudges, I was influenced by Daniel Goleman's work on emotional intelligence (EI) as it related to the FEEL Nudge. Goleman presents EI as a parallel to the intelligence metrics of an Intelligence Quotient (IQ). Before Goleman's *Emotional Intelligence*, Howard Gardner's model of multiple intelligences may have set the stage for Goleman to expound on emotion as an intelligence. A fundamental proposition of EI is that an individual's emotional intelligence can be assessed by demonstrated social skills, self-awareness, self-regulation, motivation, and empathy. According to these models for behavioural change, benchmark skills can contribute to a person's wellbeing and success. Undoubtedly, the development of these skills can deliver as promised.

The reason I opted for a different path from EI with the FEEL Nudge is that layers related to emotion include mood and feelings. Creativity is not solely an emotional reaction to a condition. While intensely valuable in the act of creation, emotion doesn't stand alone. Creativity demands an action for a creation to be brought to life. An emotion, on its own, cannot do that. Whether an emotion simmers for a time or is an immediate reaction, it needs the traction of feeling to interpret and act. Demonstrated creativity is the desired outcome of the Nudge

Principle. Mood also plays a part in its effect on the creative's perspective and execution of the creative process.

Perhaps the most daunting obstacle in building an emotion-oriented case for the FEEL Nudge, as it relates to EI, is in the implementation of those five EI skills promoted by Goleman. The one ability that bothered me for a few years of contemplation was empathy. Arthur Koestler wrote in *The Act of Creation* that 'Empathy is at the source of our understanding of how others think and feel.' Although I can appreciate Goleman and Koestler's views, I can't say I entirely agree as empathy relates to the creative process. Does a creative need empathy in the process of creation? Not really. It can be a useful source of motivation, but it is not essential. History is smeared with artefacts of creatives that used their creativity to drag civilisation through our darker chapters. Cruel torture devices crafted in the Dark Ages or tools of mass destruction in the twentieth century bookend a long shelf of volumes on the rotten things people do to other people. Of the five skills required for a high EI, the EI skill of motivation would score high for those people that trade in suffering.

In searching for another approach, I decided to frame the FEEL Nudge in the context of emotional awareness. Being aware of your emotions, mood, and how they affect you and others can lead to a conscious decision on how to respond. A feeling is that internal flag activated by an emotion and contextualised by a condition. In a sense, it is like having an inner signal person using flag semaphores to bias your decision-making process. Consider this scenario. An emotion is triggered by an event or thought, and your signaler will raise flags to catch your attention. Typically, there is a precipitating physical reaction. Quickened heartbeat. Sweaty hands. Nervous twitch. If your emotional awareness is honed, even slightly, you will recognise the signals and be alert for what is likely to follow. With your feeling identified, you act.

We are going to take a page from the emotional awareness aspect of the creative process in the FEEL Nudge. To accelerate a creation from PLAY through FEEL to the next stage of BE, we want to put our stamp on it. Harness the power of your emotions to ensure success becomes engrained in your creative experience. Recognising how mood, yours and others, can affect your emotions beckons us back to the SEE Nudge. Our observations become the first filters for understanding. Also, don't lose sight regarding the influence of mood. A turn in mood can seriously set back a creative endeavour. Energised by emotion and complimented by mood, a feeling can be an incredible asset in your Nudge Principle toolbox.

Emotion

You are probably going to think that I am favouring Irving Stone by starting out this section with another mention of the author. It just so happens that he wrote numerous biographical fiction novels over his career. His first significant published work was *Lust for Life*, a novel about the life of Vincent Van Gogh. We know the artist for his famous paintings that are now merchandised on everything from refrigerator magnets to socks. I can't begin to imagine what he would think to see his art used in such widespread commercialism.

Van Gogh was, to say the least, intense. Today his art is appreciated worldwide, but in his lifetime, his view and execution frequently fell short of his vision. Looking through the window of time, it seems that Van Gogh was a poor manager of his emotions. We view Van Gogh as tortured by an unyielding internal emotional conflict. He experienced depression, delusions, and psychosis. The torment eventually boiled over with an infamous moment of self-harm and the taking of his life at 37-years of age.

Emotions are a powerful force. Managed and channelled for good, they are the source of every great human achievement. In terms of artistic creativity, you'd find it a challenge to prove that an emotion is not at the core of inspiration. The euphoric physical reaction that occurs at the point of awareness, enlightenment, or inspiration is a feeling that you sense in your body. That is why emotions are often associated with the heart. "I feel it in my heart" is more-or-less an acknowledgement of a physiological occurrence activated by an emotion. Provoked by a condition, internal or external, an associated emotion fires a chain reaction in the brain to provide a foundation for your feeling. You then associate that feeling to the corresponding emotion. At that stage, the conditions of the emotion and the feeling appear to be one and the same. Thus the confusion.

As cited earlier, there is significant research available on emotions. I find Robert Plutchik's wheel of emotion the most stable, flexible, and friendly model. At the core of his model are eight primary emotions: joy, anticipation, trust, fear, surprise, sadness, disgust, and anger. The brilliance of the model is in the way that it is organised. Primary, secondary, and tertiary dyads enable practitioners to identify root relations between mild and intense emotions, opposites, and feelings. The reason I qualified that sentence by mentioning practitioners is that mental health professionals must be aware of the root emotions behind feelings. Especially those practitioners that apply Cognitive Behavioural Treatment (CBT) in their treatment of patients. Using a reverse engineering style approach, a practitioner will begin a patient's treatment by helping him identify feelings. For many patients, a sense of ambivalence makes it difficult to label a specific feeling. Let alone identify an emotion. Muddled by habituated thought patterns, the patient, put simply, can't find their way out of the emotional woods.

A creative in touch with his emotions is better positioned to manage his emotional state. We risk venturing into some dangerous open waters with emotion and creativity. The water is safer closer to the shore of feelings where the conditions for feelings are more manageable. A rogue wave of emotions on the open water can easily overwhelm the most balanced of persons. Sudden loss, death, a situation that evokes rage, or winning the lottery can come with such intensity that the affected are unable to cope with the change.

Subsequently, we may consciously react to an emotion and not the feeling that it arouses. With the filter of the prefrontal cortex bypassed, we are prone to make poor decisions. Do that frequently enough, and it creates a pattern. Patterns become habits. That, in a nutshell, is the essence of addictive behaviours so often observed in artists. A dependency on emotional sensations, unchecked by a cognitive awareness and mismanagement of the associated feelings, can lead to augmented sourcing of those emotional sensations. The casualty list of artists, musicians, and performers that pacify their emotional demands with substances like drugs and alcohol is long and punctuated with sadness.

How do emotions relate to the FEEL Nudge and creativity? Use your emotions as a litmus test for how you respond to an observation. Perhaps others may not emotionally react in the same way as you. You may, nonetheless, find that a similar emotion is activated in other observers. If your creation is designed to evoke a desired range of feelings, then focus your efforts on those basic emotions that are most likely to achieve your goal. To achieve feelings of optimism and courage, work toward evoking the emotions of anticipation and joy. For love and friendliness, focus your efforts on the underlying emotions of joy and trust.

On the flip side, if during your creative process you sense anxiety or dread, be aware that the feelings come from the emotions of anticipation and fear. Perhaps you get a gut feeling working on that research project that you are running for the umpteenth experiment. You need to run the experiment objectively to ensure the purity of your data, but you feel anxious about the outcome. Will it lead to disappointment or open a new channel of curiosity? Your emotions are your frontline internal check for categorising a creation by its value.

Most of Van Gogh's work was completed during the last two years of his life. Over a decade he created 1,300 paintings and 850 drawings. What was the battle that Von Gogh fought and lost? I've wondered what it felt like to be in his head.

To see such beauty and yet be tormented trying to find his place in the world. I theorise that he was subject to his emotions—a fragile ship on the crashing waves of his mind. I read several of his letters to his brother Theo. I suspect Vincent was acutely aware of his emotional state. He just didn't know how to manage it.

Besides, I wouldn't have the courage to begin again outside. I once went into the village — accompanied, at that. The mere sight of the people and things had an effect on me as if I was going to faint, and I felt very ill. In the face of nature it's the feeling for work that keeps me going. But anyway, that's to tell you that there must have been some over-strong emotion inside me that brought that about, and I have no idea what could have caused it.

Letter to Theo 9 June 1889

Mood

Blank canvas. White canvas. Empty canvas. I use those phrases interchangeably when I get stuck in the creative process. Writing from personal experience, I can make excellent strides when I am in the zone. Words flood from my consciousness organising coherent sentences that encapsulate precisely what I intend. I must say, that is a good feeling. I don't want to stop, but instead, I press on until I reach a logical stopping point. I am aware that scenario doesn't happen all the time. Most of the time, my writing spits and sputters in spasms of inspiration. I get to where I want to be, but the journey is less than fluid. Then there are those times when my creativity reaches a point in the process where I plateau. Like the *Little Engine that Could*, I struggle to get to the top of the hill. I find myself chanting inaudible affirmations to the rhythm of "I think I can, I think I can." I toss shovelfuls of thought material into the firebox of my mind intent on maintaining steam. I will reach the top.

The toss-more-material approach works sometimes. I run out of steam because I've spent all the readily accessible material in the creative process. Desperate not to lose ground, I mine my research and external sources for that piece of information that will heat up my momentum. Other times, there is no amount of materials that I can stuff into the experience to free my mind from stalling. My emotions are fully engaged with anticipation and trust. Anticipation in that I know inspiration will come. Trust, in that I am relying on myself to break the deadlock. Plutchik's dyads of anticipation and trust suggest my associated feeling will be either of a hopeful nature or lean toward fatalism. I've experienced both. Not just in writing, but in work, relationships, and creative processes.

Sometimes hopeful wins out. Sometimes fatalism. The key factor for which succeeds over the other is my mood.

From a top-down layered view of emotion, I find the definitions and examples of mood to be overly simplistic in its binary orientation. On or off? Hot or cold? Positive or negative? I am certain that mood is more complex. Consider mood like a 3D sphere that you want to draw. On its own on a sheet of white paper, a drawn sphere just looks like a circle. To give that sphere dimension, you need to add some shades of grey. When working with charcoal or graphite, an artist can achieve amazing results using a variety of shadowing effects. Hatching, cross-hatching, blending, stippling, smudges, and other techniques. What gives that sphere a 3D appearance, and a more realistic perspective, is the combination of positive and negative on the composition. Dividing up mood into either category feels like a person can only get one dimension of mood at a time. Ours is not to attempt a scientific study of mood. I primarily want to identify how mood affects your emotions and feelings.

If you were to think of your emotional landscape like a painting, your emotions would be the subject, the use of light would be the mood, and the colours applied are the feelings. Sticking with the positive/negative orientation, the lighter the painting the more positive, the darker the more negative. That is an apparent generalisation, but it illustrates the idea. An observer of your landscape is likely to regard your mood by an either-or assessment. That initial assessment may linger as a characterisation.

Even after a single, brief meeting, a person may conclude "What a happy (nice, pleasant, cordial, etc.) person she is." You can probably see the hazards for misunderstanding and misrepresentation. Wrongly developed characterisations may factor later when you are expected to demonstrate those perceived characterisations as part of your social personality. The occasional observer of your emotional landscape won't recognise the layers applied to your canvas that make you who you are.

A good quality of mood is that it is manageable. I mentioned earlier how I experience plateaus in my creativity. The stalls in my creativity can be categorised as petite-stalls and grand-stalls. A petite-stall is a temporary state. With that, I can usually alter my mood with a change of music, a smile, a diversion, a variation of my environment and those type of quick fixes. I may have to take a nap or eat something. I know myself well enough to recognise when my mind hits that plateau, and I fall into a creative petite-stall. Most of the time, I play ambient music in the background while I work. It keeps me on a steady pace and isn't a distraction. While writing this chapter, I found myself falling behind on my schedule. I changed my playlist from ambient to an instrumental orientation. Then I changed it from instrumental to classic country. The music time signatures of the country music energised me. I also find myself nodding while I work. We all know what that means. Get more sleep!

There are other easy fixes for mood that you can perform like maintaining a nutritious diet, exercise, sleep, reducing or eliminating the use of depressants like alcohol. What makes it easier is if you are the master of your environment or are engaged with others that foster a positive environment. Adversely, the lack of sleep, exercise, a nutritious diet, excessive alcohol, a depressive environment, and stress brought on by toxic people will also influence mood.

Time is another factor. I can snap out of a petite-stall by taking specific actions to jar myself out of the stall. The longer I remain in a stalled state, the more effort it takes to reengage. A long-term stalled state is a grand-stall. The key to mood management is to recognise your mood concerning your emotional reactions. Be aware of how the bearing of various conditions guides your moods. You may not be able to effect change in your environment, but you have a choice on whether you allow that environment into your head.

Feeling

For seven seasons and ninety-two episodes, advertising executive Don Draper amused and charmed audiences of the AMC series *Mad Men*. Set in the 1960s, *Mad Men* fictionalised the lives of those guiding the competitive climate of the American advertising industry. Draper sums up advertising in one of his many quotable commentaries when he says "Advertising is based on one thing: happiness. And do you know what happiness is? Happiness is the smell of a new car. It's freedom from fear." He expands his definition to "a billboard on the side of the road that screams with reassurance that whatever you're doing is OK. You are OK." Advertising, therefore, is the tool used to create a triad between the primary emotions of joy, anticipation, and trust. The goal of such a triad is to engender the feelings of optimism and love. Those two feelings set the stage for a sale.

The FEEL Nudge empowers you to manage your emotions for effective decision-making. Any creation that you envision will encompass a range of feelings that your creation generates. Frontline feelings are your own. After you pencil that drawing in preparation for a portrait, do you respond with disgust because it doesn't reflect your vision? Do you then succumb to that disgust and toss the crumpled drawing into your wastebasket? Or do you display it with your other attempts like a storyboard to observe the evolution of an image? How you respond to that basic emotion with a feeling will put the reins in your hands to direct your thoughts in any direction you choose. Let go of the reins, and your feelings will lead you. Some prefer to live like that as a lifestyle choice. All of us yield to our feelings in different ways. How much so is entirely personal. How much so will be a determinant of your creative style.

We can look around and witness the results of a creative's emotional response to a condition. You may not know the specific source of a creative's emotions or the associated feelings that ignited the inspiration, but they are there. Marked in the chronology of the creation's development is a narrative emphasised by a creative's investment. Even if you are in a relationship with that creative, being exposed daily to her creative processes, you will never know the intimate ebb and flow of her feelings. At best, you can generalise from the common ground of basic universal emotions.

My workspace is an organised eclectic. I could pick up any of the seventy-six or so items in arm's length and imagine the emotional narrative of its creator. What emotional investment was deposited into the hand-painted stone that I purchased off a doorstep in Clovelly, North Devon? What feeling did the creator have when he selected 'Be Original' to be stamped on the blue eraser resting at the base of my monitor? Feelings help you choose between options. With each successive experience, you develop a familiarity with those feelings and associated emotions. Over time, that familiarity becomes the basis for your intuition. Given a set of conditions for which you must decide, you will first apply what you know about the conditions and the likely outcome.

Mixing a red tint into a blue tint will darken the combined tints on your palette. You know that, so you know the results. The more experience you have in mixing colours provide an expanded foundation for making an educated decision about a colour mix. With a limited knowledge base, you will either augment your knowledge or rely on intuition. After a time of using your feelings and intuition in decision processes, you may discover how it begins to be integrated with your emotions. Your reaction to an intuitive experience being reinforced by a familiar emotion. All of that happens with or without your conscious engagement. Awareness of these processes and your response to them is to act on the nudge.

We can't exit a conversation about feelings without viewing so from the perspective of others. How does what we do or create affect others?

Understanding another person's emotional state is empathy. There is a considerable degree of emphasis placed on empathy in the development of emotional intelligence. Success, according to some EI proponents, is wrapped up in your ability to relate to others. High empathy being the critical factor of that success. I won't quibble over the role that empathy plays in social conditions or the importance it can play in personal success. The spanner in the empathy works is when the concept of empathy is applied to the creative process. You can be creative, but not express a drop of concern for others. The creative process can ultimately be self-serving and the antithesis of caring for fellow humans. We may be hardwired to demonstrate empathy, but that is wholly a choice.

I've been through so many emotional twists and turns the past decade, that I've lost sight now and again. Battered by disappointments and postponements, I frequently felt like quitting. There were times I felt the despair of Van Gogh. Yet, I still see beauty all around me. I do photography as a hobby to capture what I see. I clumsily attempt a variety of artistic expressions to dispense the treasures in my mind. Deciding on a worthy receptacle to deposit those treasures was a challenge. Ignoble qualities of humanity sneak into the everyday to sully the beauty of the world and life. Should I, you, or anybody surrender to the feelings that ignobility breeds, then we are vulnerable to a blindness that tarnishes the transmission of beauty to our brains.

The final episode of *Mad Men* closed with Don Draper meditating on a cliff overlooking Big Sur California. During his lifetime he pulled off the penultimate creative action. He started out in life as one person, transformed himself into another person, and then found peace with himself. The closing scene implies that Draper was participating in an encounter group popularised in the 1970s. Encounter groups were intended for members to get in touch with their emotions and feelings in a group setting. Corporations signed up to the concept throughout the 1970s and into the 1980s. Traditionalists dismissed the activities as "touchy-feely" and broad-brushed participants as gathering to imbibe in group hugs and sing *Kumbaya*. The trend petered out as the popularity attracted less and less qualified practitioners to conduct effective group therapy. The movement progressed from feelings to self-awareness. For the most part, that is where we are today.

Why Your Feelings Matter in Creativity

People appreciate being valued. We demonstrate valuing others in all sorts of ways. At the top of the value expression list is the feeling of being respected.

Essentially, to be respected is when others attribute to you a quality that demonstrates that they get you. The encouragement to "Do to others as you want done to you" sums up the simplicity of being valued. That is probably why that passage is plucked from the New Testament and most frequently cited by non-religious people. We know it as the Golden Rule.

What I've discovered in life is that a sense of value and respect is best delivered from an orientation of recognising the feelings of another person. Dismissing the way somebody feels is equal to saying, "I don't care what you feel." Translated in the mind of the rejected, dismissal of this nature is equivalent to "I don't care about you." Whether we are practiced at valuing others or not, we can learn to be alert to our own and others' feelings.

We want to capitalise feelings by using the FEEL Nudge to test, measure, and propel our creation forward. Your feelings are an emotion check and a broadcast signal to others of your state of being. By expressing feelings, you let others know, by intent or accident, your receptivity to communication and conditions. When you ignore or dismiss feelings, you stand to lose valuable ground in the hard-earned arena of understanding. Since your creation communicates a message to others, you want to ensure that the message arrives with a minimal amount of confusion. Your appeal to reason, logic, and common associations may work up to a point. Beyond that, you have to reach the heart.

To be aware that emotions and feelings are a constant in the creative process is fundamental to a FEEL Nudge. How do you feel when you present an idea, and it is shut down by a dominant personality? What is the emotion you experience when you receive recognition for an innovative proposal? We cannot isolate emotion and feeling from the creative process. Creatives should not only be alert to their emotions and feelings, but also of those of others. If communication is an essence of your creative goal, then you'll want to communicate across a broad range of people types. Appreciating feelings—yours, mine, and theirs—is going to enrich your understanding of self and others.

As part of the creative process, we recognise how emotions can produce a variety of responses. Some responses bear a positive quality, whereas others tip toward a negative. We've also explored how emotions and feelings permeate every aspect of creativity. There is something else feelings do. They make us feel. Have some fun with your emotions. Let your feelings run the show now and then during the act of creation. Allow the impetuousness of your feelings to alter the path you've marked. Explore bold, brash colour or sweeping gestures when you'd typically work in subdued, neutrals, and measured movement.

When you are mindful of your feelings in the flow of creativity, you can open a new catalogue of creative tools from which to play. During the application of the PLAY Nudge, you will have experienced successive emotions. A concept arrives in the theatre of your mind. An emotion flashed a physical sensation. To keep the play going, you respond with the first feeling to connect. Reject or accept the concept? Turn the creation in a different angle to change perspectives. What kind of an emotional reaction did that evoke? How do you respond to that switch? Try not to look at exploring your emotions through your FEEL Nudge as "Playing with your emotions" in a negative sense. Instead, embrace the playfulness as a pathway to self-discovery. Where you can go with your discoveries will clear the way for you to see new opportunities.

Before I close this chapter to let you play around with the freedom to explore, I need to introduce another variable to the emotion and feeling equation. How you perceive the world, the actions that happen around you, and your response to them is regulated by your values. Remembering our childhood, we all know kids whose parents appeared stricter than any of the other kids' parents. They may have been the centre of stories by a childhood friend or the myths passed around when a peer is disallowed from participating in a social event. The parents being the "bad guy" source of the restricted playtime. Given the diversity of people from different backgrounds, faiths, nationalities, and experiences that gather in populated areas, we are bound to have witnessed a wide range of approaches to parenting. While one family may be friendly and welcoming, another may be aloof and private.

Expressing feelings in the first family may be demonstrated with ease. For the second family, the demonstration of feelings may require some learned behaviours. Why a person embraces a set of values may differ from ours. Recognition that not every person experiences the same emotional reaction or feeling response is a step toward understanding others and improving your cultural awareness.

10

BE

Minnesota beautician Peggy Blumquist dreamt of bigger and better things for her life. Married to her high school sweetheart, Ed, the two settled in for a life of normalcy in the small rural community of their childhood. For Peggy, exploration of the world beyond the county line was a fantasy realised through travel magazines. To satisfy her longing for travel, she filled her head with visions of seeing the world and imagined herself as being somebody. Peggy collected thousands of travel magazines so that her hoard flowed from one room to the other in her and Ed's humble two-bedroom home. While seeking a means of escaping the mundane nature of her day-to-day existence, she was introduced to a self-help programme. The goal of the programme was for participants to achieve a state of self-actualisation whereby the person could live life in their fullest potential.

Life isn't known to lay down a linear path for us on the journey to someplace. Obstacles, diversions, changeups, and traumas tend to materialise out of nowhere to keep us on our toes. Such changes happened to Peggy. An event of such magnitude that it would change her life, Ed's, and the lives of quite a few other people. At the height of the drama, Peggy sat on a step of her basement stairs, contemplating her dilemma in existential reflection. Her deliberation spills out as a delusional conversation with an imagined psychologist.

Psychologist: Have you actualised fully?
Peggy: What?
Psychologist: Have you actualised fully?
Peggy: I don't know. I mean, I'm trying.
Psychologist: Do you feel cold sometimes, even when it's hot?
Peggy: Sometimes.

Psychologist: Do you understand the difference between thinking and being?

Peggy: What do you mean?

Psychologist: Do you understand the difference between thinking and being?

Peggy: I—

Psychologist: To be is simply to exist. Try it. Try simply being.

Peggy: I'm sorry. But how is sitting here gonna help me be the best person I can be?

Psychologist: Ah. You want an explanation.

Peggy: Well, kinda.

Psychologist: The human mind, aroused by an insistence for meaning, seeks and finds nothing but contradiction and nonsense.

Peggy: Okay. It's just practically, I'm saying. Uh, as a person, a married person, a woman who's worried she's not living up to her full potential.

Psychologist: Think or be. You can't do both.

Peggy: You're saying, don't think about the person I want to be. Just be that person. Don't think about the person I want to be. Just be that person. Just be that person.

Peggy and Ed Blumquist are characters from season two of the FX series *Fargo*. The names have not been changed because they are fictitious. Although the season was set in 1979, Peggy's search for her identity is played out today consciously and unconsciously by people of every walk of life. The weight of life choices and conditions that stretch your internal resources will lead you to attempt balance by fitting your perceptions into an expanded reality. Often, that stretching process involves nudges that you've already explored such as FLOW, PLAY, and FEEL. Finding balance ends up with adjustments that you perform without much thought. Big questions like "Who am I?" are reserved for philosophers or intimate conversations shared with a lover or friend under a canopy of stars.

The BE Nudge is not going to take you down that route. Peggy's enlightenment to "Just be that person" could have been reduced to "Just be." Further reduction will eliminate any sense of demand to a pure state of being. Our imaginary psychologist from Peggy's delusion clarified that "to be is simply to exist." How do you practise a nudge of existence or being? To desire such a nudge feels like the antithesis of the state for which you seek. From the resources in your mind, your creation is going to germinate from existing thoughts. Your consciousness is defined by the interactions of immeasurable connections made in a lifetime. These establish the basis for who you are. You know this as your identity. Others also recognise this of you as your identity. Identity adjustments are made regularly by the choices we make. Some are easy. Some are hard.

For the most part, we've looked at the Seven Nudges from an individual orientation. Pragmatically, a specific act of creation is actualised by an individual. Complete creations may be the result of acts of creation by several people, a team, or an organisation. Take, for instance, the level of creative collaboration required to produce a blockbuster film. Every contributor listed in the IMDB credits for *Avengers: Endgame*, bar special thanks, totals two-thousand seven-hundred sixteen creatives. Each person added their bit of creativity to make that film complete. What you see as an outcome is their collaborative work. You have your personal identity, but you may also associate with a broader identity in the organisation you represent. That identity may be to your employer, a client, or the public at large. While fulfilling that latter role, you are expected to conduct yourself based on the expectations of the entity that you represent. In other words, to 'be' or exist in accord with the identity of that organisation.

We are not going to explore the existentialism of who you are as a person. I'm not too concerned whether you feel a sense of self-actualisation by applying the BE Nudge. Although a worthy subject to study, we are going to allocate the complexities of consciousness for after-dinner conversation. What we want to develop in the Nudge Principle of BE is an awareness of how it affects the creative process. Once realised, we want to ensure the BE Nudge is etched into our final product. Your creation is a mark of who you are, and who you represent. A creation is the legacy of your existence. That legacy started when you began developing your values, and the legacy that continues in the evolution of those values.

Values

A reference book that stands within arm's reach of my desk is *When Cultures Collide: Leading Across Cultures* by Richard D. Lewis. Part One of the desktop reference is Lewis' chapters on cultural diversity. There are few experiences where your daily existence is not in some way touched by those of another culture. In fact, in the increasingly globalised world it is becoming more challenging to distinguish root cultures without surrendering to a stereotype. To an extreme, such stereotyping will earn you a badge of dishonour as you are labelled with an anti-social moniker that better describes somebody else's restricted thinking than your own. From that perspective, *When Cultures Collide* lacks one culture as it grows in presence and characteristics– the Global Culture. I make that notation not to expose a gap in this excellent material, but to raise questions. What are the roots of a globalised culture? What are the values of that culture? What motivates a person that identifies with a global perspective?

The reason I ask those questions is that at the bedrock of a culture is a stratum of shared values. For most of the nations listed in Lewis' book, each national section has a subsection entitled Culture or Cultural Values. Culture and values being so closely associated, give the impression that they are synonymous. They are not the same but are part of a whole. Something like the fact that your physical body is composed of around 25,000 protein-coding genes that shape your outward appearance. While each gene contributes a slice to the whole, a single gene doesn't represent the entire body. Its influence is restricted to the combined 30 trillion cells that make up your body. Despite its apparently minuscule contribution, a single gene adds a unique quality to the whole. Similarly, a single value doesn't comprise who you are but supports the full version of you.

A collection of people that share a similar gene pool make a racial group. Ethnic groups may or may not be members of the same race but will share some commonalities in terms of history and cultural orientation. National groups typically represent the majority population of an ethnic group. Race is probably a secondary factor because in many cases a nation may host a majority race but host multiple expressions of ethnicity. Consider the two most populated countries in the world: China and India. The combined populations of these two nations are 2.8 billion, which is 36% of the world population. As ethnic groups are numbered, China has fifty-six ethnic groups, whereas India has more than two thousand. Playing with numbers a little more to drive a point, if you include overseas or diasporic Chinese and Indians, the total reaches an estimated 3.6 billion of the global population. Against the backdrop of a 7.7 billion comprehensive estimate, people of Chinese and Indian nationalities comprise 46.7% of the world population.

Let's make a shift in thinking now. The Indian population is about 1.67 billion or 21.6% of the world. Although there are some cultural and certain ethnic similarities, those similarities are unlikely to be based on values. Cultural values stem mostly from environmental memes. Ethnic values stem from the dominance or subordination of an ethnic group within a culture. Personal values will include influences from both of these sources but are tweaked by inherited values and its interpretation by personal experience. Each form of value tags a sort of viral genetic code that permeates the disposition of its host. Why and how you respond to given conditions or stimuli is going to be filtered by that code. A values code. Imprinted from an early age and carried throughout life, your values code will significantly dictate how you interact with others. That code can and will evolve to varying degrees, but the foundational coding will always be there.

You cannot isolate a single value any more than you can a gene to understand the entirety of a person. Yourself included. You can add labels of a demonstrated value, but the core value is a compilation. As a Baby Boomer, my generation is known by numerous stereotypical behavioural values. Born at the end of World War II, Boomers are goal-oriented with a fundamental drive to change the world or at least the world they can influence. Traditionally, a Boomer is identified as conscientious and hard-working. Are all Boomers built that way or demonstrate those values? No. But like the study of cultures, generational studies are also based on generalities and statistical samples.

The dogged determination to see something through to the end, regardless of the personal cost, might be a value born of my generation. Those of other generations exposed to that determination may or may not catch the viral nature of the value by proximity, but they might. This is demonstrated in our creativity. Creativity, for me, is intrinsically connected to pragmatism. Filters for my own creative work check and recheck the pragmatic value of an activity against the investment of time. Sounds like a crippling cycle of procrastination. I am acutely aware of my paradoxical view of pragmatic idealism. Knowing that my ideas must work, I spend more time ensuring that they do. I get there in the end.

Back in chapter nine, I introduced how feelings are used in the decision-making process. Values, as well, play a significant role in arriving at a decision. When a feeling arrives on cue from an emotional reaction to a stimulus, the first filter for that feeling will be your values. Somebody with a hedonistic value set may seek immediate gratification by default. Where that is the case, the hedonist's feelings at the moment will trump any deep-seated values in favour of the moment. Decision-making then becomes an autonomic response to a stimulus without value checks. For anybody else, there is at least a modicum of "Should I?" involved in the process.

In your creative engagement, as an individual or part of something bigger, awareness of your filters can liberate you to explore. Alternatively, your awareness may lead to disappointment if your values conflict with the established norms of your culture or society. Expectations and demands both realised and assumed will influence your creative energy. You'll have more power to choose which path you want to explore in terms of implementation from the position of an individual.

The struggle may be bitter, but it will be internal. Should your struggle for creative expression be with the establishment, such as in an organisation, you'll find that your creativity is tested in different ways. A seed of inspiration from your gift to an organisation must find fertile ground on which to prosper. Any conflict that you experience will invariably be related to contrasting values. You can mitigate some, others are stubborn, and others only exist in your imagination.

Introspection

Thumbing through my stack of comics and Mad magazines was once a regular way for me to while away time on rainy afternoons. Growing up in a wet coastal area like Seattle and Southeast Alaska obliged me to find things to do indoors. As a 12-year-old, I preferred to be outside. Stuck inside, I watched old films, listened to music, or read comics. I can vividly recall one of the oddest comic panels I came across. The image was that of a person watching his umbilical cord protrude from his belly button. The caption included something about navel-gazing and meditation. I had no clue what any of that meant. My only association with meditation was my Mom's reference to an uncle travelling to India to "smoke banana peels." I remember having a lot of time for wandering thoughts in my adolescent and teen years. Fortunately, my reading diet included more than the edgy material of magazine mascot Alfred E. Neuman.

What I didn't know then was that navel-gazing has a deep spiritual meaning and is known as omphaloskepsis. Hinduism views the navel as the third chakra called the Manipūra. Associations of a person's wellbeing emanating from this energy centre include self-esteem, a sense of purpose, personal identity, individual will, digestion, and metabolism. A goal of yogic practice is to achieve Supreme Consciousness. The Manipūra chakra is a required destination for self-actualisation. Some reading this book are going to be inclined to the level of commitment required to explore their chakra, soul, or spirituality. For anybody else, let me assure you that introspection does not demand a spiritual quest. What introspection will expect is thoughtfulness regarding questions about you.

Have you ever been asked "Which famous person, living or past, would you like to have dinner with and an evening of conversation?" This is an icebreaker kind of question asked at team-building events and social gatherings. Most of the responses I have heard fall into a pop celebrity category or family member. Sometimes there are other historical figures noted, for reasons of asking specific questions. Notables of that ilk may include Oppenheimer, Einstein, Kalishnikov,

Loghman, Farnsworth, Nobel, Galston, and Zuckerman. These are a few names of inventors that created or contributed to a specific invention or discovery.

During the creative process, each of these inventors would have had ample time to consider the ramifications of their creation. Few would have weighed the subtle or savage results of their inventions applied to extremes. If you were to open conversation with any of the inventors mentioned above, would you raise the topic of their infamous regret? They will have been asked countless times and introspected the implications ad infinitum. How would you phrase your conversation starter in such a way that would empower your inventor guest to be open and relaxed to reflect with you? Would you even care about his or her feelings? "Let's get to the nitty-gritty" would be the starting point for some folks. Your approach, whichever path that may be, is going to reflect your values.

The creative process, flash or intentional, is going to include an element of introspection. A moment or journey of self-examination that measures your mental and emotional processes against a condition. In the moment, that condition is an act of creation. You might argue that purposeful introspection is unnecessary to creativity. That creativity just happens. A child with a box of crayons, sheets of paper, and imagination doesn't reflect on the meaning of the universe before she draws a flower. Then again, apart from its nostalgic value to Mum or Nana, that precious piece of art is temporary. If you want your creation to have longevity, you want to ensure that it has meaning. Besides personal meaning for you, you'll likely want your creation to appeal to others. Ideally, for that creation to have meaning or purpose.

On a personal level, the values influencing your creativity will be displayed regardless of your efforts to mask them. Let's say that you embrace pacifism as a core value. "Do no harm" is your life motto. Yet you work for an organisation that produces and internationally distributes machetes. The images of machetes being used in the harvest of sugar cane and other agricultural products give you a sense of pride that you are helping people in developing nations. You ignore news reports of machetes being used nefariously by roving gangs in the same country. Although the core value of pacifism rules your heart, choosing to ignore the other uses of that machete your company just shipped reveals a values compromise. To achieve a values balance of ideology to actions, you'll need to spend time in introspection. That is, if resolving a values conflict is meaningful to you. To be fair, resolution may be meaningful, but life places you in a position where you have to choose expediency over conscience.

Tied to values, but deeper in its impact, are morality and ethics. Morals are how a person distinguishes between good-bad or acceptable-unacceptable behaviour. Whereas ethics are based on community, social, or legal expectations of acceptable and unacceptable behaviour. News reports for any week of the year will contain one mention or another of an ethic related breach. Sometimes the lines blur when an individual's or group's morality become superimposed over a criterion for ethical behaviour. The display of Robert Mapplethorpe's *The Perfect Moment* at a public art gallery, film distribution of *The Last Temptation of Christ*, or international restrictions on genetic cloning of humans experienced moral opposition at the root of their ethical arguments. Does my creation deserve public support? Even if that creation is contrary to the moral and ethical code of the society in which it is to be displayed?

I've asked myself a variation of that question for countless scenarios over and over. In respect to a definitive response, the question is meant to be rhetorical. I don't want an answer. What I want for myself is to formulate a value set that doesn't contradict with my core values yet allows room for personal evolution. That would be my value. Not to be superimposed on others, but rather a coping mechanism for all the probable variations to what may at first glance be issues of contrast. Introspection, the questioning of morals, ethics, standards, and expectation of your mental and emotional processes contributes to resilience that gives your creation sustainability. All it takes to prime the pump of introspection is a straightforward question, "Why am I doing this?"

Viewpoint

During a recent Toastmasters meeting, the impromptu session question I was asked was far too easy to answer. "What is your idea of a personal heaven?" was the question fielded in my direction. "North Devon," I replied. More specifically, I continued, my personal heaven would include "an ocean-facing cottage on a bluff where I could write and practise creativity." Let it be known that I love all types of landscapes—including some cityscapes—but the sea has a calming effect on me. I could watch the pulsing rhythm of the sea for hours. Gazing out across an endless body of water, my mind becomes soothed in contemplation. The experience feels like I am in tempo with the universe. Salt air, warm sun (when available), and clouds to provide a panoramic display of billowy dancing shapes and colour. Core values of autonomy, independence, and creativity fuel my imagination of writing by the sea. From that vantage, I am sure I could see into eternity.

Perhaps that is a romantic notion of writing, but it is mine. I grew up being close to the ocean and mountains. Toss in the dynamics of a nearby cosmopolitan city, and I had it all. Strictly in terms of landscape variety, my perspective of the world afforded me different scenes. I appreciate the physical beauty I've seen in the world. My viewpoint of appreciation is not relative to how many feet I stand above sea level or observations of a blanket of blue sky and ocean waves. They are pictures to my frame. We can call this our frame of reference. My enjoyment of a seascape may be shared by millions of others. I am also aware that not everybody appreciates a view of open water. For those, the vast expanse may be intimidating and even frightening. Others, being from a landlocked arid country, may have no perception for that much water. My view of a personal heaven will most certainly differ from the latter.

Over a lifetime of interactions with others, you also develop a landscape view of people. Some of those landscapes are beautiful. You observe them with admiration and may even adopt a perceived value or two from them. Their character resonates with you as a shared value. You spend time together, and value sets seem to blend in harmony. Those people become part of your life as trusted friends, partners, or colleagues. Interactions with these groups of trusted people may influence your perceptions of all the big questions people ask in life. That landscape is one that you enjoy and seek to experience as often as you are able. Other landscape views of people become tainted by behaviours that contradict your values. Whereas the first group of people afforded an invitation for interaction, the second lot produces an aversion. You'll find that you tend to gravitate toward those people that think and act as you do.

As values and viewpoints go, a value is likely to be more concrete. A viewpoint, conversely, is more fluid and suspectable to the power of the influences working on that viewpoint. Anybody that has raised a child through their teenage years knows what I am talking about. You instil values in your child by your actions and direct influence such as parental advice and boundaries. As the child matures through the stages of youth, she will be exposed to differing points of view from her peers. A change of taste in music, a desire for make-up, style, and a plethora of other changes you hoped would never arrive show up all at once. Your values may not change, but your viewpoint on how to parent through your daughter's transitions may require adjustments. Such is life—a series of modifications designed to cope with change.

If it were not for a delineation between values and viewpoints, we might never experience innovation in the creative process. Dogma would dictate societal norms. Change would be relegated to weather patterns and not human dynamics. Being able to position yourself to see from a different perspective incorporates each of the other nudges we've covered. Translating the culmination of the creative process into the language of your values and views will strengthen your resolve to see your creation fully realised. All of that will depend on the nature of the creative effort. Are you looking to create something of permanence? Are you wanting a legacy creation that leaves a stamp of your existence or a flash creation that acts like kindling for a bonfire? We've already established how values factor in as a contributor for your decision-making. A viewpoint adds a spectrum to the value set by introducing flexibility or reinforcing intransigence.

The scale of a creation is also a consideration as it relates to your viewpoint. A temporal creation requires minimal investment from any of the nudges. Small by design, the temporal creative effort may play a part in the collective experience but lack the investment of an extensive creation. The nudges of the creative process will no doubt be engaged, but in a temporal creative effort activity, they will appear seamless, unidentifiable. A large-scale creative effort, like a project or product development, will benefit the most from the detailed processes of the Nudge Principle. Moving from one stage to the next with purpose will deliver a sustainable outcome because of the resilience built into the application of each successive nudge. Creatives exercised in BE will adopt viewpoints that encompass possibility alongside pragmatism. The two forces, together with being, are essential elements of innovation.

Awareness

> *Where ignorance is bliss, 'tis folly to be wise.*
> Ode on a Distant Prospect of Eton College, Thomas Gray

For the final push of the BE Nudge, I want to give you a good ol' nudge. The creative journey on which the Nudge Principle is based may begin with SEE, but there is a pre-existing foundation already laid on which to build. Literally, everything you experience with your creativity and the stages therein is formed on the groundwork of BE. You cannot escape it. You cannot alter its reality. The layers that comprise who you are is a complex integration of values, experiences, genetics, memes, and the infusion of your interaction with a lifetime of stimuli. How you choose to play with possibilities, invest your faith, and act on your thoughts is the remarkable outcome of years of creating you. Yes, you. You are your most magnificent creation. Whether you did so by intent or accident, with the power of choice activated, you become the creation of your design.

You can move forward in life passively being acted on by the conditions that assail you. Being a victim is easy. All it requires is ignorance of the unique gift that you are and perhaps a willingness to blame others for your state. Ignorance is only bliss where wisdom is considered foolishness. Let me remain in my state of ignorance. In that state, there are no demands. No expectations. No ambition. Applying that mindset, we can make an assumption. Bliss is achieved by ignoring the obvious, quarantining reality as a disease to safeguard you from being infected by life. The most idyllic of scenarios cannot guarantee perfect happiness. Ignorance only avoids the inevitable. One day the inevitable will arrive at the door. "Do you hear that Mr Anderson?" growls Agent Smith, "That is the sound of inevitability."

Alluding to a scene from the 1999 sci-fi masterpiece *The Matrix*, Mr Anderson is subdued by Agent Smith on a subway line with a train rapidly approaching. All appears lost for our hero protagonist. Amidst rising tension, Mr Anderson musters a burst of energy and proclaims that his name is Neo. With that exclamation, Neo lurches free from Smith's grasp and escapes certain death. Meanwhile, in the real-world Neo's mentor, Morpheus, asserts that Neo is "beginning to believe." Neo's awareness reached a critical stage wherein he began to understand who he is and what he can achieve. Self-actualisation on a sci-fi scale of one to ten, Neo rolls in at eleven. Being a victim or remaining in ignorance does not lead to bliss. All ignorance does is to dismiss wisdom as noise.

Individuals are not the only entities to fall prey to ignorance. Organisations can do so, as well. Understandably, there are examples aplenty of organisations that have buried their head in the sand with damaging consequences. One such organisation was the massive British company Carillion. The company had interests in support services, project finance, and construction services. Carillion markets spanned the United Kingdom, Middle East, North Africa and Canada. The 2016 Carillion annual report projected £41.6 billion in the pipeline. Stocks for the company traded at £370 on 26 February 2015. Despite glowing projections, the annual report also noted 'Given its business model and the nature of its markets, the degree of confidence that can be placed on the Group's future revenues diminishes significantly for periods beyond the next three years.' In other words, we can't promise what things are going to look like after three years, but it doesn't look good based on our current business model and the market.

Two years, four months and fourteen days later on 10 July, 2017 company stocks were trading at £117. On the next trading day, 12 July 2017, the stock value crashed to £57 a share. One hundred eighty days later, stocks plummeted to half the price at around £23. On 15 January 2018, the giant Carillion stopped trading and entered compulsory liquidation. An employee base of approximately 30,000 was out of work. Before the fall, Carillion management hailed a values-based culture for delivering company objectives. Values for the company espoused the ability to care, achieve together, improve, and deliver. What happened? How did a company the size of Carillion spiral to disaster without changes being implemented to save the behemoth? Companies of this size don't crash without warning. Indicators flag the attentive and the inattentive. The critical factor for staving off disaster is whether the right people listen and act in time to implement a turnaround.

Awareness is one aspect of the equation. We can plead ignorance or plausible deniability, but that doesn't change reality. As a nudge, something which you can develop and measure, BE is hard to pinpoint except by its consistency. Deviations from the norm can be identified and corrected to ensure that root values are reliably demonstrated. Neither companies nor people crash because they stayed true to their values. Values act as a high-level filter for your actions and the way you interact with the world. Individuals that hold to their values find the challenges of life easier to navigate than those whose values are undefined. Organisations that retain their employees and can withstand most challenges are accountable to a set of values and foster a culture where those values are demonstrated.

On a personal level, I find the creative process a preferred approach to developing awareness. When I exercise my creative core, I regularly discover the range of my strengths and weaknesses. Functioning from that realisation, I can make frequent adjustments to facilitate my goals better. Since I started practising the Seven Nudges over a decade ago, I found the BE Nudge to be the most rewarding of all. No matter what I develop as a creative expression, the fact that I do so emerges from a set of values. That I challenge my viewpoints through introspection and remain aware of my state of mind and emotion has been immensely liberating. I've been in this place a few times in my life. Apart from a physical location that I can call my personal heaven, the posture I create through awareness is by far the most rewarding. I like this place. It feels good.

Sheriff Hank Larsson and the Aliens

Back in the small Minnesota town of Luverne, townsfolk are trying to put aside the ugliness of the past weeks. Where possible, they will work to get back to normal. The bad guys are either in graves, prison or are hiding under the floorboards of society. Life struggles of the average family come back into view as the echoes of unparalleled local violence are silenced. Minnesota state trooper Lou Solverson, his wife Betsy, and her father Sheriff Hank Larsson relax in the living room after Sunday dinner. The recent happenings in Luverne, Fargo, and Sioux Falls have left the family exhausted but thankful for having survived.

While her father was away dealing with the criminal factions of the story, Betsy stopped by her father's place to feed his cats. Upon opening Hank's office door, Betsy is confronted with layers of alien-type symbols written on sheets of copy paper blanketing the walls and cabinets of the room. In the typical "Okay then" attitude of the region, Betsy closes the door and leaves. Only later, during an after-dinner conversation, does Betsy query her father's activity.

Hank: So, after your mother died, I got to feelin' pretty low. We all did. And I took, well, you remember I took some time off. And I started thinkin', which I know is dangerous. But, you know the things I've seen, you know, in the war and at home, on the job so much senselessness, violence, you know? And I got to thinkin' about miscommunication. Like, how isn't that the root of it? Conflict, war, does, doesn't it all come down to language? Right? The words we say and the words we hear, which aren't always the same thing. So, I thought, you know, what if there was one language a universal language of symbols? 'Cause pictures, to my mind, are clearer than words. So that's what that is.

Betsy: Mm. In your office? You're making your own language.

Hank: Well, it sounds crazy when you say it out loud, I know. But you know, when we see a box with a roof on it, well, everyone knows that means "Home," right? You know, and my six-year-old granddaughter, she draws a heart. It means love. No question. Anyway, that's where I started, you know, with simple ideas. And the more I worked on it, the more it became all I could think about.

Betsy: (Reaching out her hand to touch her father's arm) You're a good man.

Hank: Well, I don't know about that, but I like to think I got good intentions.

Characters of *Fargo* season 2 frequently commented on how society was changing for the worse. The loss of innocence struck deep into the heart of the small traditional values Minnesota berg. With that loss, norms of behaviour were shaken. Incursions into the community by bearers of contradictory values represented change. How long would they be able to hold onto to their values? Would they be capable of passing those values to the next generation? Secure a future for them that is safe and promises hope? At what point in the scale of change does the balance tip toward a shift in values? Solversons, Larssons, Blumquists, and Gearharts are each vessels of their unique value sets. Contrasts between them are deep, but nonetheless valid. The names and locations of the characters will change befitting your experience. Change is the inevitable that comes for the unprepared. Those preparing for change are the creatives that make a difference and participate in change.

I mentioned in Chapter Eight, how promoting love and good works are values underlying this book and any development associated with the Nudge Principle. Mindful of those values, I feel the mandate to apply these principles to every aspect of life. To live and always demonstrate them. I know my values. I am aware of my viewpoints. I am mindful where there may be conflicts of interest and contrasting values. By holding onto who I am and maintaining my commitment to conduct business with my values gives me a sense of assurance that my creativity will bear the mark of those values. I don't know what the future brings. I prepare by exercising my creativity. It empowers me with flexibility. Although I have a crystal ball on my art table, I don't use it for peering into the future. Mostly I keep it close by to show me what the world looks like from a different perspective. But that is just me.

11

DO

The moment I decided what I wanted to do for a career came in a flash of inspiration when I was about 10-years-old. Playing outdoors in a fort that my neighbour Luke and I created, our afternoon idle chatter landed on an odd topic: "What do you want to be when you grow up?" Kids are regularly asked that question, even though nearly all of them haven't a clue whatsoever. Luke's family owned a petrol station, so it was assumed he would take up the family business. After leaving the area to live in Alaska, I lost touch with Luke. Last I heard, he was once elected to the State senate. I don't recall Luke mentioning his dream of politics. I think sometimes things just develop that way. As for me, the sound of my dream job chimes loud and clear through time, "I want to be an archaeologist."

Looking back, I can surmise several childhood influences that may have contributed to my fanciful career selection. Those influences fall into three categories: books, movies on television, and imagination. I was fascinated with Greek and Egyptian mythology throughout my youth. Any reading material I could find regarding myths was devoured with an appetite. I've mentioned how the rain frequently restricted my outdoor activity when not in school. With nothing else to do, I might be found watching old films. My favourite movies were adventure films like *King Solomon's Mines* (1950), *The Mummy* (1932), and any film with Bud Abbott and Lou Costello. When I could stay up late on Friday nights, my interest turned to B movie horror films broadcast on the local station KIRO-TV for *Nightmare Theater*. Adventures into mysteries of the past arrested my attention—even if it was just the silliness of Bud and Lou being chased by Boris in wraps.

Lastly, my imagination fed the vision of travelling the world. Discovering lost cities. Mingling with other cultures. Seeing places that otherwise nobody else may have recorded before. Holding pieces of history in my hand that may have seen epic battles of Biblical fame. When Spielberg and Lucas produced *Raiders of the Lost Ark* in 1981, my romanticism for archaeology experienced a resurgence. All the exciting parts of archaeology came alive with action from the opening scene to end credits. Had I missed my calling? During my high school years, I decided to investigate what it meant to be an archaeologist. Did it hold the promise of travel and adventure I held so dearly in my heart? Yes, under the right conditions. However, I also discovered that I lacked one quality that is essential for all archaeologists. Without that quality, I'd scarce be able to achieve the title but would also be unfit for the work. What was that missing quality of such gravity? Patience.

Our youngest is at university and considering his career options. When we are asked by friends what he plans to do as a career, my mind reflects to the afternoon conversation with Luke. I didn't pursue archaeology. After graduation, I thought I'd have a go at what was then called commercial art. That didn't happen. I tried junior college, but at that point of my maturity, I found it to be an empty experience. I admire those that take the further education route to secure their career choices. Professional career paths are more easily defined for the university graduate. Or at least that used to be true. The escalating growth rate of technology, economics, and the shifting status of the political landscape are game-changers for university students. Although a candidate for the job market in four years, a first-year university student may not have a notion of what he wants upon graduation. A lot will change in three to four years. What we tell people about our son's career destination is "What he will be capable of doing is a job description not yet written or conceived."

The combined percentage of graduating 18-year-old sixth form entrants to university in 2018 from England, Wales, Northern Ireland, and Scotland totalled 27% of all leavers. That means 73% of those leavers are going down a different path than university and perhaps a formal education. University graduates in three to four years are going to apply the tools they've gained to carve out a future using those tools. Hopefully. Regardless of which speciality they study, they will have to apply creativity to secure their job and succeed in their lifetime.

What about those that didn't go on to university? They too will have to apply creativity to secure their position and succeed in their life path. In either camp, they are going to be reliant on their ability to be creative. I hope that they will apply the Nudge Principle to their choices so they can find fulfilment in their respective outcomes. Just as it is my hope is for you. Instead of a career path, I chose employment opportunities. Appraising my life choices, I don't regret the roads I've chosen.

What distinguishes those that apply creativity to their journey remains the last and most critical of the nudges: DO. Without a corresponding action to a creative thought, there is nothing. No permanent mark. No evidence. No reinforcement or check for you to validate your idea. That's all I'll mention about the downside of not acting on a creative idea. If you have pondered or procrastinated a creative concept until it disappears into vagueness, you have your own story to tell. Instead let's talk about what you can do to change things for the better, the potential risks, and how you plan to get there.

Solo

Converting your concept to a creation sounds like a straightforward proposal. Within some expressions, it probably is a simple process. To initiate a blank sheet of paper or canvas with a medium is by its nature an uncomplicated task. A seasoned artist will probably have a ritual preparation process he goes through before the first stroke is laid. Perhaps a wash or texturing must be first applied. Larger scale projects on non-traditional platforms like sidewalks and walls may require some prep as well—or not. If you've done the pre-check nudges of the Nudge Principle, you should be poised to dive in. All of that engagement, be it for a microburst or saga, is ready to be applied.

When you tip the creative bucket out to draw from the mix, your first challenge is to apply the medium. Just get it on the surface. I like that approach because it subverts the legalistic boundaries of your prefrontal cortex with its linear restricting demands. Unless you are still developing in the other six nudges, it is best to take an action. Once committed to an action, the creation is freed to take on the organic nature of flow. At the forefront of how you are going to perform an action are questions for your creation. Is the creation ready? Are you ready? I guess that you have experienced at least once in your life what happens when you delay an action. The longer the delay, the increased likelihood of procrastination. That can have all sorts of unfavourable influence on your creative energy. As the pithy superhero Sphinx admonished his team of misfit superheroes, "When you doubt your powers, you give power to your doubts."

Most of the previous sections flowed with relative ease. For some reason, I hit this section and with it that proverbial brick wall. After a day or so of agonising over my writing plan, I decided to go back to square one. I needed to refresh myself and regain perspective of where I wanted to take you on this journey. For the past few days, I've been editing previous chapters. I hoped that would be enough to prime the creativity pump. Feeling anxious that I was getting behind, I identified that issue in FEEL. I restored my inspiration in the BE Nudge. This is my third attempt. The risk to not complete this section with the same engagement as the other ten chapters is not acceptable. By going through FEEL and BE again, I identified my hang up.

Working on a creative project at an individual level is wrought with obstacles. I know mine. In fact, I am painfully aware. I am fortunate in that regard. Being intimate with those issues that surface in the process helps me to identify them quickly. Once identified, I can act. A gnawing doubt has been festering in my head for days, perhaps a week or so. I can look at my writing schedule to see where it first occurred. Doubt is one mental condition that so many creatives experience when they start out. Regardless whether that starting out is in a new medium, a new audience, style, formula, it doesn't matter. Nobody is exempt. What is that doubt that cripples so many creatives? "Is my work good enough?" or a variation like "Will people like it or reject it?" At its worse, "What criticism will I receive for my work?" I mean, come on, as a creative you put a lot of work and emotion into your creation. You didn't set out on the creative journey to purchase criticism. In all likelihood, you want to share with others your gift, and in the process, receive some sort of recognition and remuneration. Getting slapped down on social media was not in your plan.

What might happen does not change what needs to be done. Your first responsibility is to your creation. I can't reiterate this enough. Your creation is anything you create. That could be a decision for dinner to developing the cure for cancer. In the sense that the source of the creation is from your mind, you own it. In legal terms, that creation may be subject to contracts of employment, but the nurturing to life is yours. You are the creative. You have something to share. Where that creation has a value or worth to another person, you also have the right to be recognised and possibly rewarded for that creation. You will never receive either unless you apply that first stroke, record that first chord, write that first sentence, and let others see it. You choose the format for visibility, but it must be seen, heard, touched, sensed, or felt.

There are risks. Out of your hands and exposed, your creation is vulnerable to public reaction. That comes with the territory. When going it alone, the focus of a creation's success and delivery feels concentrated all on you. Rightfully so, you are after all the author of the object of attention. Where you need to come to terms is that unless you manifest your creation, you will have no measurement of its success. By success, I don't mean whether it nets that mythical one million pounds or some other arbitrary monetary value. What success means, as it relates to a creation, is whether it demonstrates the creator's vision and that it can be understood as intended. Yes, probably a broad generalisation but accurate in most instances. At the root of the creation though, you want your audience to get it. If they get it, they will want it. With that, your cycle is complete. Job done.

Never underestimate the power of testing a creation across of range of its development. Take the risk. Every time you run through the Nudge Principle applying the Seven Nudges, you improve on your creation, build depth into your creative core and integrate creative processes into your conscious thinking and decision-making. I hope that you aren't tired of reading this. The necessity to reinforce the principle warrants to write it again: The Nudge Principle and Seven Nudges apply to every single act of creation you can imagine. The creative process may be a flash of inspiration that last seconds or can involve years of development. At the end of the day, the only way you or another will experience that creation is by you acting on it. Every creative process must end with an action—without exception. Otherwise, you don't have a creation.

Partner

Point to any domain or industry, and you will find at least one example of a successful partnership. Some co-founding partnerships are engrained in corporate history by their brand name. Hewlett Packard, Marks & Spencer, Rolls-Royce, Dolce & Gabbana, Hall & Oates, Torvill & Dean, and Ben & Jerry are several examples. Expand the list of successful partnerships to those brands that do not include surnames in the brand name. Prominent companies to mention are those of the most celebrated partnerships between co-founders of companies like Apple, Google, and Microsoft. With the right combination, a business partnership or a collaboration in the arts can produce history-changing results.

The multiplication of effort, an increase of resources, and synthesis of creativity are clear advantages of a partnership. Where a partnership is reinforced with a solid relational orientation, the bond can propel the creative thoughts of two individuals into a reality not imaginable by a solo creative. We can praise the advantages of a good partnership, but you also need to be aware that a partnership increases the risk factor by at least two-to-one. If your creative effort is business-related, you will do well to perform a thorough risk analysis before entering that partnership.

What does a partnership have to do with the creative process? What does a partnership have to do with the Nudge Principle? Both have a significant impact on the creative process and outcome. A direct connection to the creative process is the eventual need for collaboration to occur for a creation to be realised. The collaboration may be casual such as in a source providing a service to deliver an end product. Writing a book is a true-to-life example of collaboration. To write a book requires hard work, but to get that book published requires multiple layers of collaboration. You can go it alone, but your results may be diminished.

Over the weekend, we visited an antique centre where I made a curious observation. A local poet had his books on display in one of the shops. The display included about twelve of his poetry books. An A4 size computer printout was his marketing tool, and a sales notice indicating the cost of purchase was £2.99 each. The unusual print size of the paperbacks suggests that he self-printed or paid extra for an odd print template. Although I applauded his action to self-publish and develop a sales outlet, I wondered if that was the extent of his marketing effort or his partnering.

Researching the world of partnerships and solo acts led me to a list of the top 100 British entrepreneurs. You won't find any of the entrepreneurs listed on a Surname & Surname filter from Companies House. There are plenty of books and resources available to fire the imagination using anecdotes of successful entrepreneurs. I can safely leave that to others. I've read those books too. If I were to generally surmise why these entrepreneurial greats took the solo route versus a partnership, I'd rank the following as the most likely reasons:

- Financial
- Avoidance of additional legal or contractual entanglement
- Differences in operational or business philosophy
- Imbalance of vision sharing, scale, or scope
- Retain control over intellectual property
- Lack of relational confidence in potential partners

Even the supremely self-made entrepreneur must partner to some degree. The differentiator between a partnership and a serial solo entrepreneur is the latter may have more confidence in their skills than those of a prospective partner. The scene is regularly played out on the television programme *Dragons' Den*. Candidates seek investment in their bright business endeavour to secure both financial and business advice from a panel of entrepreneurs called Dragons. Using a keen eye, we can observe each Dragon apply the Nudge Principle.

- First up is the **SEE** demonstration. Black notebooks opened, the Dragons make notes paying particular attention to numbers and listening for a unique selling point.

- Next up is the **TELL** interaction when Dragons dialogue with the candidate to validate the basis for their perceptions on a candidate's claims.

- With the essential TELL established and an interest piqued, the Dragon will look for a **FLOW** between the proposed product and the Dragon's strengths and assets.

- Should a Dragon recognise a potential profit-making opportunity (FLOW), the Dragon will **PLAY** with the candidate's offer through negotiation and simultaneously evaluate the mettle of the candidate.

- Having relied on their instincts time and again, the Dragon has learned to trust his or her intuition. A fine-tuned **FEEL** Nudge empowers the Dragon to determine whether a partnership with the candidate can be productive.

- If a candidate achieves enough confidence in a Dragon to make an offer, he or she has arrived at the inner sanctum. The Dragon has assessed the situation and is ready to associate their reputation (**BE**) with the investment.

- Once a Dragon is committed, he or she is ready to act—to **DO**. At that point, he or she is prepared to partner and ideally make money for all— the entrepreneur and investor.

The intent of going down the *Dragons' Den* route was not for a commentary on the programme, to analyse the success rate, the pitch-to-win ratio, or recognise those businesses that have succeeded or failed. I want to demonstrate the tracking of the Nudge Principle and the Seven Nudges with a narrative reinforcement of partnership. If you are a creative and are partnering with somebody, that relationship is going to turn to business or take on a business orientation. Art, music, literature, business, politics, service, interdepartmental collaboration, it doesn't matter. At the culmination of a Nudge Principle engagement, your creation will demand action. That action will have consequences. In a partnership, the implications of those consequences increase your risk ratio.

Don't let the prospect of risk dissuade you from a partnership. In every creative endeavour, there are risks. Does the benefit outweigh the potential risk? A positive is that within the extended boundaries of a creative partnership, you can build a relationship of trust. With a partner, you can double your outcome of the Nudge Principles of SEE, TELL, FLOW, and PLAY. Together you can get to new places in the creative process that would generally take much longer. The two-heads-are-better-than-one axiom comes into play and promotes a dynamic creative alliance. Be selective, activate the Nudge Principle in your decisions, and ensure that you perform your due diligence. In a business-related partnership, it is better to err on the side of caution than to correct in retrospect. Build connections that complement and amplify the best of both partners.

Team

Have you been on a team that was dominated by one or more personalities? Perhaps one or more people vying to wrest control at the expense of the team objective? Hopefully, you've had good and bad experiences so you can tell the difference. If you've watched the television programme *The Apprentice*, you have witnessed a first-place battle unfold with each new task and appointed leader. Teamwork is essential to winning the Apprentice game. Should you be allowed access to *The Apprentice* candidates' applications, I wonder how many times you'd come across the word team or team player in a candidate's pitch. Anybody that has watched the programme will recognise the importance of playing as a team.

Viewers are acutely aware of how difficult effective teamwork is to attain where personal ambition dominates and exacerbates the tension. Tasks are crafted for each episode to ensure maximum entertainment value and edited to highlight conflict. None of the obstacles devised can minimise the need to function as a team. Of the sixteen Apprentice contestants, only one will earn the coveted role of *The Apprentice.* The season finale requires teamwork from fired contestants to demonstrate that importance. Getting things done to win demands teamwork for our wannabee business tycoons. Strangely, they have to work together as a team with only one person rising to the top. A prospective winner will do well to have behaved along the way so not to have damage relationships. I am dubious of whether that corresponds to a real-world scenario or purely set up for televised drama.

How do you get the most of yourself and others on a team? Contextualised as it relates to creativity, a team's purpose is the same as any team. The goal is to work together toward an objective while integrating the strengths of each team member. To do so in a creative environment, let's say project management, means that each member is responsible for being attentive to the nudges of the Nudge Principle. When a threat to the team's success is identified at any stage of the project, a member should raise the alarm that something is or may be amiss.

During a SEE, TELL, FLOW session, team members have the opportunity to note their observations, dialogue on the observation, and work toward synchronising with the team objective. A team that values and demonstrates creativity is going to achieve unparalleled results. Especially if they use the Seven Nudges in their measurements for creating sustainable outcomes. Team members check each other's blind spots. You get the most of a team when you minimise internal competition. Instead of spending energy on self-promotion, expend effort identifying the strengths of others on the team. You will get more out of the experience yourself, your team members will benefit, and the work will get done with higher quality results.

My son and I attended a Little League baseball tryout when he was 12-years-old. The building was full of boys, a few girls, Dads, Moms, coaches, and Little League officials. Devon, my son, gave his all through every stage of the tryout. Sports tryouts are tough. Most coaches look for the biggest, strongest, and the most skilled kids to recruit for their team. At the end of the day when the selections had been made, Devon's group of hopefuls waited with anticipation to meet their coach. The physical diversity of the gathering of boys was visibly smaller, larger, or lankier than many of the players selected for other teams. After waiting for what seemed forever, the boys and parents were told that a coach was not forthcoming. Unless one of the parents wanted to coach, the boys would not be playing that year. I spoke up and said something to the effect that within our group of parents, somebody could coach the team. I didn't stop to think that commenting before anybody else was a declaration of a critical leadership quality. As you might gather, I was nominated as the coach.

Fortunately, I had help from a couple of other dads. Our pre-season practises tested the kids in each position to identify their strengths. We worked those strengths, drilled fundamentals, and played the game as part of every practise session. I didn't have one kid on that team that didn't give his or her best effort. They were all eager to do well. We also had the only girl in our division, and could she ever play.

One of the things I made clear to the players' parents before we got started was that our coaching was to be focused on the players. Winning games was secondary. Their development and wellbeing were paramount. There would be no favouritism, and everybody played, regardless of how well a kid played among peers. No exceptions. Our players spoke well of each other. They encouraged each other, rallied around other teammates, and accepted losses with dignity—even if their heads did hang low. They showed up for practise and played their hearts out. The only time that I had trouble was with parents who thought their child should play out of order. I stood by my terms. We would play each kid in rotation, even if it meant we might lose a game.

What do you imagine happened that fateful season for that group of boys and our girl player? They got better and better. They won games, missed the ball, hit the ball, cheered each other on, and made a small group of volunteer coaches very proud. Several of our players were selected for the All-Star match against the team led by that one coach who cherry-picked all the bigger, stronger, and faster kids. I was elected the coach of the All-Star team because our Devil Rays players had earned first place in the win category. For the entire game, my kids held their own against a much more technically skilled team. We were outscored, but we didn't lose. Those older boys treated our players with respect at the end of that game because our players deserved it. They earned it. As the round-robin tournament advanced our team against one opposing team to another, our players' confidence rose with each score and win. Who would have thought at the end of the 2004 Colorado Springs Little League season that the group of kids nobody wanted at the sports tryout would end up being the champions?

Comparing the dynamics of teamwork between twelve-year-olds may not be a like-for-like comparison to adults. What it was meant to demonstrate is that when you focus on the strengths of every team member, they will feel valued. Empowered with a sense of self-worth that team member will give his or her all to help the team win. That is human nature. Without question, some players play better in some positions than others. If I had a weak pitcher in the rotation, I had to adjust the outfield to have the fastest kids that can throw and an infield that could play with confidence. They covered for each other. Whether weak in an area or strong, they played as a team.

That is what you want to achieve on your team. Where you need to perform as a team won't matter, regardless of the domain or context. Business, politics, sciences, creative collaboration, any and all endeavours that require a team to work together will gain the most from your contribution and the value you attribute to your team. If your team environment doesn't produce that kind of loyalty, then it is up to you to find a way to create it.

Community

We accomplish what we achieve on our own, in partnership, as a member of a team, or as a community. Your creative vision may encompass any or all of these configurations as your path to achieve your desired results. Starting from a solo position, you may want to work through partnerships and teams until you reach a pinnacle of collaboration with community. What will that look like when you arrive? Granted, the view at the destination will differ for each person and journey. If building, participating in, or sustaining community is part of your vision, then we should consider what that means.

One of our sons has a vision of building a communal group based on peace, harmony, self-sustainability and being ecologically responsible. To do so, he and his envisioned community, besides living in proximity to each other, will need to have likeminded people that share the same attitudes and interests. The level of creative engagement for a vision of that magnitude demands a high degree of creativity, commitment, and investment. Values must be deep-rooted for such a venture to succeed. Knowing him, I can imagine a discussion over a campfire on the subject of community would eventually lead to a yearning for global adoption of his envisioned community values.

Near where he lives is a small community of artists that share a common area for studio space. The artists' degree of community is partially defined by the financial benefits of shared expenses and that they share a common bond of artistic expression. Living or working in proximity, as a standalone quality for community, is an expression of location-based community.

Forgive me, but I am going to digress again and share another pop culture anecdote. Simon Pegg and Edgar Wright's dark comedy *Hot Fuzz* depicts an idyllic fictitious village in Gloucestershire. A group of elite locals are so obsessed with maintaining their village status as Village of the Year, that they go to extreme lengths to secure the repeat honour. A fanatical love for their community, geographic and shared values, is the impetus and excuse for their unethical behaviour. It should be noted that not all of the people in the community share the group's approach to maintaining order. Those that express dissent do pay a costly price of exclusion. What we observe from this behaviour is that sharing proximity to one another doesn't make a community. It may compose the physical elements of a community, but not the commonality.

From a more global perspective, we are all part of the worldwide community. We share space on the Big Blue Marble and have a mutual responsibility for its wellbeing. Arguably, that wellbeing should also extend to its inhabitants, all living things, and everything necessary to ensure life and a quality of living. Apart from the human-defined boundaries that segment and divide our planet, what we do within our boundaries affects those in their boundaries. Interconnected across overlapping layers of commonality, the unyieldingness of our human-made boundaries continue to dictate our rate of progress toward unity on issues that affect us all.

We have a universal community regarding a place, but not universality for the cause. In the plus column, the number of international volunteer organisations spreading the benefits of altruism is an incredible testament of collaboration and the human spirit. If your creative passion involves participating with or creating such an organisation, you'll find it an effective path for exploring your creative self. At the same time doing good for others and bolstering your own wellbeing is a win-win all around.

The Internet opened another universe in terms of community of place. Social media alone, while being the radioactive affected, steroid bulked up beast of Japanese legend, is a segment of a greater community. For all the coverage social media attracts, a person might conclude that the entirety of the Internet is comprised of social media platforms. Use of the Internet certainly is heavily tipped in favour of social media, but there is much more. Not unlike the stars in the heavens, the Internet is a vast array of sites and data sources. Some sites are high profile and shine brightly; others are harder to spot and require a systematic approach to aid discovery.

Using a different allusion, imagine the Internet as a pile of sand. Your site or site of interest is just one grain. Getting your grain to the top of the pile is dependent on numerous factors. The most important being the size of your community and their engagement. Each site garners its own community of followers and interested parties. That you navigate to where your community meets via an address is like visiting a neighbourhood brick-and-mortar without the hassles of parking. The Internet is an excellent example of a community of place.

Another type of community is the proximity community which draws members together due to their proximity to each other. The importance of a proximity community is valid in a lot of ways. Belonging and safety are two qualities of community we covered in chapter one with a veiled Maslow hierarchy parallel. A group of people that rally to protect the basic needs and ensure security for that community doesn't need a deep connection between community members for that community to function. Superficiality can suffice. Should an external or internal influence threaten that community, a metaphoric beacon is lit, and a rallying cry uttered to gather community members to thwart the invasive threat.

We have to be realistic in terms of creativity. There are times when the invasive threat may be perceived as you and your creative ideas. Generally speaking, people are uncomfortable with change. A segment will embrace change, a majority will tolerate change, and an active proportion will resist change. I would not dare suggest who is right or wrong in disputes regarding change. Perception is going to drive either campaign for the heart of the community.

Applying the Nudge Principle will undoubtedly enable you to define your approach and navigate the feelings of stakeholders. A key for winning over a proximity community is to convert them to a community with purpose.

If you want to create a community that is passionate, committed, and engaged, you need to foster meaningful relationships. That community will need to feel they have an investment in their mutual success. To achieve that kind of investment demands a creative approach that integrates every aspect of the Nudge Principle. Your community will need to SEE the intricacies that interlace with their own interests. You will need platforms where you can stimulate dialogue (TELL) to ensure the community shares a common understanding. Beyond that, you will need to encourage a FLOW of ideas that integrate multifaceted solutions.

By the time you reach this level of investment, the members of your community should feel empowered to PLAY with possibilities and cycle through the first three nudges until a consensus is reached. Invariably, the PLAY process will stretch some members of the community outside their comfort zone. To secure community commitment, you will need to be attentive to your members' emotional mood (FEEL). If they rallied around a purpose (BE), then you should work to reinforce the genuineness of that commonly shared value. With all that safely navigated and a community working together, there is an increased likelihood of success when they DO what they set out to DO.

Showing DO to Your World

You, being the action-oriented person that you are, probably thought when it came to the DO Nudge that the chapter would be quite short. Perhaps you thought all that was needed by way of encouragement in the DO Nudge was a branded swish and a famous slogan instructing you to act. Wouldn't that be simple? I expect that you've adopted the premise that acting is a non-negotiable condition for creativity. Now standing on the end of high dive board pondering to decide whether to step off, we can shout "Go for it" and it would be appropriate. Unless of course you are known to be a sinker, not a swimmer. Instead, I wanted to demonstrate how the DO Nudge is an integrated part of life and the creative process. No matter which path you choose to engage in the delivery of your creative energy, the outcome will create consequential footprints. A creation is hard to isolate as a sole event. The most sterile and secure environment cannot stop the viral nature of a creation. Once manifest, something will happen.

Being at the lead of delivering a creation places you in charge of the creation's destiny. The dynamic of nurturing your creative thought from inception to completion relies on you to guide the process to ensure delivery. Yes, there are those creative flash moments that will materialise from what appears to be nowhere. The entire Nudge Principle and each nudge may pass through your consciousness with such rapid speed and intensity that it will feel fluid. The degree of comfortability you enjoy with your creative awareness can accelerate the process.

Arriving at DO, you may be ready to go, go, go! Aware that your next action will be impossible to retract, you take that decisive step forward. Never lose the sense of wonder that comes with doing. Protect it and use the momentum to build positive experiences. Every risk that you take is a conversion of a creation into reality. Regardless of the outcome, you will notch a mark in the win column and secure an investment of experience that will contribute to a future risk's success. If you developed a goal before reaching this stage, you now have a measurement of assurance that you are on the best course.

You naturally need to consider how best to show your creative moxie to the world. Where do you want to go with it? With a goal in sight, you stand a far better prospect of arriving at your desired destination with your creation intact and fresh. Building that support infrastructure of the other nudges along the way reduces a back-and-forth approach. Allow me to give you an example. When I shop at a supermarket, I prefer to start at one end, usually the entrance, and shop aisle to aisle to ensure I don't miss what I came to purchase. I know a lot of thinking, planning, and marketing go into floor design for shops. They have experts advising experts and some corporate person making floorplan decisions based on the most up-to-date customer traffic and purchasing analysis.

Food aisles near the shop entrance carry produce and refrigerated products like meat and dairy. Organised for the first part of the shop, you are expected to trolley your refrigerated product for the remainder of the shop. At the far end, or close to it, you have your frozen products. In between is aisle after aisle of dry goods. Almost without exception, a shopping experience does not end with a logical start-to-finish line of action. I have to travel back and forth at least twice. While annoying, it is a necessity by design if I want my refrigerated products to remain fresh during a shop. Applying the Nudge Principle, you are going find yourself frequently returning to previous nudges to keep your creativity fresh. When you are ready to check out, move to DO and make it happen.

The speed at which you engage the Nudge Principle is up to you. Some creative bursts will make the process fast and easy. If your creative solution requires a minor proposition, like deciding whether to use chalk or pastel, then make it easy on yourself—test both. Enjoy that you have the liberty to choose. Set yourself a goal to engage in regular freestyle creativity. Allow yourself to move impulsively with a medium. Step outside the confines of your standard patterns of thinking by shaking it up with some randomness. The way to break down barriers and open your creativity is by doing.

You may have heard somebody being referred to as a "free spirit." The moniker transmits images of Woodstock, hippies, and a lackadaisical approach to life's problems, daisy chains and macramé. Allow yourself designated times and space to feel your own free spirit with creativity. Do your best not to overthink or analyse. Give your best effort to create. Plain and simple—create. That way, when you need to draw on your creative juices, you can easily tap into your reserves. You know what it feels like to be free, or to be restricted, and to produce.

You will need your creative capital for so many experiences in life. In a workplace environment, you are unlikely to have a carte blanche pass to be a free spirit. If you do, congratulations. You are in a rarefied world of freedom. How fortunate are you? Workplace scenarios are often slow burns for creative success and demand more of your attention. Should that be the case, use the same condition as the earlier chalk or pastel scenario, test your options. Craft a proposition for action. The complexity and layers of your proposition will affect your approach to the solution. As will it require different layers of engagement with others.

I've been mulling over an interdepartmental scenario for several days. With limited information, and that biased by the source, advising a successful path falls into the PLAY category. I recognise that I don't have all the pieces. Best practises meet speculation as to the dynamics of the affected employees, and their organisational roles must be considered. This scenario is the opportune situation to employ the Nudge Principle for a solution. When I do so, a missing piece will manifest that makes my choices clearer.

Countless times in a day, you have choices. Some choices will demand an autonomic response. You choose without a thought or concern for the consequence. Other choices demand that you think through to an action. You will apply creativity so many times in a day, that you probably don't even notice when you are doing it. Nudge after nudge gently pushes you along. A soft whisper that comes by way of an encouragement. "You can do it." "I believe in you." A feeling that puts a smile on your face as you consider an action. Other times, a nudge comes at you boldly like a bull in a china shop. Messing up everything in sight, disrupting the norm, and leaving you to do a clean-up. Creativity is an exploration of the person tasked to answer a nudge, and produce something— somebody—new.

Three

Exploring the Uncharted

12

Discovery

Growing up in Alaska, I frequently pondered whether there were any areas of the state that had not been visited by a human. Southeast Alaska, where I lived, doesn't have a road system that joins city-to-city. A sense of remoteness is a contributor to the pristine quality that attracts people to visit and stay. To think that there are areas unvisited by humans is hard to imagine, given humanity's insatiable curiosity. As the Last Frontier, Alaska has virtually hundreds of thousands of square kilometres of undeveloped land. Much of that land is accessible only by foot. From Eagle Beach, 27-miles outside of the capital city is an inspiring view of the Chilkat mountain range. A visitor to Juneau can complete the drive to Eagle River from the airport in about thirty minutes. You may have to share the beach with some eagles and a few other people. If you wait long enough, you will likely find yourself alone to appreciate the magnitude of the landscape and its beauty. The eagles will probably hang around too.

There are other places in the world like Alaska. Polar caps, dense forests, deserts, mountain ranges, the ocean, and space call the intrepid searcher with their taunts of untamed nature. "Will you come to me to test your grit?" and "Do you dare to venture within?" Where shod foot has not trodden, satellites can offer a desktop view of almost any place in the world. Plug in a search request to Google Earth, and you can follow the path of squiggly shaped rivers of the Sakha Republic in Russia or view rooftop gardens near the Trevi fountain in Rome. In terms of places, there are very few undiscovered locations given our aptitude to adapt. An exception is where a person has chosen not to venture or explore. That includes the unexplored reaches of the land called You.

Nearly every day, I am astounded to learn how another human being has discovered or honed a talent that I will see for the first time. On some occasions, it will be my only time observing their discovery. I don't want to trivialise the creative journey with an overload of examples or to offer contrasts at the expense of one example over another. I believe that our brains automatically differentiate one creative act over another by attributing priorities or rank. That comes when our culture-value system kicks in to ascribe a creative act to a category based on its perceived worth over merit. Instead, let me just tell you what I randomly discovered so far today:

- I watched a video of a guy combining bubbles to create a variety of shapes and selectively inserted vapour to design kinetic displays.
- I listened to and watched an Animusic performance called Resonant Chamber.
- I learned about the grey-headed albatross' nesting issues, the increased hazards for king penguin chicks due to early thawing of the ice shelf in Antarctica, and a short history of the right whale from David Attenborough on BBC iPlayer cast to my Google Home hub while I was doing dishes.
- I drew several figures of a wooden model on sticky notes.
- I learned the term for something I introduced in Part Two is called analogical thinking.
- I applied the Nudge Principle to thinking through the merit, challenges, and application of the inclusion buzzword *microaggression.*

There are discoveries to be made every day. Moment by moment, we are poised to add something to our character that enriches our existence. Small things. Big things. Mixed up things. To get the most from life, partner with the random. Be ready to convert experiences into something that becomes yours. We are going to use the Nudge Principle to stimulate a sense of exploration and self-discovery, that should excite a sense of adventure.

SEE

Some of the examples I just mentioned arrived via social media. An image might catch my attention, and I will deviate from what I am doing to investigate. I have to watch myself, as the Internet is rife with interesting stories, images, and sounds that I could become trapped in a perpetual learning mode. My proclivity is to absorb as much information as I am able. Therefore I limit myself to snippets of time where I can draw inspiration from browsing. To help me in this regard, I filter my searches with some tools and randomise others. For a deliberate season,

I have to be content with some desired real-life discoveries by proxy experiences and my imagination.

What excites me when I browse the Internet is observing the boundless possibilities to anybody willing to apply effort. The Internet gets a bad rap at times, but we can't deny the positive attributes that it brings into our homes and into the palm of our hand. The depth and width of inspiration that is available is a testament to the human story. At any moment in the world, somebody is doing something creative, ingenious, innovative, or pushing the limits of their mental and physical capacity. Extraordinary is a relative term as it has become a standard across the globe. So many people are proving to themselves that there isn't anything they can't do with a mind set to do so. The Internet is saturated with examples of our ability to create, that a rise of extraordinary can't be a coincidence. Our common denominator is that we are human. Nestled in that broad category rests the quality of creativity. How can that not be exciting?

Where are the most tantalising and mysterious unexplored places in the world today? Don't look to far off landscapes or scientific discoveries for answers. The uncharted territory lies within you. Imagine a jungle explorer of the nineteenth century hacking away at the underbrush, trudging through thick forests to make small gains every day. The image evokes an appreciation for the idiom, "can't see the forest through the trees." When you are in the thick of a situation, it may prove difficult to see clearly or that an end is in sight. Each step forward exposes a new viewpoint and marks an achievement. A SEE Nudge will lead you to ask questions that lead to more questions. Curiosity builds with increasing expectation all the while demanding a response. At some point, that curiosity has to spill over into a nudge or an action. Be proactive in that process. Direct the flow toward something that enables you to learn more about yourself, your capacity for growth, and ways you can expand your experience. Use questions to gain understanding. The principle applies to every aspect of life.

Are you keen to explore your potential? Push the limits of a skill or test the boundaries of your influence? Your expedition preparation begins with asking questions. Work with what is known and work toward what is unknown. When it comes to self-exploration, your destination is what you envision. You will know which questions to ask or develop questions as you go along. To provoke you a bit, consider these questions as a launching point.

- What are the best parts of your day? Why is that so?
- Which factors most frequently affect your mood? How do you typically respond?
- What captures your attention and imagination? How do you express yourself, creatively?
- How do you interact with others? Is it draining or energising?
- What are your preferences toward your lifestyle? What would you like to change?

If those questions don't fit your situation, ask questions that are relative to you. What I hope for you to experience is more than just a question and answer exercise. Look beyond the factual and perceived responses that arise. An often-ignored aspect of observation is paying attention to your me-centric flags. If you are asking questions that do not evoke some kind of emotional response, then you have not touched the core of your person.

A clinical response is okay for fact-finding, but in terms of self-discovery, you are probably only brushing the surface when you focus on facts. Superficiality breeds superficiality. Real change, the kind that makes a profound long-term impact, comes with challenges. Pushing through a difficult problem to come out victorious on the other side leaves a positive imprint in your mind. The commitment and hardships to arrive at a destination are past events, milestones on your journey to where you want to be.

What an exciting proposition it is to embark on an expedition to the unknown corners of You. Perhaps I am too enthusiastic. Writing from my journey, I am deeply motivated to do more at sixty and continue my lifetime with unfinished exploration. The frequent daily reminders I set myself range from doing something with art, playing the guitar or a simple woodwind instrument, micro exercises, learning a phrase in another language, and to doing something for others. My day is disrupted over and over with reminders from my phone to engage. I have the choice to accept, postpone, or ignore the prompting. I do my best to comply with those self-instigated calls to stretch myself. Small gestures build confidence and skill, strengthening my character for more difficult tasks. I don't know where this effort will lead me. I am confident that I will pull more from life. As I venture forward, I can see that I am making progress. I am an explorer. My domains for exploration can only grow larger. As will yours when you branch out.

You don't need to read a book about Stanley and Livingstone to stir up the imagery of an explorer. What does an explorer look like today? English explorer Ed Stafford can give you an idea. Stafford holds the Guinness World Record for being the first to walk the length of the Amazon River from the source to ocean. His expedition took 860 days to complete. Shortly after his journey, he set out on an expedition to find his biological parents. I suspect that a need to know is behind the inquisitiveness that motivates Stafford onward. Be deliberate in your expedition of self-discovery. Create your own story. Journal the adventures of you. Above all, get new experiences. You'll surprise yourself with what you are capable of achieving.

TELL

A few years back, I watched a video of a speaker that did something with her audience I'd never seen before. In truth, I have not seen it since. Standing among her audience members, she calls out for somebody to express a need. The audience responds as if on cue. There are a lot of needs. Some are small, others are substantial. The speaker then asks if there is anybody in the audience that can fulfil a need or has a resource to offer. I expected that somebody would respond with a matched solution or a money-fix. To my surprise, that is not how the solution was meted out. One person replied with what he had as an available resource, another person suggested she had something that might fit but was uncertain. As the audience listened to needs and resources being called out, a design started to emerge. The way needs were solved was like watching a human version of a mystic square. Resources were being allocated along an invisible track until the puzzle was solved. Eventually, all the needs were met, and the audience was thrilled by the experience.

That was about ten years ago when I discovered that speaker and her video. Despite my best efforts, no search combination that I plug into my browser returns with her name. My curiosity is stoked with wonder about whether her programme continues and the impact her paying-it-forward type activity had on her participants. What captivated my attention was a notion that her activity could be expanded to a broader audience, like a community, town, or city. The logistics of such an effort could be managed online with verification processes and collaborative delivery systems. To be honest, I don't even know if a proposal like that is feasible. It worked in that room, with that audience, under those conditions. Under its own weight, the concept liberates the imagination to think well of one another. As long as that concept remained a concept, without an action, it was no more than a good idea.

When an idea is conveyed, it takes on a life of its own. With exposure to the conditions of interpretation, the idea is tested in some version of an open environment. What comes with that exposure is a degree of vulnerability. Engaging in a purposeful path of self-discovery will require that you allow you, your ideas, and your feelings to be exposed at times. Expressing who you are, or who you want to become, opens you up to a wide range of mental and emotional variables. The potential for rejection is that unknown that lingers in the shadows. In the example above, a participant would have to be quite brave to express a non-material personal need. For instance, being lonely, feeling frightened of failure, or paralysed by indecision. A solution is available, but only as a need is revealed. Start by getting comfortable asking yourself probing questions and listening to the resulting self-talk.

- What are the existing outlets I have for expressing my thoughts?
- What is the tone of dialogue I have with myself?
- How do I acknowledge those areas in my life that I want to improve?
- What do I perceive to be the obstacles hindering my progress?
- What are the emotional indicators that surface when I attempt something new?

Risk is another word associated with vulnerability. The theme of risk is unavoidable in self-discovery and creativity. There is no getting around that reality. You can create a sense of control regarding your risk-taking, but you'll never fully control an outcome. Otherwise, it wouldn't be a risk. Whether standing in an audience and proclaiming that you have a need or contemplating your life in the security of your mind, both carry an inherent measure of risk. That you are willing to have that dialogue is not only courageous but essential to your wellbeing.

Have you heard somebody say, "What in the world were they thinking?" when commenting on a behaviour? From my observations, the most frequent reply to that question is "They weren't thinking." For whatever reason you might suspect, that person's actions appear to those on the outside as risky, stupid, or ill-informed of the consequences. I am an active proponent for independent thinking. I believe that if you can think independently, and hopefully express yourself in that capacity, you can build a degree of resilience for change. I am not talking about being dogmatic or obstinate. Those ways of thinking will eventually suffer from their fragile nature as opposed to a robust or anti-fragile mindset. As the word intimates, fragile infers that something is breakable. Allowing others to think for you may pacify a social need, but it is of little value to your character development. Independent thinking, especially in a TELL scenario, means to weigh feedback and have the good sense to accept differences. Adopt change where appropriate. Think for yourself and gain confidence in the discourse of change.

A danger of relying solely on TELL for decisions is that you may become dependent upon another person's perception while dulling your own. Comparisons are also a terrible malaise to fall into regarding self-talk. When either happens, you can skew otherwise balanced independent thinking. I've mentioned in a previous chapter about my straight-out-of-high school interest in commercial art, graphic art, and design. I didn't pursue that path due to a single sentence of doubt sewn by somebody I trusted. In retrospect, the comment was fairly innocuous. As an unsettled teen, I interpreted it wrongly and thought my skills were being questioned. Using the awesome power of 20/20 hindsight, I'd say that it is unimportant whether I was ever gifted or talented in art. The damage was done, and I took an alternate path.

What did matter to me was that I had a good eye for artistic expression. Perhaps there was something there to build on. Had I not allowed that single dissuading comment to influence my passion, I may have pursued something related to graphic design as a career path. Looking back from my today perspective, I can see how that single directional change would have altered my entire life. However, in the grand scheme of things, I wouldn't change any of my life decisions because of who I am today. The slightest shift may have set me on a trajectory to another place, to another timeline, and another reality. A lesson for life? Ensure that your TELL Nudge has plenty of affirming dialogue. At some point, you will need the reserves.

FLOW

"Everything happens for a reason," is a phrase I hear when people attempt to make sense out of something that doesn't make sense. Whether intentionally or not, the well-meaning person is implying that there is design behind every action. I don't agree. I'd offer an alternative such as, "Everything happens from a consequence." Unfortunately, that comment doesn't offer much solace if the situation includes grief. There being a reason behind an event denotes either a Divine or deliberate human intervention. I accept neither proposition.

A similar claim is that a person subject to an accident or crime was "Just in the wrong place at the wrong time." Such a claim suggests that by an incredible coincidence, the collision of two people could have been avoided had only one or the other made a slightly different course correction. Chance being the guilty party, not the consequence of another person's actions. These instances are not flow. They are examples of Newton's third law, whereby every action has an equal and opposite reaction. Flow, in the aftermath of an event, is what you make out of a situation.

I haven't played with the concept much, but I don't see why flow can't also apply to mixing in a non-existent condition as well. Introduce some chaos. Let's hold off on that for now until we get to the PLAY Nudge. Until then, what I'd like to ask you to do is reflect on pivotal events of your life. Not just the event itself, but the flow that ensued. What did you gain in terms of experience, knowledge, skills, character, and relationships? Accumulation of wealth, or the lack thereof, is inconsequential for this reflection. You can save the inventorying of stuff for a different activity. Material things are vulnerable to decay, devaluation, and an endless list of other factors. Character, built on the flow of your story, stays with you regardless of conditions. I can't vouch for what kind of character a person may develop, as that is an extremely personal judgment. If you take good care of that character, it will remain a constant for you. Trauma and extreme situations tend to put a person's character to the test. This is the type of reflection I hope that you will give yourself.

Get ready, I am going for a bit more forceful nudge than I have been doing. When asked who the target audience is for this book or any of the aspects of Nudge, I never quite know what to say. The orientation of my age, background, gender, and race certainly have a weighty bearing on how I've written Nudged. Consequently, I'd suspect that a portion of those reading this book may have that as a common connection. As I write, I try to think of readers across a wide range of demographics. The core attributes of creativity are blind to age, colour, social or financial status, education, or anything else in our outward measurements. So, in a sense, Nudged is relative to anybody.

What I suspect, however, is that a reader that will read Nudged is looking to be more creative and is willing to go to different lengths to demonstrate their creativity. You are probably well exercised in SEE and observant to the world around. I'd bet that you communicate well (TELL) within the context of your influence. You are also likely to demonstrate the other actions of the Nudge Principle but may not be aware of its day-to-day contribution to your life. Expanding awareness of your creative capacity with the Nudge Principle is an invitation to enhance your experience with purposeful creativity.

On the other hand, I'd be surprised if this book will find its way into a bundle of essentials carried by a person risking life and limb to migrate to another country. I suspect that it won't make it into the hands of that homeless person living rough in the town centre. A small crop farmer struggling to find solutions for their drought-ravaged orchard in Central Chile is unlikely to turn to his copy of Nudged to look for inspiration. You, on the other hand, may start to see a connection between your experience and that of the challenges other people face. The power of the FLOW Nudge is its flexibility to interject any condition, issue, or topic into your equation to test whether it fits in your solution for a positive outcome. You may have a small piece of the puzzle or have the influence to make a difference. The person that first reports a problem is not always the person that delivers change. There is more likely to be a string of contributors, each adding to the flow until the momentum reaches critical mass. At which point, another Nudge flows over, and an action is delivered.

You may think that discovery is all about you. Without question, the exploration experience is yours, and the qualities it embeds in you are yours to distribute as you see fit. Discovery does not end with the results pooling in a reserve tank someplace in your mind. Discovery leaks. No matter what a person might try to do to block the flow, what you discover about yourself is going to leak out. When it does, it touches other lives with elements for their experience. This is FLOW in a broader sense. Consider the following questions in your FLOW reflection.

- Where does your life intersect with those issues that you consider important?
- Reflecting on your life experiences, where might you apply your skills to other areas or domains?
- What interests you enough to draw a commitment? A cause, a hobby, work, leisure, learning, or a grab bag random idea?
- Are there common elements in the activities that interest you? What are those common elements?
- Can you envision yourself doing something different with your life? How does that look?

You can either let the random happen to you, attempt to dodge it by playing safe or absorb the happening into your story. At first glance, you may attribute overlapping features of your life to a series of acting out each of those three risk responses. Reality is that you regularly do each of them. You can't stop the random. You live life, greater or lesser, with some caution while hedging risks in the decisions you make. If you were not curious and willing to take a risk, you would not be reading this book. Last, but most importantly, you've used bits and pieces of your life to be where and create who you are. The differentiator is the level that you are willing or able to engage.

PLAY

The adventure of discovery is deeply rewarding. A satisfying quest is especially true if speaking about self-improvement, self-discovery, or self-actualisation. You are ultimately the beneficiary of a discovery realised. Any of these destinations require a mandatory passage through the process of PLAY. With playful exploration, your quest for meaning is given a dash of exciting and splash of spice. Finding alternatives to an existing plan, by exploring nonrelated or extended possibilities, exponentially expands your options—and it's fun! You happen to live in an era of such rapid growth and changing conditions that choices aren't dependent on decades-long investiture. The mindset that holds to the virtue that your dues are paid relative to a series of decades is a career trait of a bygone era. Having established that it is acceptable to incorporate PLAY in a work orientation in chapter eight, let's go ahead and use the context of work for this Nudge.

Although we are experiencing a multi-generational workplace, the employment map changes with each successive generation and the retirement of the former. The next-generation workforce refuses to be bound by commitments that don't produce outcomes that satisfy their lifestyles. What that means, in plain terms, is that inbound generations to the workforce allow themselves more latitude for exploring their potential and value. Influences advancing that attitude aren't solely due to generational angst but also vulnerable employment opportunities, a tectonic shift in technological advances, and sweeping economic factors. Don't be too fast to broad-brush the conditions affecting the newest generation in the workplace to only youth. Similar conditions are changing the way we all work. Age is only as restrictive as you allow it to be.

Where do you want to go? What do you want to do? Sort out what you can't do later. Imagine the accumulation of your skills set, interests, likes and dislikes, education, goals and the whole of what you are as similar to pieces on the game board of your life. If you draw from the Chance deck occasionally, there is a good possibility that you will need to deviate from an established course. There's nothing wrong with that. To alter your path along the way, can provide new areas for observation and experience. PLAY is your idea sandbox for alternatives.

Somewhere in my reading from about 2007, I read an anecdote regarding a new employee to W. L. Gore & Associates, the makers of GORE-TEX. According to my recollection, an associate arrived for his first day of work. During his orientation, he was introduced to the company in a non-traditional approach to organisational structure. Instead of saying to the new associate, "Your job is to do X, and your position title is Y. Therefore, you will proceed in a manner that is in the alignment with Z," the organisation did something different. In place of relying on a hierarchical system for assigning roles within the organisation, the company adopted a freelance approach.

Instead of plugging a person into a position and title, the new hire was encouraged to use his skills to create a role. For the life of me, I can't find that reference. I hope that I am not imagining the story. Nevertheless, the corporate values and organisational philosophy outlined on the Gore website indicate that the company does hold these values within the organisation. For some, the idea of this level of team-oriented autonomy might be a terrifying prospect. To those folks, boundaries, barriers, regulations, and structure create a degree of comfort that keeps life in order. A venture outside the lines is disconcerting.

PLAY does not necessarily mean that there are no boundaries, structure, rules, or the safety net of regulatory expectancy. In fact, within PLAY, there are quite clear rules. The new hire of this lost anecdote found the prospect of playing with possibilities in terms of his new employment status as liberating. Unfettered from stale organisational compliance, the new hire was loosed to create possibilities where he might not otherwise have explored. His guidelines, or rules, was that he was responsible for shaping his place in the company. So even in a freelance environment, there is a measure of guidelines. If you are looking for companies that embrace your kind of values, you may want to go back to the SEE stage and search out companies that demonstrate versus espouse those values. That may be a tough call, so don't get bogged down with that research.

Instead, play around with possibilities versus what currently exists. Why not envision the optimum employment or self-employment environment? Use your imagination to create the structure, the bilateral collaboration, the target audience, product, service, the rewards, all of the factors that you want in employment. Create, in principle, a company for whom you would give anything to work. Working with that company, you would give your all and find personal satisfaction in daily life. Stir up your thinking about what you wrestle with by pondering some of the following questions:

- Are you satisfied with what you are doing?
- What is the worst-case scenario you can imagine if you were to break away from your current ways of thinking?
- How would you overcome in that worst-case scenario?
- In your predisposition to play it safe, what opportunities might you miss?
- Where can you stretch yourself to gain more experiences with a reduced level of risk?

When I was seventeen, my Dad taught me and my friend Jerry how to play backgammon. Every match I played was a wipe-out. I got clobbered. Later, alone in my room, I played match upon match until I understood the dynamics of play and the nature of the die. I both lost and won each time I played. Four decades later, I continue to play hundreds of matches of backgammon to keep a single concept of loss fresh in my mind—I win far more games than I lose. When I play a real person versus my well-learned algorithm, I am guaranteed to win some and lose some. Those matches that I lose I attribute to two factors: bad rolls or what I perceive as random play by my opponent. PLAY teaches you more about yourself, the nature of the game, and uncontrolled conditions than any other action you can take. But it does call for taking a risk.

FEEL

You may have been told not to "go by your feelings," by somebody in your life. Perhaps the caution came from somebody important to you, maybe not so important. The encouragement to disavow your feelings feels counterintuitive to your nature. You know it because that feeling is smack dab at the forefront of your person. I'd suggest in place of a complete disconnection of feelings from your decisions that you strive for balance. Instead of repressing your feelings, partner with them. While you may fall into all kinds of entanglements by going solely on your feelings, you should not deny them either. If the feeling is strong enough, denial of the associated emotions is left to creep around in your mind for a long time. You owe it to yourself to at least explore the possible outcome of a satisfying feeling. You don't have to take action on it, just allow the feeling to arc through to completion.

What you feel has a significant role in the shaping of your perspectives. Your wellbeing, in one state or another, is going to have an impact on your creative capital. As creativity goes, the actions related to emotions may be the most challenging. This may be especially valid if others extend influence over your decisions. In some cultures, the choices you make are perceived as a reflection on the entire family. For those in that dynamic, the support you gain from your family may be a non-negotiable priority for you and weigh heavily on your decisions. For those with a flying solo independent approach, you might believe that those type of influencing dynamics exist only in movies and historical conditions. Let me assure you that this is not the case. Whichever side you fall with external influences, be conscious of the fact that others may not share your orientation. Feelings will materialise like it or not.

You may be in an environment that demonstrates unwavering support for your decisions. Whatever you do is perceived as a learning experience for which you are the primary beneficiary. Your happiness, your fulfilment, your development as a person is of utmost concern. Then again, other people may not factor into your decision-making processes. You may have retreated to an off-the-grid lifestyle and are a candidate for an episode of *New Lives in the Wild* with Ben Fogle. Influencing dynamics set aside, there are also other relational questions to consider. How do you feel about the impact your decision may have on any of those for whom you care? I'd like to make a generalised statement and say that we are all equipped with a good set of tools in our emotional toolbox to help navigate the question of relationships. We do not. We have to use the tools we have on hand.

Conditions and self-preservation can do strange things to people. We don't want to be blindsided, so we have to be alert to our feelings. I hope that you will use your tools to become more alert and comfortable with your feelings and those trigger mechanisms that can set off a chain of relational situations. Prepare yourself for subjects that can potentially set off a sense of conflict, such as career choices, business opportunities, employment, or interpersonal relationships. Consider some of these probing questions:

- Which stimuli evoke a response from any of my root emotions? Joy, anticipation, trust, fear, surprise, sadness, disgust, and anger.
- How do you respond or react to those emotions?

- What role do you allow feelings to play in your decisions?
- Where or with whom are you emotionally energised?
- What methods do you use to manage your emotions and awareness?

Every summer across the United Kingdom around mid-August, GCSE and A-level results are released. Students waiting for results are asked with annoying regularity what they intend to do. Most of them have no idea. Their choices, like forks in a road, are dependent upon their results. Furthermore, their options are bound by earlier decisions to apply for university, work or employment, internship, take a gap year, or choose a non-traditional path. Up to this point in their formal education, students have been absorbing information. Their world for decisions is comprised to a large extent, by the SEE Nudge. What they've observed, accepted, or brought into their being via education arrived through a lecture-oriented learning environment. Although educational delivery methodologies are advancing in incredible ways, few formal processes are in place to help students discover their talents and passions. Therefore, most students arrive unprepared at the fateful crossroad in August, where released exam results can impact a successful launch into adulthood.

Decisions related to career are not limited to the school leaver. With an ever-changing economic landscape, experienced adults are also at risk of having to make work choice decisions based on what is equal to a grade. Do you have the right certification? Do you have specific experience? Have you worked in this industry before? Does your signature block have twenty-five characters arranged in acronyms to indicate your qualification pedigree? Questions like these seem to be insurmountable in the mind of an applicant seeking new opportunities when their otherwise stable employment has dissolved.

For those experiencing life changes, one emotion will undoubtedly make an appearance—fear. When it comes to your crucial decision of what you want to do, fear will stalk you relentlessly. The emotion is fuelled by the what-if speculation. What if? If you find yourself paralysed in a cycle of what-if when you reach the FEEL Nudge, confront it head on. You can change the orientation of your fear and emotion to one of the other primary emotions and continue to make progress. You can even use fear to propel yourself forward. The damning issue is not that you are fearful but that you might allow fear to paralyse you. Should you decide to take a risk, you can exchange your emotional state of fear and trade it for one of anticipation.

BE

Dorothy Gale was swept away by a tornado and hurled across time and dimension to crash onto the landscape of Oz. As Dorothy steps from her black and white world and into the vibrantly coloured Munchkinland, her first words to her four-legged companion are "Toto, I've a feeling we aren't in Kansas anymore." What she would have to experience to get back home, would teach her as much about who she is as what she holds dear. The young girl from Kansas didn't ask for the adventure, nor could she appreciate how it would alter her life forever. For her, the only thing on her heart was to get back home. To do so demanded a visit to the Emerald City to meet the Great and Powerful Oz.

Francine Evans, on the other hand, could not wait to escape the little town blues that starved her creative hunger. Her path to break into show business was one that led straight through the toughest place in the world to get a start in entertainment. Not only did Francine want to get to the empowering metropolis of Dreams Come True, she intended to take it by storm. She aimed to be queen of the hill and top of the heap. Start new. In her mind, she knew with absolute certainty that if she could make it there, she literally could be successful anywhere. Francine wanted adventure, sought it, paid for it, and nothing was going to stop her from achieving it. Dorothy and Francine are fictional characters. Both started their journeys from the familiar and worked their way through challenges to reach their destination. Dorothy returns happily to the care of her Auntie Em while Francine creates a legacy under the glittering canopy of stardom.

Two stories of two adventurers, both guided by an internal sense of who they are and what they want to become. Knowing what you want to do, hinges upon quite a few factors. I think there is one factor that stands out more than any other. Some may disagree with me, and I am happy to entertain that there is are alternate views. I am confident that to be assured of who you are is intrinsically tied with what you want to do. I'll not commit that as a sole factor, but it is a significant one. I am not talking about a lifetime ambition, career selection, or pigeon-holing yourself into a forever category. Instead, I aim to encourage you to harmonise your mind with your motivations. What makes you want to get up in the morning to do what you do? In our confused world, it is sometimes difficult to know who we are apart from what we do. Why not instead, do who you are and from that position know what you do?

We've discussed at length or nudged toward questions related to our being and values. Social media is the anomaly, the wild card in the development of the human psyche. We see its influence capturing the minds of people of all ages. We can also witness the shallowness and subsequent dangers that it produces.

Without a doubt, we can propose a good argument that there are career and moneymaking opportunities within social media. We can point to the seven-year-old earning millions of pounds reviewing toys or the endless queue of buffoonery posted as online videos. I could not do what I need to do without the use of the Internet. I am a massive fan and proponent. But like driving a car, you must drive the Net responsibly. More so, businesses that drive the industry do so with some accountability.

A common theme that permeates the entire social media infrastructure is voyeurism. We are obsessed with peeking into the lives of other people, frequently without invitation. Governments and companies do so as well. Peeping Toms with sheriff badges or a vampire's invitation. It is the in which we world we live. These are the conditions that we find ourselves. At any restaurant, public place, or where people are gathered, you will see the affected with their smartphones, snapping photographs, texting, speaking loudly on the phone. All the while, the value of genuine community is losing ground. Before you think I am just going on a rant, I should preface that I use social media. I use it as a tool for information sharing, for storing moments of my life, and for interacting with people with whom I choose. There has never been in the history of humanity so much information available with such astonishing accessibility. The Internet has changed the world and how we navigate that world.

Asking the question of who you are is not going to be fully answered at this time. One thing is for sure, you won't find the answer on the Internet or on the apps that cull from social media feeds to post a pre-designed cliché of who you are. To find the core of who you are requires reflection through observation, communication, working things out, exploration, your emotions, what you've done, and how you behave in various conditions. Whoa! That is a lifetime of work. I know I get it. You are not looking for mercurial answers or epitaphs chiselled in granite. You want to shoot for a simplified version. One that empowers you to be and do what you want and need to do. Use the BE Nudge and glean from the process those precious strands of truth that affirm your identity.

Arriving at a port of call on the journey is the next launching point to someplace else in the discovery of You. A final destination, of self-actualisation or a state of Nirvana, should only open doors for more exploration. Awareness intensifies who you are and ushers in a personal dynamic that lives and breathes in the changes that occur in your person. Where you allow that to shape you, you will find greater adaptability for your choices. You've gotten this far in the Nudge

Principle having advanced from what you see, to having communications that flow into something new. You've played with an idea and reflected on how it made you feel. Now in this being (BE) stage, I think what you want is a confirmation— a knowing that what are doing is right. Primarily right for you. Nobody else writes the goals for your life. Nobody can be successful for you. Your choice and the consequences thereof are yours to own.

DO

Ready to launch your expedition, you need some idea of a destination. A minimum requirement is a starting point. Where and how are you going to demonstrate the incredible talent of you? Applying limitations of where you live, is a good place to start. I don't mean live as a location or vocation. Rather where your mind is at a given time. Your first step, no matter where you want to go, begins with where you are. Think big, act small. (I just discovered that is a book title by Jason Jennings—and is now on my reading list.) In other words, cultivate big ideas, but find ways to take small actions to make big things happen. There are opportunities aplenty to put that principle to use.

Living in the United Kingdom, a person cannot help but sense the momentum of imminent change. Wherever posterity leads, whatever will happen will have happened by the time you read this book. Some other change will be quick on its heels. To be fair, you can plug the name of any country and come up with some topic that threatens life-altering social change. The wise words of Agent K come to mind: "There's always an Alien Battle Cruiser or a Korlian Death Ray, or an intergalactic plague about to wipe out life on this planet, and the only thing that lets people get on with their hopeful little lives is that they don't know about it." Change is on the way. In one form or another, it is coming. Which is great because it provides an endless supply of opportunities to apply creativity, innovation, or to make a difference.

The inevitability of change is why companies and governments build resilience into their strategies and plans. If a perceivable condition happens that might have a negative impact on the company's wellbeing, they can resort to plan B, C, D, or E in response. You, too, must build resilience into what you want to do. Naturally, that will take you back to the SEE Nudge to where you can collect and collate relevant information. A thorough plan integrates all the facets we've been discussing. To keep the momentum of our current course, we will leave that diversion for another time and focus on now. What are you going to do?

With all you've collated to this point, I'd expect that you have come up with a semblance of a creative notion that you can test. Your commitment to an action doesn't necessarily mean it's going to be the only action. Every scientific endeavour or experiment that has produced a sustainable solution or product was not created with one attempt. No, the phrase "Try, try, and try again" is common amongst inventors and entrepreneurs. For your DO Nudge, I'd expect that you are ready to test what you've created. To do so, you will need a condition where you can practise it. This may be difficult, depending on the context of your proposition statement.

Find a legitimate format, where you can test your concept. I realise that not everybody is comfortable with being entrepreneurial. That does not mean that you can't develop entrepreneurial skills. "Me an entrepreneur?" Yes. If not full-blown at least in attitude. You might say, "There are only 24 hours in a day." That is true. Boy, don't we all know that. You also realise that your ability to action your proposition can depend on time, resources, and energy. You stated correctly when you declared that you only have 24 hours in a day. We just have to measure the use of that time as a non-renewable resource. If the proposition that you formulated energises you with anticipation and a sense of creative flow, you will find the process easier and less cumbersome.

Before I stepped out into full-time writing, I did a lot of writing. I wrote a blog every day for a year. At an average of 300 words a blog, in that one year, I wrote an estimated 109,500 words. After that, I wrote a hundred-page book on mentoring. I also completed about 40,000 words toward this book and four unpublished screenplays. Add work done in producing training material or writing proposals, and my body of written work represents an above-average start. Aware that I was unable to complete the book in the timeframe that I hoped, and within my constraints, I chose to take a risk. The level of that risk is yet to be realised but will soon be tested as I work through the processes of publication and marketing. With the actions that I have taken relative to the Nudge Principle, my risk will either be vindicated or vilified. Either way, I will have accomplished what I set out to do in this stage. Chalk up another learning experience, creative engagement, and the pushes I needed for my creative self.

"What do I want to do?" That is your question in this activity. You need to adopt a posture that there are limitless actions for you to explore. What you can do, where you explore, how you explore, with whom you explore, and when you do so is mostly up to you. The actions that you take will pitch all of these factors into your consideration. The all-or-nothing proposition is high risk. Unless you know, with 100% confidence that you have the winning hand, the winning combination, go back for a SEE Nudge. Otherwise, your risks may have consequences that will affect your creativity and your willingness to take risks again. Focus on an area, look for opportunities. If opportunities are not available, make them. Test out what you can do in a variety of situations. One way or the other, you're going to learn something about yourself and the environment that you are working in, the people with whom you'll interact, and create something that will last in the end.

Wrapping it up

You were encouraged to consider your journey of discovery as an expedition in this chapter. To explore the unknown. That will mean different things to different people. You are already on the journey. You may as well be purposeful in your quest. Settled and on a path of your choice, you may think that ruminations on a grander scale are a waste of time. That is okay. We didn't set out on a quest to solve a question of urgency. What you were invited to do was ramble with me through the Nudge Principle and the Seven Nudges. For the ordered mind, the trip may have seemed arbitrary, almost aimless. More of a wander than purposeful. Where we travelled together was down paths of provocations, random as they may feel, to nudge you to think, feel, and stimulate your sense of wonder. With each successive nudge, you were presented with conditions and a variety of anecdotes or observations. Even if those nudges took a scattered approach to stimulate your creative mojo, your mind was making associations.

An average adult reads between 200 – 250 words a minute. At 225-words per minute, you could have read this chapter in about 45 minutes. Your mind will have darted side trails, entertained personal reflections, felt a range of emotions, and perhaps sparked the basis for a new neural connection or two. If I did my job well, you should have experienced all of these conditions and more. Had we been sitting face-to-face, the dynamic nature of the Nudge Principle would have pushed us into all sorts of directions. You and I may have felt like paint on Pollock's brush. Swept intentionally from one point to another in fractal casualness. Standing back to look at what we created, we may not be able to define what we see. But we know something remarkable occurred.

I am not a proponent of list-making or how-to activities when promoting creativity. These are great where needed. I think lists are useful for contrasts and data collection. How-to activities are also valuable for demonstrating a step-by-step procedure. But if you want to stimulate lateral thinking, you have to apply principles that harmonise with lateral thinking. Allow for deviations. Build risk and anomalies into your process. Seek to become exceptional at the Nudge Principle, not as a list of actions about a method activating your creative core. When it comes time for you to make a decision that relies on a creative outcome, you will be ready and confident. Now, let's put that to work.

13

On the Ground

In a wood, barely a stone's throw from a small lake somewhere just off the M20 to Dover was a cottage. The home was that of a former Royal Commander that lived with his wife and two small children. Having travelled the Empire established under Queen Victoria and surviving the Great War, Commander Caractacus Pott settled down with his family and turned his attention to invention. Given all that Pott had seen during his naval career, he had an abundance of ideas to stoke his imagination for innovation and creativity. Where he lacked resources to propel his inventions into the marketplace and be listed among the great inventors of the century, he was rich in family and freedom of thought.

Locals viewed Pott as an eccentric, perhaps a little away with the fairies. He paid little attention to what others thought of him. Day after day, he gathered bits of metal, leather, and any other scrap he could find to convert refuse into creations. Working with available resources enabled Pott to apply ingenuity from countless failed ideas to improve on his concepts. Getting into his mind, you'd recognise that he had his emotional highs and lows. Yet, he never allowed that to dissuade him from his mission to create something unique and secure his place among giants. Eventually, his patience paid off when he succeeded to build a magical car. That vehicle of dreams could take Pott and his family anywhere. To those that questioned the practicality of proposed spontaneous travels, Pott would reply "That's no way to treat adventures. Never say 'no' to adventures. Always say 'yes'. Otherwise, you'll lead a very dull life." Commander Caractacus Pott is the creation of author Ian Fleming. The magical car, as you may have already sussed, is Chitty Chitty Bang Bang.

Explorer and inventor. The two seem to go together like a hand in a glove. Across time, inventors have explored possibilities using imagination, available resources, and frequently the fuel of hope to inspire generations of dreamers to dream. Leonardo da Vinci envisioned a flying machine, that although it couldn't fly, was a concept four hundred years ahead of its time. Interesting how the Wright brothers Kitty Hawk aircraft shared so many similarities in structure as da Vinci's concept. Thomas Alva Edison was well-positioned for an era of electricity and with his prolific inventing held the international patent record for decades. With the dawn of personal computers, the number of patents in that domain have skyrocketed. Every new patent allows for variations and new concepts to rise. The world record holder of patents, Shunpei Yamazaki, surpassed Edison's record in 2003 and has gone on to quintuple that record.

A major differentiator between these inventors, as with countless others, is the difference of being a dreamer and a pragmatist. A dreamer formulates ideas and enjoys the vision. They may even share their vision in the hope that others will catch the sight and jump on board the Dreamland Express. A dream without traction, where ideas are turned into something that can be observed, might be special to the dreamer but has little external value. For a dream to become a reality, there must be a measure of pragmatism to make the dream work. Let's explore how that may occur with four scenarios: interests, interpersonal relationships, industry, and institutions.

Interests

Last week I listened to a person describe the musical talent of his partner. The way he described her inferred that she is capable of picking up most instruments and very quickly creating something with a pleasant chordal tone. Shaking his head in wonder and with a sigh, he confessed how he would like to be able to do what she does. I've felt the same about any number of artistic and linguistic talents I've observed of others. Perhaps you have as well. Maybe not in the arts, but in some discipline. Although I surround myself with opportunities to practise an interest, I find that I gravitate to those activities that most demand my attention. To give yourself to those activities that you want to learn, you could devote similar dedication to achieve better results. There is solid evidence to support the encouragement that "Wherever your treasure is, you may be certain that your heart will be there too."

Making time to expand your interests comes down to what is important to you. Keep in mind also that what may not have been possible yesterday may be very much possible today. That can apply to external and internal conditions. Availability of resources may have changed. Your perception of what resources are available may also have experienced a paradigm shift. Relationships, mood, mental wellbeing, and a plethora of other factors can shift the balance to give you a different way of looking at your abilities. If you remain in a don't-believe-it mindset, you need to get around those that do

Somewhere in this vast world, is somebody that has gone through what you have or are experiencing. Not like-for-like necessarily, but enough to make a connection. Say, for instance, you want to take up a form of art, like drawing or painting. No matter which age you are, there is a group nearby or online for newbie painters. People like you are also trying to get started as a painter. Who cares whether your interest may turn professional or not? You are just getting started. Start with a mix of paint and an application to a canvas. Even small experiences reinforce your effort. When you get stuck on a technical skill, ask somebody. Ask a more experienced person or post your challenge on a forum.

All over the country, community singing groups are springing up. Singing is one of those skills that most people claim, "I can't sing." Worse yet, they may disparagingly refer to their singing as akin to a screeching cat or being tone-deaf. Apart from a physical disability, most people can learn to sing. The trick is to involve another person to help you discover your vocal range. Community singing groups are great for that kind of help. You just need to find the one that fits your personality and lifestyle. Art, dance, literature, music, the list of groups you can explore are limited only by the range of your thinking.

Once you plug in with other people, you'll find the encouragement you need to pursue your interest. Something happens when you interact with others. Social environments tend to propagate a form of interpersonal cross-pollination. One person's experience, mixed with another's, combined with yours during a conversation, will transfer ideas that deposit ideas and inspiration. The social environment, for whichever interest you pursue, nurtures a commonality that, when interpreted in your mind, says "If she can do it, then...."

Suspend judgments, of yourself or that perceived of others, from your mind. They corrupt creativity and are the destroyer of new adventures. Don't expect to walk out of an audience on to a game panel and be an expert. Enjoy the journey. Think of any learning experience as a brainwash. Not in the traditional spy novel definition, but more so as a cleansing. Immerse yourself in the moment to allow yourself an optimum experience. If you are fortunate enough to have a group, a friend, or a professional with affirming values as a guide, then your best option is to ride the wave of new discovery. Do your absolute best to give it your all and reserve judgment. If at all possible, omit judgment altogether. You will have so much more fun.

Breaking free of the biases you have toward your ability is the passport to discovering latent skills. Following on from the singing illustration, let's say that you discovered your vocal range is E3 (female) or G2 (male). As a recently freed singer, your goal is to find songs written for your range and to practise them. You will gain confidence as you test your newly discovered gift across a catalogue of range matching songs. You should probably stay away from *I Will Always Love You* (Whitney Houston) or *Can't Get Enough of Your Love* (Barry White) unless you are suited for either extreme. You don't want to break your new toy.

On my artist table, I have several mediums that I am learning to use. The most basic and classical are pencils, charcoals, pastels, acrylic and oil paints. Then there is the box of felt pens, Boya crayons, and a bag of corks for stamp making. Within arm's reach are various clays for modelling and an acoustic guitar on a stand. I don't expect to be expert in any of these mediums or to play like Segovia. With stolen slices of time, I slash a stroke of colour or strum a chord. Just adding the tidbits of something different enriches my soul. Creative activity germinates life. Flash moments like that keep me loosely connected to my creative core.

When you plant a creative instant in your mind, there are immediate and rewarding consequences. Your brain can release a batch of neurochemicals and transmitters, including dopamine and endorphins. Toss in some norepinephrine, serotonin, and anandamide, and you've got the makings of a feel-good cocktail. If allowed to take effect, the brain produces good feelings that are all-natural, in ample supply, and are 100% effective. If you were selling creativity on that unique selling proposition, you'd assume that all creative actions produce happy, balanced, almost euphoric conditions. Standing alone, maybe. All the time? Unlikely. There are just too many things that transpire moment-to-moment that can circumvent good feelings that are produced. The chemical balance of your brain is affected by your consciousness, and therefore subject to your thinking. Be proactive in managing your thoughts, and you'll enjoy more of the benefits of your creativity.

You may have concluded that your pathway to happiness is the route of pursuing your interests. Without question, there is merit to that view. The discovery phase of every creative connection is like meeting somebody and having an immediate attraction. You get all giddy, butterflies, and your creative mind ignites with ideas about how to get to know that person better. In the short term, every moment you are with that person is a series of energy boosts that fire your neurons into a new year celebratory firework display. After a while, you will have to decide about the longevity of that relationship. Was the connection deep enough to bridge significant differences? Did the discovery expose opportunities to build on the base of your life or erode foundations?

Truthfully, you will never really know the full, long-term impact of anything you do. There are just too many variables, past, present, and future. You can count on one certainty with creativity and exploring your interests. If you do nothing, you gain nothing. Alternately, if you do something, you gain something. That can be your glass-half-full/empty challenge.

Interpersonal Relationships

Have you ever observed somebody in conversation that struggles to make small talk? Then watched a transformation occur when a topic with which they are knowledgeable or comfortable is introduced? Get another person talking about something they enjoy and is of interest to them, and you can open floodgates for conversation. The banter that can develop from such conversations can lead to new friendships, associations, opportunities. The possibilities are endless. One question you might consider to get things started may be as simple as "What do you do for a hobby?" Not only do you learn about other people, but their experience trickles into your lifeline. You'll be amazed at the doors this opens.

Whenever I find myself truly engaged in conversation with somebody I've just met and get past the initial niceties, I look for an opportunity to make the conversation personal. With information on the table, you can ask loads of questions. The fourth principle of *How to Win Friends and Influence People* by Dale Carnegie is to be a good listener. The footnote of that principle is to encourage others to talk about themselves. Even the most seemingly resistant person wants to talk about themself. They may not want to talk to you, but they do want to talk. Finding that balance is the work part. Not everybody is comfortable talking about their life with others. I've come across a few that feel that asking questions is intrusive or that their life is too private to share. Even these attitudes can reveal something about their personality. You just need to know when to pull back.

People are an unknown factor in creativity. You never know what you are going to get. Your life is going to, like it or not, intersect with others numerous times in a day. You may prefer to be alone or the centre of attention, but human paths will inevitably cross like game trails in the wild. We tend to drift toward others like us in a group setting, pooling in cliques for ease and comfort. Back in a working environment, where the conditions and expectations change, the reserve may be traded for more extravert engagement. Regardless of the setting, we will adopt and adapt as needed to satisfy our sense of belonging. We are, by nature, survivalists.

To be successful in that flux of uncertainty (people), the best place to start is to understand yourself. Regardless of the situation you are attempting to navigate, all the bits that contribute to your person can be used for that purpose. Bringing your collage of self to any situation can feed you with talking points to stimulate conversation. Get any communication barriers down early. Yours first, then others. Go for a win-win, where both parties gain from the experience. If that fails due to conditions like receptivity, go for a win-lose outcome. With the latter, at least with that scenario, you can chalk a mark in the lessons learned column. Get really good at listening.

Can we be candid about interpersonal relationships and the impact they may have on creativity? Some relationships can take on a muse-like quality. Being around that type of person fills you with enthusiasm, inspires action, and generally makes you feel good about you. On the opposite end of the spectrum is the dodgy ground. That is where energy leaks, slowly or fast, from being in proximity of people that drain you of life. To maintain your creative, and mental, equilibrium, you need to spend more time with the muse type and less time with the drainers. When the drainers are allowed to chip away at who you are as a person, it will take deliberate effort to recover. Sadly, I think the main reason there is so much brokenness in the world is due to people behaving badly toward other people.

The solution to that dilemma is also people. Where one person can do damage, another can offer healing. I am prone to spend long periods by myself. I write and create in an environment of isolation. Extended times of isolation are not good for me as I come out the other side and feel a diminishment in my oral communication skills. When that happens, I have to reach into my reserves and find the energy to make an extra effort. People confuse me. Maybe not people per se, but their behaviours. That drains me. My counterbalance to that is not to spend more time alone. Instead, I seek to find people with whom I can be energised.

Industry

Of all the places where creativity should be elevated, the workplace ought to be number one. A workplace, workshop, studio or wide-open spaces is that location where you should have the tools to create something. As it relates to a product or service, create something that another person is willing to purchase or invest. Working solo or as part of a team, you want to produce a win-win condition for all participants. If your work environment encourages and facilitates creativity, welcome to the future. You are living a trend that will lead to global commerce.

From that front row seat, you will have the opportunity to observe change, transformation, and innovation with anticipation instead of fear.

Where businesses are going to struggle is in their delayed response to a wide range of interconnectivity challenges and the demand for innovation. When it comes to connecting, chaos theory is alive and well in the business setting. Every business is influenced by various industries or are themselves the influencers. What affects industry in one area can have a roll-on effect on others. For instance, amplification of information generates massive public awareness, which in turn drives purchasing power. Although industry is woefully slow to respond to the purchasing power of everyday people, they eventually have to come around.

The issue of plastic use in the retail setting is a good example. We don't want to be more complicit in the plastic issue. Neither do we want to contribute to the rise of organised crime by the products we purchase. If the blind eyes of industry don't become open and act, the purchasing power of the public is left with few options but to boycott or go without. What does business do about it? Being a slave to expediency and convenience breeds greed. When an industry is incapable of implementing effective change, the public and its elected officials must be the custodians for accountability.

You, me, we have to find solutions to what ails us as a society. Industry will continue to produce to feed the demand, until either a resource is depleted, or an alternate solution is created. Allow me to illustrate the concept of global demand. For argument sake, let's assume that the worldwide consumption of sugar per day per person is four grams. Roughly a teaspoon. That equates to about 30,000 metric tons of sugar a day. Now, visualise The Shard building in London. Imagine a mound of sugar piled around The Shard flowing a half-mile away from the Shard in all directions with only 200 feet of building exposed at the top. Consider that as one day's global sugar consumption. I used four grams as an arbitrary amount. I suspect that is a grossly low estimate.

The critical challenges of business today are that of being ready for changing conditions and scaling for those changes. The image of central London buried under a mountain of sugar should stimulate all sorts of questions that easily relate to your business orientation. Where is the sugar being grown? What are the environmental conditions of the land where sugar sources are produced? Is there a more nutritious product than can be grown? What is the long-term sustainability of sugar production? What is the health impact of sugar consumption and the cost to the medical industry? If nothing else, a nudge in this direction can be the basis for a great innovation question for an interviewee.

As much as I'd enjoy pontificating about business management practises and the Nudge Principles, I must refrain. Lessons in business success are reserved for another day and comment. Getting your feet on the ground with business means getting to know the territory and discovering what is possible within the constraints of the corporate culture, the market, and organisational flexibility. Generally, that type of data analysis is collated during the early stages of Nudge. Given the Nudge Principle's organic nature, that means you can regularly cycle back to the collection stage for more information. Your observations are combined with new data, adjusted for improvement, and tested in your evaluation and adaptation phases.

You may be an influencer in your workplace or are influenced. Either way, you can contribute to your mutual success timeline. Everybody should be working toward the same goal. Press the flexibility of the systems and search for areas to improve. Small improvements can lead to cost reductions, enhanced safety procedures, new product and services, and energised morale. Ideas cost nothing. Even if your ideas are rejected, you might find yourself positioned with a voice. We all want to feel valued. Appreciating our opinions and that we feel that we can make a difference is one approach management can contribute to that sense of value.

If your company is serious about staff engagement, staying ahead of the competition, and fostering resilience, then expect the management to encourage openness and creativity in the cultural framework. The words may not precisely match that description, but something in the values statement will be your opening for suggestions. Don't surrender to the malaise that your opinion doesn't matter. When you come up against opposition or obstacles, either find a way to overcome them or save your ideas for your next employer. The next company that you work with may value your dedication as evidenced by your discretionary effort. You may be the missing piece to their success—great or small.

Institutions

A decade and one day before I was born, a revolutionary book was published by Eric Arthur Blair. The author lived through the Great War, the Great Depression, the Second World War, and the beginning of the Cold War. Not that these credentials are unique or qualify the author to any more insights than others that lived during that era of upheaval. As a writer, his skills were plied as a journalist, essayist, critic and novelist. His personal and professional world was consumed with observation. Communicating what he observed and translating his worldview for readers became his mark in life. His writings and thinking expressed the weariness and frustration of a generation exposed to the most unthinkable behaviours of humanity. Blair's pen name was George Orwell. When listing transformative literature, Orwell's *Nineteen Eighty-Four* (1984) is often credited as being one of the most influential books of the twentieth century.

As I was contemplating how to approach the topic of institutions and institutionalism, I struggled to find a balance that didn't point fingers. Orwell saved me. How so? The basis of his novel, 1984, describes the raw side of unchecked institutionalism. Our protagonist is Winston Smith. A common man subdued in the bleak world of a totalitarian government. Antagonists of the novel include the Thought Police and a series of ministries with double entendre titles. One such ministry is the Ministry of Plenty that doles out rations and issues false reports to maintain appearances of competence and compassion. 1984 is riveting, but a dire representation of a dystopian society.

Before we jump to the conclusion that I am equating contemporary institutions to those manipulating the public in Orwell's book, allow me to assure that I am not. What is relevant to observe are the parallels of behaviours. You don't have to read or know details about 1984 to recognise restrictive policies within an institution. Note any major social breakthrough of the past two hundred years. Behind that change, you will see the dissolution of institutional mores. Institutional change occurs when there is sufficient momentum of independent thought and legitimacy for change realised in a climactic pivot. That is restricted where an institution's activities are veiled in secrecy. To raise awareness that change is possible, demands change-makers to foster communication. Without communication, any chance of change is held captive by the institutionalised. In many instances, that group is not motivated to change as change will upset the status quo and balance of power.

Recognising the personality of your institution is your first step to understand how to succeed in implementing change. Every institution has a personality. Acutely familiar with several personality type assessments, I thought I'd conduct a non-scientific personality assessment based on my experiences with an institution. For my purpose, I chose the Keirsey temperament sorter. Instead of responding to the sixty questions from my personal orientation, I answered according to how I view trends observed within that organisation. If my theory were correct, I'd have a generalised profile of the corporate culture. The results came back as Guardian. An accurate assessment of the personality type fostered in that organisation. Although this was a non-scientific assessment, the outcome was not a surprise.

What I gained from that exploration is an understanding of how that culture operates. Change does not come easily in a Guardian culture. The organisation with this personality will have staff dedicated to protecting the norm. Instead of adopting a posture to implement transformative concepts, their approach is to do so only as the requirement of law, regulation, or necessity If you are in an organisation with a Guardian personality, you are going to have to find ways to secure loyalty and trust. To create a culture that demonstrates a future version of itself, you need to saturate that culture with what you want it to be. Since the Guardian recognises authority, that means you'll need a top-down demonstration of leadership. Be what you want to become, others will follow.

Wrapping it up

Introducing a new concept in a summary is not generally acceptable for a chapter closure. Then again, I kind of tossed out conventions when I started my book-writing endeavour. So I guess it is okay for me to continue breaking a few rules. Getting your feet on the ground was the premise for this chapter. You were encouraged to dream big, but then put that dream into some form of action. I presented four sample environments for you to consider. Truth be told, you are likely to have your feet grounded in multiple scenarios. Another reality is that the samples I presented may not relate to you in the least. The journey you have chosen may not tread any of the nuanced trails I described. Perhaps you walked into my mind space, but there was nothing to catch your attention. Although I may not have caught your attention, there was treasure available.

Long before we had multi-player interactive games, video game pioneers played interactive fiction (IF) on their 128-byte RAM Atari consoles. Players explored castles and tunnels using text prompts to look for treasure, tools, and exits. Entering strange lands with fantastical characters required two things (besides a 5" floppy and a console): an active imagination and lateral thinking. An adventurer had to frame questions in simple terms to satisfy the game's limited vocabulary. The more frequently you played the game, the more vocabulary you gained to support your progress. The game became a narrative of your journey. A map of the early IF game Acheton reads like a flowchart of decision trees. Not unlike your navigation of creativity on the ground. Paths determined by decisions. How long it takes you to complete a level is mainly attributed to the questions you ask.

14

An Expedition Journal

Every once in a while, an opportunity comes along that changes your life. Or at least has the potential to do so. For Charles Robert Darwin of Shrewsbury, Shropshire that extraordinary opportunity came on 29 August 1831 with an invitation to join the crew of the HMS Beagle. Botany professor John Stevens Henslow invited the 22-year-old Darwin on an expedition to South America. Over the ensuing five-year voyage, Darwin collected specimens and nurtured observations that would develop into his seminal work on evolution, The *Origin of Species*. For the next twenty years, Darwin continued to collect specimens and to work on his theories. On 24 November 1859, John Murray published *On the Origin of Species by Means of Natural Selection, or the Preservation of Favoured Races in the Struggle for Life*. When the title was released, Darwin must have concluded that his decades of work reached a state of confidence for public release. Once published, he could never take it back.

Such is the nature of creativity. Once out, you can't really take it back. No differently than travelling somewhere, setting foot on that soil, and then denying it is so. While there may not be evidence that you've walked on foreign soil, the mark of its instance in time is undeniable. Where you have been, whom you have intersected with, and what you are today is the summation of all that and more. As it is with me. My metaphoric foot has walked many miles on this journey. The voyage of publishing a book is nearly over for me. I'd like to tell you how I arrived here. Maybe, just maybe, you might find something in it useful.

I'd describe myself as an average guy. Generally speaking, I am easy going and have an optimistic outlook on life. Not always, but I work on it. Some things get me down. When they do, I tend to retreat. But I don't like that state of mind, so I set goals and frame my solution in activities that energise me. I enjoy giving and contributing. I dislike confrontation. When pressed, I will let another person "win" as I think a battle is not worth surrendering my peace. I am sure that my idiosyncrasies and intense need for independent thought make me difficult at times. I have to be okay with that, as it is who I am. Overall, I say I have a good handle on who I am as a person.

With full disclosure, my journey of self-discovery was a long time coming. During my twenties through to my forties, I was actively involved in my faith. Overall that was a good experience for me and provided an excellent moral code that shaped so much of how I handle my external world. The seeds of a personal revolution were also sown during that time. Thwarted by the sacred square metre, I encountered the glass ceiling of institutionalism that would lay the foundation for a mandate of self-expression and independent thought.

I married, raised a family, changed careers, made good decisions, and made bad decisions. Nurtured good relationships. Lost relationships. Struggled through job losses and two recessions. Earned two university degrees mid-life. Said goodbye to beloved family members. I passed through the lowest of lows more times than I can count. Lost everything and started over at the age of fifty. I moved to England. Married again to a vision of my dreams who shared a passion for winning the world together. Our mantra was "I don't know who brought us together whether it was God, the Divine, or the Universe, but it is to love, live life, and make a difference for other people."

In June 2019, I left regular employment to write this book full time. Once published, I will move on to the other aspects of Nudge and fulfil our vision of the life we set out to achieve. I live by the principles of Nudge. Writing a book enabled me to document what has been percolating inside for over a decade. This is my stamp as it were. Looking over the landscape of all the contributing factors that made this possible, is more rewarding than I expected. What seemed negative at one time, will actually turn out to be a contributing positive. Challenges I faced, while monumental in my mind, were relative to the intensity I allowed. Recognising that early is a key to contentment.

The next stage of this journey is making me nervously excited. I step off that ledge into uncertainty. I know I have something of value to give. Telling people about my discoveries is the fun part. The vision of Nudge is to share the Principles with those eager to tap into their latent creative skills, businesses that are open to exploring possibilities, and institutions that want an external source to prod them toward change. I want to talk about Nudge all the time with anybody that will listen. Once I figure out how to work the Xenyx mixer on my desk and become proficient with Adobe Audition, I will throw in my lot with 700,000 other streaming podcasters. I also need to get on with building a web site for Nudge Creative Labs and selling images of stock photos. Then there are the workshops.

Fortunately, I have a lot of experience in professional training. A catalogue of curricula and training lessons are anxious to be born as they've been postponed for far too long. To appease my need to SEE Nudge Principles in action, I must apply them across numerous domains and an array of participants. I want to be a witness to the transformation that I know possible. New insights and expanding possibilities are being formed in the lives of other people who are potential participants. Unlocking the creative power through products and services is certain to have a positive knock-on effect. What adventures await all of us that make Nudge a regular part of our creative routines?

Over a decade ago, I formulated a marketing strategy and prospectus for the initial version of the Nudge Principle. I called the company Paroxumos based on the inspiration of a Greek word that intimates spurring someone to action. The marketing strategy includes a board game, an interactive live game, small and large venue events, and several products. Getting any one of these products off the ground requires some creative play. Remember, I see myself as an average guy. The obstacles I face for getting something off the ground and into success status are not much different than any other person of my age. So, as the adage goes, if I can do this, anybody can. To do so is going to require stepping out of my comfort zone to try things that might make me uncomfortable. To stretch myself, discover my limits, and then push myself beyond those limits. It will be fun and at times, scary. But I am ready for that rollercoaster ride.

What concerns me most is how I will manage my emotional wellbeing through the next stages. Will the changing season invite scrutiny and open the door to a flood of rejection? How will I navigate the upward slope of the introduction stage of this product life cycle? People are always going to be the unknown factor. Success with people demands a degree of emotional pliability that enables you to absorb impacts through deflection rather than a straight-on collision. Things break in collisions or they eventually will. What is true in nature is true of life. You just have to find the right application.

Embarking on the expedition of a purposeful life, demands that you are proactive in the process. I know. I have used the word or forms of the word demand quite a few times since we started this Nudged exploration together. I may have used far too many forceful type words to describe the importance of an action or consequences. You may not have been aware of it as I tried to keep it out of tone. Forms of demand were used 63 times, require 55 times, need 144 times, and must 76 times. All in all, a form of those words were used 338 times. Most of the time, the words were chosen with the intent of describing a prerequisite for an action. If you want to do this, then you will have to do that. Your and my lives are chock full of examples that fit that criteria. Even though I have Nudged you with provocative language along our journey, let me take this last bit of time to change direction.

The world and domains to explore most certainly have their boundaries, entry points, expectations, and conditions. Just because that is the case, doesn't mean you should be restricted in your thinking. You are a powerhouse of thought, innovation, and creativity. Literally, everything you see apart from that which is natural had its source as a creation by a person. Our collective accomplishments are mind-blowing. I think it is safe to say that we easily forget that fact as we go about a daily routine. The immeasurable number of created things you'll interact with moment by moment is regularly lost in your unaware use of those creations. Each creation is an artefact of another person's creative mark. You live in a magnificent living museum of a species' achievements. Set aside for a moment value-orientation of those creations, the fact that they exist is astonishing. The person or persons that created them were equipped with the same raw materials as you. What they did with those materials made the difference.

Being Nudged is a prompting to be and do more than you are. Your make up is so that a creative response is empowering and natural. When you recognise something is not working as well as it might or identify a lack and a possible solution that is your Nudge to own it. When you feel the inspiration to capture a vision or sound through your own interpretation, that is your Nudge to act on it. It doesn't really matter how good it is or whether it works. Nothing came out perfect on the first attempt. You push on, nudge and being nudged until what grows inside of you can be realised. If you get stuck in one medium or discipline, you try another until you strike the best solution to complement your unique creative identity. Successive discoveries pave the way for the best version of you that you can create. Regardless of the outcomes.

Creativity, in all its boundless possibilities, is not so much about the creation. Rather, creativity is about the creative. There is a lot of fanfare for great works of art and music, lifechanging technology, and new approaches to living and managing societal challenges. That fanfare is just and deserved in the majority of situations. Behind the accolades is a person that worked to make that creation a reality. You or I will never fully appreciate what was entailed in that creative's journey. That is their story. The sleepless nights wrestling with a mind that can't rest as it tosses and turns with the sparks of ideation. Which sacrifices were made? What were the actual and emotional costs to develop the person so that the creation could be realised? Every step trod. Every relationship entered or departed. Every idea that flickered to a flame or fizzled into forgetfulness. All that has transpired since their infancy, contributed to the creation we enjoy or use daily. From the cave of Theopetra to the street where you live and work, evidence of the creative power of people is forever celebrated in everyday use items. You are surrounded by the what began as a possibility.

That is why the greatest exploration of all time is the discovery of yourself. There is no more meaningful challenge than that of seeing what you are capable of accomplishing. Your mind is a rich source of knowledge and experience. Why settle for the passive entry and exit of a day when you could be a powerful influence on your world? That designation is not just for elite people with some particular skill, deep pockets, power or authority. Every person has that potential. Without exception. What differentiates one person from another is how they invest in the discovery process. That doesn't require a special gift or even a specific IQ. As a catalyst for self-discovery, creativity is not a respecter of class, income, or physical attributes of the creative. It is colour blind, status ignorant, ability adaptable, and inviting to all. The challenges differ from creative to creative equivalent to the person, conditions, and creative demand. Differences attribute dimensionality to the creation. For that, we can be grateful we live in such a diverse and sometimes confusing world.

With an increased degree of difficulty of a challenge comes the potential for a higher degree of reward. Applaud the inventiveness of a person seeking to find what they are capable of doing. Enable them with tools that they may realise a vision that benefits others. I believe every job interview should contain a hefty proportion of dialogue that includes a screening for creativity. A series of "what if" questions that afford the interviewer to observe (SEE) how an interviewee might tackle challenges in the workplace. Expose the interviewee to challenges that enables them to demonstrate their creative spirit. With a metric for creativity as a hiring criteria, companies can introduce staff into their mix that are flexible and liberated to grow. Naturally, the infrastructure must be accommodating to that expectation. A corporate culture with creativity as its core is empowered to achieve great things.

What if that same company took a step further? What if they partnered with the community to tap into the richness of the community's creative strength? Imagine what might happen if a company opened its doors to the community to attend creative labs? The company could foster goodwill and nurture new staff. Assuming that a criterion for creativity was a deciding factor in hiring, those that did not make the grade could attend company-sponsored workshops. Youth, elders, unemployed, homeless, disabled, people of all walks of life would welcome the opportunity to participate in programmes that stretch their creative capacity. The individual benefits. The community benefits. The company benefits. Creativity as a catalyst for change is not just an ideal, it is the answer to all the problems we face.

As people, we are not meant to be sedentary. Everything about us is designed for mobility. Muscle and sinew are for moving our skeletons. Electric pulses fire through our bodies as blood courses through our veins. Our brains work 24-hours a day, either keeping us alive or interacting with the inner world of our awareness or the outer world of stimuli. We are creatures of mobility of mind, body, and spirit. If there is a lesson from the world of nature it is that we remain in a cycle of create and rest. The rest part is just a transition for the next creative action. Then, when you achieve a goal, stretch beyond that milestone with new goals, explore broader possibilities, and open new vistas for your vision. Imagine a world where we work together and apply principles that lead to the betterment of others.

All said and done, the journey you embark on must be one where you are true to self. As we all must conclude. Nobody else can live your life for you or through you. The choices you make and the paths you follow will create their own stories of success. If you are true to yourself, then you can relish a sense of accomplishment when you reach landmarks toward your destination. What will you see? Who will you tell? How will you make it flow? Where will you play? How will that make you and others feel? What will enhance your sense of being? Most importantly, what will you do?

Index

www.ingramcontent.com/pod-product-compliance
Lightning Source LLC
Chambersburg PA
CBHW030911060726
47591CB00005B/1503